STRATEGIC NEWSPAPER MARKETING AND MANAGEMENT

STRATEGIC NEWSPAPER MARKETING AND MANAGEMENT

K. C. Thakur

CYBER TECH PUBLICATIONS
4264/3, Ansari Road, Daryaganj, New Delhi-110002 (India)
Ph.: 011-23244078, 011-43559448 Fax: 011-23280028
E-Mail: cyberpublicationsdelhi@yahoo.com
Website: www.cybertechpublications.com

STRATEGIC NEWSPAPER MARKETING AND MANAGEMENT

K. C. Thakur

First Edition 2010

Published by :

G.S. Rawat for **Cyber Tech Publications**
4264/3, Ansari Road, Daryaganj, New Delhi-110002 (India)
Ph.: 011-23244078, 011-43559448 Fax: 011-23280028
E-Mail: cyberpublicationsdelhi@yahoo.com
Website: www.cybertechpublications.com

Printed at: Asian Offset Printers, Delhi-53

Preface

The years have multiplied the problems of newspaper management and placed a growing premium upon its basic soundness. Lately there has been a marked acceleration in both directions with new problems and with a still greater need for sound management. Some newspapermen even were not fully aware of all that transpired, or, if they knew what had occurred, they were sometimes at a loss to account for it or to understand it. It is not strange that the layman should lack an appreciation of the importance of the business side of publishing or an understanding of its problems. Indeed, to the lay mind, journalism invariably means only the editorial side of publishing. Many readers, in fact, have too limited a conception of even the editorial department. As a rule, the business aspects of publishing are beyond their ken, except in a vague and general way.

For newspapermen and public alike, it is important that the newspaper should be viewed as a whole. The day is past when the editorial department is sufficient unto itself, or when the advertising department can be conducted without regard for the circulation or production departments. There are no longer separate watertight compartments in the scheme of newspaper organization and management, if, indeed, there ever really were.

What has been attempted here is an analysis and appraisal of the functions and workings of the daily newspaper other than editorial. Special effort has been made to note and to evaluate the changes that came about during or as a result of the depression. How permanent they will be can only be guessed, but there appears to be no question but that many of the effects will be lasting.

This is not intended as a technical treatise on any of the subject matter covered, nor is it presumed that all the answers are here. This is designed, rather, to present the rounded picture of daily newspaper publishing from the standpoint of management. In controversial matters, such as, for example, the questions relating to advertising rates, every effort has been made to give both sides fairly. Unless otherwise indicated, the author must be responsible for such opinions and conclusions as are expressed, as well as for any errors or misstatements. No book of this sort would be possible without advice and help from many sources.

—Author

CONTENTS

1

INTRODUCTION

Strategic management can be used to determine mission, vision, values, goals, objectives, roles and responsibilities, timelines, etc.

Definition: Strategic management is that set of managerial decisions and actions aimed at the generation of sustainable competitive advantage that determines the long-run performance of a corporation. It includes environmental scanning, strategy formulation, strategy implementation and evaluation and control.

OVERVIEW

An organization's strategy must be appropriate for its resources, environmental circumstances, and core objectives. The process involves matching the company's internal resources (*e.g. IT*)and capabilities e.g. (*quality management)* to the *external business environment* the organization faces. **Strategy formulation** involves:

- Doing a situation analysis: both internal and external; both micro-environmental and macro-environmental.
- Concurrent with this assessment, objectives are set. This involves crafting vision statements (long term view of a possible future), mission statements (the role that the organization gives itself in society), overall corporate objectives (both financial and strategic), strategic business unit objectives (both financial and strategic), and tactical objectives.

- These objectives should, in the light of the situation analysis, suggest a strategic plan. The plan provides the details of how to achieve these objectives.

This three-step strategy formulation process is sometimes referred to as determining where you are now, determining where you want to go, and then determining how to get there. These three questions are the essence of *strategic planning*. *SWOT Analysis: I/O Economics for the external factors and RBV* for the internal factors.

Strategy implementation involves:

- Allocation of sufficient resources (financial, personnel, time, technology support)
- Establishing a chain of command or some alternative structure (such as cross functional teams)
- Assigning responsibility of specific tasks or processes to specific individuals or groups
- It also involves managing the process. This includes monitoring results, comparing to benchmarks and best practices, evaluating the efficacy and efficiency of the process, controlling for variances, and making adjustments to the process as necessary.
- When implementing specific programs, this involves acquiring the requisite resources, developing the process, training, process testing, documentation, and integration with (and/or conversion from) legacy processes.

Strategy formulation and implementation is an on-going, never-ending, integrated process requiring continuous reassessment and reformation. Strategic management is dynamic. It involves a complex pattern of actions and reactions. It is partially planned and partially unplanned. Strategy is planned and emergent, dynamic, and interactive. Some people (such as *Andy Grove* at Intel) feel that there are critical points at which a strategy must take a new direction in order to be in step with a changing business environment. These critical points of change are called strategic inflection points.

TIME SCALES

Strategic management operates on several time scales. Short term strategies involve planning and managing for the present. Long term strategies involve preparing for and pre-empting the future. Marketing strategist Derek Abell (1993), has suggested that understanding this dual nature of strategic management is the least understood part of the process. He claims that balancing the temporal aspects of strategic planning requires the use of dual strategies simultaneously.

Strategic Management is actually a solid foundation or a framework within which all the functioning managerial operations are bundled together. This is the highest level corporate activity that sets the terms and goals for a company that it should follow for prosperity.

General Approaches

In general terms, there are two main approaches to strategic management which are opposite but complement each other in some ways:

'The Industrial Organization Approach'

- o based on *economic theory* — deals with issues like competitive rivalry, *resource allocation, economies of scale*
- o assumptions — rationality, self discipline behaviour, profit maximization

The Sociological Approach

- o deals primarily with human interactions
- o Assumptions — bounded rationality, satisfying behaviour, profit sub-optimality. An example of a company that currently operates this way is *Google*

Strategic management techniques can be viewed as bottom-up, top-down, or collaborative processes. In the bottom-up approach, employees submit proposals to their managers who, in turn, funnel the best ideas further up the organization. This is often accomplished by a capital budgeting process. Proposals are assessed using financial criteria such as *return on investment or cost-benefit analysis.*

The proposals that are approved form the substance of a new strategy, all of which is done without a grand strategic design or a strategic architect. The top-down approach is the most common by far. In it, the CEO, possibly with the assistance of a strategic planning team, decides on the overall direction the company should take. Some organizations are starting to experiment with collaborative strategic planning techniques that recognize the emergent nature of strategic decisions.

THE STRATEGY HIERARCHY

In most (large) corporations there are several levels of strategy. Strategic management is the highest in the sense that it is the broadest, applying to all parts of the firm. It gives direction to corporate values, corporate culture, corporate goals, and corporate missions. Under this broad corporate strategy there are often functional or business unit strategies.

Functional strategies include marketing strategies, new product development strategies, human resource strategies, financial strategies, legal strategies, and information technology management strategies. The emphasis is on short and medium term plans and is limited to the domain of each department's functional responsibility. Each functional department attempts to do its part in meeting overall corporate objectives, and hence to some extent their strategies are derived from broader corporate strategies.

Many companies feel that a functional organizational structure is not an efficient way to organize activities so they have *reengineered* according to processes or strategic business units (called SBUs). A strategic business unit is a semi-autonomous unit within an organization. It is usually responsible for its own budgeting, new product decisions, hiring decisions, and price setting. An SBU is treated as an internal profit centre by corporate headquarters. Each SBU is responsible for developing its business strategies, strategies that must be in tune with broader corporate strategies. The "lowest" level of strategy is operational strategy. It is very narrow in focus and deals with day-to-day operational activities such as scheduling criteria. It must operate within a budget but is not at liberty to adjust or create that budget.

Operational level strategy was encouraged by *Peter Drucker* in his theory of *management by objectives* (MBO). Operational level strategies are informed by business level strategies which, in turn, are informed by corporate level strategies. Business strategy, which refers to the aggregated operational strategies of single business firm or that of an SBU in a diversified corporation refers to the way in which a firm competes in its chosen arenas.

Corporate strategy, then, refers to the overarching strategy of the diversified firm. Such corporate strategy answers the questions of "in which businesses should we compete?" and "how does being in one business add to the competitive advantage of another portfolio firm, as well as the competitive advantage of the corporation as a whole?"

Since the turn of the millennium, there has been a tendency in some firms to revert to a simpler strategic structure. This is being driven by information technology. It is felt that *knowledge management* systems should be used to share information and create common goals. Strategic divisions are thought to hamper this process. Most recently, this notion of strategy has been captured under the rubric of dynamic strategy, popularized by the strategic management textbook authored by Carpenter and Sanders

This work builds on that of Brown and Eisenhart as well as Christensen and portrays firm strategy, both business and corporate, as necessarily embracing ongoing strategic change, and the seamless integration of strategy formulation and implementation. Such change and implementation are usually built into the strategy through the staging and pacing facets.

REASONS WHY STRATEGIC PLANS FAIL

There are many reasons why strategic plans fail, especially:

Failure to understand the customer

o Why do they buy

o Is there a real need for the product

o inadequate or incorrect *marketing research*

Inability to predict *environmental reaction*

o What will competitors do

 * Fighting *brands*

 * *Price wars*

o Will government intervene

Over-estimation of resource competence

o Can the staff, equipment, and processes handle the new strategy

o Failure to develop new employee and management skills

Failure to coordinate

o Reporting and control relationships not adequate

o Organizational structure not flexible enough

Failure to obtain senior management commitment

o Failure to get management involved right from the start

o Failure to obtain sufficient company resources to accomplish task

Failure to obtain employee commitment

o New strategy not well explained to employees

o No incentives given to workers to embrace the new strategy

Under-estimation of time requirements

o No *critical path* analysis done

Failure to follow the plan

o No follow through after initial planning

o No tracking of progress against plan

o No consequences for above

Failure to manage change

- o Inadequate understanding of the internal resistance to change
- o Lack of vision on the relationships between processes, technology and organization

Poor communications

- o Insufficient information sharing among stakeholders
- o Exclusion of stakeholders and delegates

Failure to focus

- o Inability or unwillingness to make choices which are true to the strategic mission (i.e. to do fewer things, better), leads to mediocrity, inability to compete

CRITICISMS OF STRATEGIC MANAGEMENT

Although a sense of direction is important, it can also stifle creativity, especially if it is rigidly enforced. In an uncertain and ambiguous world, fluidity can be more important than a finely tuned strategic compass. When a strategy becomes internalized into a corporate culture, it can lead to *group think*. It can also cause an organization to define itself too narrowly. An example of this is *marketing myopia.*

Most theories of strategic management seem to have a lifespan less than that of the popularity of the latest teen music idol. Many critics claim that this is because most of them generally do not work. Keep in mind that this article describes only the 50 or so most successful theories, thus exhibiting survivorship bias (ironically, itself an area of research in strategic management). For every theory that gets incorporated into strategic management textbooks there are many that are quickly forgotten. Many theories tend either to be too narrow in focus to build a complete corporate strategy on, or too general and abstract to be applicable to specific situations.

The low success rate is further fuelled by the management lecture circuit in which hundreds of self-appointed gurus, many without serious academic credentials or substantial expertise, attempt to sell books and explain their "revolutionary" and "groundbreaking" theories to audiences of business executives for a sizable fee.

While there are undoubtedly inspirational ideas contained in these seminars, the theories expounded therein have not, for the most part, been subjected to serious study. Some critics take the opposite approach claiming effectively that there are not enough theories, and when they arrive they are too late to help managers make any important decisions.

These commentators remind us that the basic, everyday purpose of strategic management is to match a company's strategy with the business environment that the organization is in. Because the environment is constantly changing, effective strategic management requires a continuous flow of new theories suitable for the new circumstances.

The problem with most theories is that they solve yesterday's problems, similar to a business *Maginot Line*. Various approaches to solve this problem have emerged, however, including Mintzberg's ideas of 'emergent strategies' and use of ideas from *complexity theory* in what is often called *complexity strategy*.

Gary Hamel (2000) coined the term strategic convergence to explain the limited scope of the strategies being used by rivals in greatly differing circumstances. He lamented that strategies converge more than they should, because the more successful ones get imitated by firms that do not understand that the strategic process involves designing a custom strategy for the specifics of each situation.

INTERNATIONAL STRATEGIC MANAGEMENT

International Strategic Management is an ongoing management planning process aimed at developing strategies to enable an organization to compete internationally. The process of developing a particular international strategy is referred to as 'strategic planning'. International strategies for multiple countries are similar to the strategies used in a single country. An organization must be able to answer the following questions:

- What products or services does the organization intend to sell?
- Where and how will the organization make those products or services?
- Where and how will the organization sell those products or services?
- Where and how will the organization acquire the resources?
- How does the organization expect to outperform its *competitors?*

COMPLEXITY IN DEVELOPING AN INTERNATIONAL STRATEGY

Developing an international strategy for an organization in a foreign country is more complex than developing a strategy for an organization in a domestic country.

In a domestic country, you only have to consider one *national government*, one *currency, one accounting system, one political and legal system* and usually a similar culture. In foreign countries, you are talking about multiple governments, multiple currencies, multiple accounting systems, multiple political and legal systems and a large variety of languages and cultures.

In foreign countries, there is the possibility of:

- local languages required in many situations
- very diverse cultures, both between countries and sometimes even within countries
- often volatile politics
- varied *economic systems*
- scarcity of skilled labor, in which case you would be talking about training or redesigning methods
- poorly-developed *financial markets* and government-controlled capital flows, in some of the countries
- problems and exorbitant costs in obtaining *market research* data

- limited *advertising,* subjected to lots of restrictions
- possible low *literacy rates,* not to mention the possibility of making mistakes in the language when advertising
- currency exchange fluctuations
- inadequate or limited communication
- mandatory worker participation in management in some countries
- Legal restrictions on lying off of workers.

International strategic management is therefore a whole lot more difficult than strategic management in one nation.

SCHOOLS IN STRATEGIC MANAGEMENT

Strategic management is not a task, but a rather a set of managerial skills that should be used throughout the organization, in a wide variety of functions.

*Strategic cross-functional managemen*t is central to capitalizing on functional excellence, and in order for functional specialists to make the greatest possible contribution, managers must take *a broader view of their functions* and understand how they fit into the web of the organizational processes and, ultimately, into the overall *strategy.*

New Systemic Approach to Strategic Management

All the above schools, often fighting between themselves, favour different single-sided approaches to strategy formulation. They represent both different approaches to strategy formulation and different parts of the same process. Today's managers have to deal with the entire business systems – as opposed to dealing with its different parts independently - not only to keep strategy formulation as a vital force but also to impart real energy to the strategic process. They must practice balanced results-based leadership strategies and apply a balanced approach to business systems.

Certain positive moves in this direction have been seen recently. Some of the more recent approaches to strategy formulation take a wider perspective and cut across the above ten schools in eclectic and interesting ways, for example learning and Design in the "Dynamic Capabilities" approach, or the "Dynamic Strategy" one based on knowledge working.

The currently dominant view of business strategy – resource-based theory – is based on the concept of economic rent and the view of the company as a collection of capabilities. This view of strategy has a coherence and integrative role that places it well ahead of other mechanisms of strategic decision making.

What is Strategic Planning?

Strategic planning is a management tool, period. As with any management tool, it is used for one purpose only: to help an organization do a better job - to focus its energy, to ensure that members of the organization are working toward the same goals, to assess and adjust the organization's direction in response to a changing environment. In short, strategic planning is a disciplined effort to produce fundamental decisions and actions that shape and guide what an organization is, what it does, and why it does it, with a focus on the future.

A word by word dissection of this definition provides the key elements that underlie the meaning and success of a strategic planning process:

The process is strategic because it involves preparing the best way to respond to the circumstances of the organization's environment, whether or not its circumstances are known in advance; nonprofits often must respond to dynamic and even hostile environments.

Being strategic means being clear about the organization's objectives, being aware of the organization's resources, and incorporating both into being consciously responsive to a dynamic environment.

The process is about planning because it involves intentionally setting goals (i.e., choosing a desired future) and developing an approach to achieving those goals. The process is disciplined in that it calls for a certain order and pattern to keep it focused and productive. The process raises a sequence of questions that helps planners examine experience, test assumptions, gather and incorporate information about the present, and anticipate the environment in which the organization will be working in the future.

Finally, the process is about fundamental decisions and actions because choices must be made in order to answer the sequence of questions mentioned above. The plan is ultimately no more, and no less, than a set of decisions about what to do, why to do it, and how to do it.

Because it is impossible to do everything that needs to be done in this world, strategic planning implies that some organizational decisions and actions are more important than others - and that much of the strategy lies in making the tough decisions about what is most important to achieving organizational success.

The strategic planning can be complex, challenging, and even messy, but it is always defined by the basic ideas outlined above - and you can always return to these basics for insight into your own strategic planning process.

What is the difference between strategic planning and long-range planning?

Although many use these terms interchangeably, strategic planning and long-range planning differ in their emphasis on the "assumed" environment.

Long-range planning is generally considered to mean the development of a plan for accomplishing a goal or set of goals over a period of several years, with the assumption that current knowledge about future conditions is sufficiently reliable to ensure the plan's reliability over the duration of its implementation.

In the late fifties and early sixties, for example, the US economy was relatively stable and somewhat predictable, and, therefore, long-range planning was both fashionable and useful. On the other hand, strategic planning assumes that an organization must be responsive to a dynamic, changing environment (not the more stable environment assumed for long-range planning).

Certainly a common assumption has emerged in the non-profit sector that the environment is indeed changeable, often in unpredictable ways. Strategic planning, then, stresses the importance of making decisions that will ensure the organization's ability to successfully respond to changes in the environment.

What is strategic thinking and strategic management?

Strategic planning is only useful if it supports strategic thinking and leads to strategic management - the basis for an effective organization.

Strategic thinking means asking, "Are we doing the right thing?" Perhaps, more precisely, it means making that assessment using three key requirements about strategic thinking: a definite purpose be in mind; an understanding of the environment, particularly of the forces that affect or impede the fulfilment of that purpose; and creativity in developing effective responses to those forces.

It follows, then, that strategic management is the application of strategic thinking to the job of leading an organization.

Dr. Jagdish Sheth, a respected authority on marketing and strategic planning, provides the following framework for understanding strategic management: continually asking the question, "Are we doing the right thing?"

It entails attention to the "big picture" and the willingness to adapt to changing circumstances, and consists of the following three elements: formulation of the organization's future mission in light of changing external factors such as regulation, competition, technology, and customers development of a competitive strategy to achieve the mission creation of an organizational structure which will deploy resources to successfully carry out its competitive strategy.

Strategic management is adaptive and keeps an organization relevant. In these dynamic times it is more likely to succeed than the traditional approach of "if it ain't broke, don't fix it."

What Strategic Planning Is Not!

Everything said above to describe what strategic planning is can also provide an understanding of what it is not. For example, it is about fundamental decisions and actions, but it does not attempt to make future decisions (Steiner, 1979).

Strategic planning involves anticipating the future environment, but the decisions are made in the present. This means that over time, the organization must stay abreast of changes in order to make the best decisions it can at any given point - it must manage, as well as plan, strategically.

Strategic planning has also been described as a tool - but it is not a substitute for the exercise of judgment by leadership.

Ultimately, the leaders of any enterprise need to sit back and ask, and answer, "What are the most important issues to respond to?" and "How shall we respond?" Just as the hammer does not create the bookshelf, so the data analysis and decision-making tools of strategic planning do not make the organization work - they can only support the intuition, reasoning skills, and judgment that people bring to their organization.

Finally, strategic planning, though described as disciplined, does not typically flow smoothly from one step to the next. It is a creative process, and the fresh insight arrived at today might very well alter the decision made yesterday. Inevitably the process moves forward and back several times before arriving at the final set of decisions.

Therefore, no one should be surprised if the process feels less like a comfortable trip on a commuter train, but rather like a ride on a roller coaster. But even roller coaster cars arrive at their destination, as long as they stay on track!

What is a strategic plan?

In strategic planning it is critical to formally consider how your organization will accomplish its goals. The answer to this question is a strategy. There are a variety of formal definitions for strategies, but everyone fundamentally agrees that a strategy is the answer to the question, "How?" "Strategies are simply a set of actions that enable an organization to achieve results." MAP for Nonprofits, St. Paul, MN. "Strategy is a way of comparing your organization's strengths with the changing environment in order to get an idea of how best to complete or serve client needs."(Jim Fisk & Robert Barron, The Official MBA Handbook.)

Essentially, there are three different categories of strategies: organizational, programmatic, and functional. The difference among the categories is the focus of the strategy:

Organizational strategy outlines the planned avenue for organizational development (e.g., collaborations, earned income, selection of businesses, mergers, etc.). Programmatic strategy addresses how to develop, manage and deliver programs (e.g., market a prenatal care service to disadvantaged expectant mothers by providing information and intake services in welfare offices).

Functional strategies articulate how to manage administration and support needs that impact the organization's efficiency and effectiveness (e.g., develop a financial system that provides accurate information using a cash accrual method).

When should a strategic plan be developed?

Strategy development follows the creation and affirmation of the organization's purpose statement, environmental and program data collection and analysis, and identification of critical issues.

It is critical that strategy development follow these steps because the information gathered and decisions made in these phases are the foundation for strategy creation and selection. Each of these steps provides the following: The purpose statement, the statement of the organization's ultimate goal, provides the direction to which the strategies should ultimately lead.

External market data and program evaluation results provide critical data to support strategy development. Without this information and insight, the organization's strategies will not be in alignment with or effective in the marketplace.

The critical issues list serves as the specific focus and framework for the activities of the organization and the pattern of these activities (developing and selecting the strategies).

How are strategies developed?

Strategy formulation is a combination of rational, scientific examinations and educated, intuitive best guesses. Many individuals are overwhelmed by the idea of developing strategies, but it can be a fun and invigorating process. The process entails: examining the organization's critical issues determining how the organization's strengths and skills can be employed to address the critical issues analyzing opportunities and strengths and looking for ways to synthesize the two exploring and choosing the best approaches for the organization. During this evaluation ask these key questions: Does the strategy meet/address critical issues? Is this aligned with our mission? Is this approach financially viable?

One effective method of strategy generation is to list critical issues and organizational strengths onto flipcharts and then have staff or board members brainstorm possible uses of those strengths or other skills to address the critical issues.

Once the brainstorm session is completed, use a roundtable discussion to investigate and evaluate the possible strategies. Remember to develop a list of alternative strategies to investigate and keep in the contingency planning file. It is important not to discount the ideas that come to people during non-working hours.

The Polaroid camera is the result of a three year olds question to her father: "Dad, why can't I see the picture now?"

What are some tools for analysis and planning?

A number of analytical tools have been developed to assist organizations with the planning process. Many non-profit organizations have adapted these tools, modifying the questions and criteria to align with their own specific services and markets. Listed below are analytical tools frequently used by non-profit and for-profit organizations?

What is SWOT Analysis?

SWOT analysis is a methodology of examining potential strategies derived from the synthesis of organizational strengths, weaknesses, opportunities and threats (SWOT). The partnering of the different elements and the extensive data collected as a result of the analysis can serve as a spark for roundtable discussions and refinement of current strategies or generation of new strategies.

What is the Macmillan Matrix?

This strategy grid, developed by Dr. Ian Macmillan, is specifically designed to assist non-profit organizations to formulate organizational strategies. There are three assumptions underlying this approach: the need for resources is essentially competitive and all agencies wanting to survive must acknowledge this dynamic given that resources are scarce, there is no room for direct duplication of services to a single constituency — this is wasteful and inefficient mediocre or low quality service to a large client population is less preferable to delivering higher quality services to a more focused population. These assumptions have implications that are difficult and painful for many organizations and individuals. It might mean terminating some programs to improve core services and competencies, giving programs and clients to more efficient, effective agencies, or competing aggressively with those programs that are less effective or efficient. Mac Milan's matrix examines four program dimensions that guide placement on the strategy grid and indicate implied strategies.

Alignment with Mission Statement: Services or programs that are not in alignment with the organizational mission, unable to draw on existing organizational skills or knowledge, unable to share resources, and/or unable to coordinate activities across programs should be divested.

Competitive Position: Competitive position addresses the degree to which the organization has a stronger capability and potential to fund the program and serve the client base than the competitive agencies.

Program Attractiveness: Program attractiveness is the complexity associated with managing a program. Programs that have low client resistance, a growing client base, easy exit barriers, and stable financial resources are considered simple or "easy to administer." The level of program attractiveness also includes an economic perspective or a review of current and future resource investments.

Alternative Coverage: Alternative coverage is the number of other organizations attempting to deliver or succeeding in delivering a similar program in the same region to similar constituents.

The Macmillan Matrix provides ten cells in which to place programs that have been reviewed in terms of these four dimensions. Each cell is assigned a strategy that directs the future of the program (s) listed in the cell (e.g., aggressive competition, joint venture, orderly divestment, etc.). One cell of the matrix, "Soul of the Agency," requires additional explanation. These are the difficult programs for which the organization is often the clients' "last, best hope." Management must find ways to use the programs in other cells to develop, piggyback, subsidize, leverage, promote, or otherwise support the programs in this category.

2

THE PROCESS OF STRATEGIC MANAGEMENT

The primary purpose of the strategic management process is to enable companies to achieve strategic competitiveness and earn above-average returns. Research indicates that companies that engage in strategic management generally outperform those that do not. The attainment of an appropriate match or fit between a company's environment and its strategy, structure, and processes has positive effects on the company's performance. Bruce Henderson, founder of the Boston Consulting Group, pointed out that a company cannot afford to follow intuitive strategies once it becomes large, has layers of management, or its environment changes substantially. As the world's environment becomes increasingly complex and changing, today's companies as one way to make the environment more manageable use strategic management. Strategic competitiveness is achieved when a company successfully formulates and implements a value-creating strategy. By implementing a value-creating strategy that current and potential competitors are not simultaneously implementing and that competitors are unable to duplicate, a company achieves a sustained or sustainable competitive advantage.

So long as a company can sustain (or maintain) a competitive advantage, investors will earn above-average returns. Above-average returns represent returns that exceed returns that investors expect to earn from other investments with similar levels of risk (investor uncertainty about the economic gains or losses that will result from a particular investment). In other words, above average-returns exceed investors' expected levels of return for given levels of risk. In the long run, companies must earn at least average returns and provide investors with average returns if they are to survive. If a company earns below-average returns and provides investors with below-average returns, investors will withdraw their funds and place them in investments that earn at least average returns. Internationally these types of companies are prime take-over targets, a concept that is picking up in India.

COLOURS OF CHANGE

At one extreme you had the internet start-ups with almost-teenagers strategising for the company. At the other, you have companies like the Godrej group — over a hundred years old, with legacy systems of managing and strategising. Now the group's infusing a little colour into those processes. Godrej's new colour-coded approach to rejuvenating the group is a careful balance between both — involve youngsters in decision-making, access all those bright young ideas, and also bring a touch of sobriety (plum, a mix of red and blue) to weigh the final approach. A young executives board, comprising a group of youngsters with functions similar to that of the company's board of directors, gives its recommendations to the board. Meet Adi Godrej, the new Chief Personnel Officer of Group Godrej, and the man behind the red and blue teams. "Post the dissolution of our JV with P&G in 1996, we did a lot of introspection, which led us to the realisation that we needed to change dramatically if we wanted to progress," he explains. Godrej isn't preaching what he doesn't practice. When you're a managing director trying to ensure people-focus and youthfulness in your group, you set an example. When he decided that all managers have to go through extensive feedback sessions — not just from peers and subordinates, but also from vendors and suppliers — he underwent one himself. Says a deadpan Godrej: "My evaluation said that I'm too autocratic and not a good listener. People also felt that I do not encourage teamwork." Adi Godrej was inspired to start the red and blue teams after a CEO's forum held by US-based management guru CK Prahalad. Godrej modified the plan, and got the guru himself to speak to his teams about the concept's methodology and relevance to the group's needs. Now red and blue are the colours of change at the lush green premises of the Godrej group in suburban Mumbai. In an interesting experiment to evolve out-of-the-box thinking, various group businesses have formed two eight-member teams called the red team and the blue team, made up of young employees whose mandate is to come up with recommendations on future growth prospects for their divisions, strategies and business directions.

Working independently of each other, the red and blue teams meet with opinion makers from all walks of life for a period of 3-4 months in order to chalk out a strategic plan for the next three years. These teams then present their plan to the 'plum team', a team of senior managers from the respective businesses, .ometimes including chairman Adi Godrej. The senior team's job is to review the two plans, distil the best suggestions, and come up with a final plan to be implemented. It was tried at Godrej Agrovet last year, and has been rolled out to the rest of the group now. So far, the teams have come up with suggestions on a variety of growth strategies — potential acquisition candidates, new categories of consumer goods to be explored, ways to improve rural thrust and how to go about globalising their businesses. "We've found a wider variety of thought processes and ideas than ever in the past," adds an enthusiastic Godrej.

Another fairly uncommon, and bold, initiative is the young executive's board (YEB), which was formed in October 2001. It has eleven 20-somethings on board (the oldest is 32). For all strategic purposes, they are supposed to behave like any senior board, and give their suggestions on strategy, human resource policies, corporate governance and ways and means to make the future brighter for the group. They have been provided access to all information, documented and otherwise, that the directors of the group's management committee have access to. Again, the idea is to get strong young perspective on board issues. Also, the group wants to strengthen communications and transparency within. "The idea is to have a bottoms-up approach in strategic planning, as opposed to the traditional top-down one in which plans are formed by the senior management and left to the managers below to implement, who grumble about not having their say in planning. It also benefits the youngsters because it is a tremendous learning opportunity for them, and it is they who will rise to be the future managers," explains Godrej.

Meanwhile a team of five business heads has been instituted, which has to come up with a group-wide strategic plan this year. It is this team's recommendations on various business strategies — which businesses to exit, which new ones to enter, and deliberations on new growth horizons — that will decide what the Godrej group will be five years from now. Why this sudden need for action on the HR front? Godrej learnt its lessons from the break-ups with its various joint ventures. Not only did a lot of managers walk out along with JV partners, the group did not attract as many talented people with the advent of MNCs in India.

Their internal surveys on HRD climate and employee satisfaction reflected that young people in the organization felt underutilised, and uninvolved in strategic decision-making. A think-tank of eight people from different functions and group companies has been formed to evaluate trends in science, engineering, infotech, marketing and management developments, that are likely to affect them in future. In the last four months, 38 top managers, including Godrej himself, have had to undergo an assessment centre evaluation where they were tested for their ability to think, relate, learn and act.

Moreover, the company's existing 360-degree evaluation programme — that so far included only peers, subordinates and superiors — has been widened to include feedback from vendors and suppliers on employees who interact with them. To ensure that all these initiatives evolve into more than just colourful exercises, Godrej has rehauled compensation too. The group has linked its variable remuneration to economic value added (EVA).

Come April, Godrej's managers and officers, including the chairman, will receive a performance remuneration that's linked to their contribution to the business' EVA in the last year. What would make the employees even happier is that there's no limit to how much they can make as variable remuneration — their imagination will be limited only by their efforts, if at all.

Godrej credits the changed focus of the group for the turnaround of his Oleo chemical business, which has gone from making losses of more than Rs 75 crore and no exports four years ago, to making a profit of Rs 40 crore and exports worth Rs 120 crore this year. Another business to have benefited is the consumer products one, which went through very bad years after its fallout with P&G. According to Godrej, the changed fortune of GPCL has more to do with the initiatives than with any fundamental changes in the product portfolio. A framework that can assist companies in their quest for strategic competitiveness is the strategic management process, the full set of commitments, decisions and actions required for a company to systematically achieve strategic competitiveness and earn above-average returns. This process is illustrated in Figure.

FIGURE: Strategic Management Process

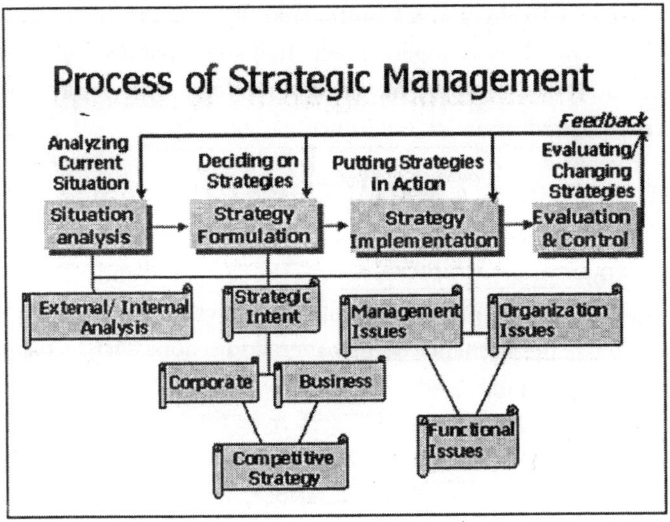

Figure above illustrates the dynamic, interrelated nature of the elements of the strategic management process and provides an outline of where the different elements of the process are covered in this text.

Feedback linkages among the three primary elements indicate the dynamic nature of the strategic management process: Situation Analysis, Strategy Formulation and Strategy Implementation.

Situation Analysis, in the form of information gained by scrutinising the internal environment and scanning the external environment, is used to develop the company's strategic intent and strategic mission.

Strategy Formulation is guided by the company's strategic intent and strategic mission, and is represented by strategies that are formulated or developed and subsequently implemented or put into action.

Strategy Implementation strategic competitiveness and above-average returns result when a company is able to successfully formulate and implement value-creating strategies that others are unable to duplicate.

Strategy Evaluation & Control links the elements of the strategic management process together and helps companies continuously adjust or revise strategic inputs and strategic actions in order to achieve desired strategic outcomes.

ESTABLISHING A MANAGEMENT INFORMATION SYSTEM

Information is a *critical resource* in the operation and management of organizations. Timely availability of relevant information is vital for effective performance of managerial functions such as planning, organizing, leading, and control. An information system in an organization is like the nervous system in the human body: it is the link that connects all the organization's components together and provides for better operation and survival in a competitive environment. Indeed, today's organizations run on information.

The term *information system* usually refers to a computer-based system, one that is designed to support the operations, management, and decision functions of an organization. Information systems in organizations thus provide information support for decision makers. Information systems encompass transaction processing systems, management information systems, decision support systems, and strategic information systems.

Information consists of data that have been processed and are meaningful to a user. A system is a set of components that operate together to achieve a common purpose. Thus a management information system collects, transmits, processes, and stores data on an organization's resources, programmes, and accomplishments. The system makes possible the conversion of these data into management information for use by decision makers within the organization. A management information system, therefore, produces information that supports the management functions of an organization (Davis & Olson, 1985; Lucas, 1990; McLeod, 1995).

BASIC CONCEPTS

Data versus Information

Data refers to raw, unevaluated facts, figures, symbols, objects, events, etc. Data may be a collection of facts lying in storage, like a telephone directory or census records.

Information is data that have been put into a meaningful and useful context and communicated to a recipient who uses it to make decisions. Information involves the communication and reception of intelligence or knowledge. It appraises and notifies, surprises and stimulates, reduces uncertainty, reveals additional alternatives or helps eliminate irrelevant or poor ones, and influences individuals and stimulates them to action. An element of data may constitute information in a specific context; for example, when you want to contact your friend, his or her telephone number is a piece of information; otherwise, it is just one element of data in the telephone directory.

Computers have made the processing function much easier. Large quantities of data can be processed quickly through computers aiding in the conversion of data to information. Raw data enter the system and are transformed into the system's output, that is, information to support managers in their decision making.

Characteristics of Information

The characteristics of good information are relevance, timeliness, accuracy, cost-effectiveness, reliability, usability, exhaustiveness, and aggregation level. Information is relevant if it leads to improved decision making. It might also be relevant if it reaffirms a previous decision. If it does not have anything to do with your problem, it is irrelevant. For example, information about the weather conditions in Paris in January is relevant if you are considering a visit to Paris in January. Otherwise, the information is not relevant.

Timeliness refers to the currency of the information presented to the users. Currency of data or information is the time gap between the occurrence of an event in the field until its presentation to the user (decision maker). When this amount of time is very short, we describe the information system as a *real-time* system.

Accuracy is measured by comparing the data to *actual* events. The importance of accurate data varies with the type of decisions that need to be made. Payroll information must be exact. Approximations simply will not suffice. However, a general estimate of how much staff time was devoted to a particular activity may be all that is needed.

Value of Information

Information has a great impact on decision making, and hence its *value is* closely tied to the decisions that result from its use. Information does not have an absolute universal value. Its value is related to those who use it, when it is used, and in what situation it is used. In this sense, information is similar to other commodities. For example, the value of a glass of water is different for someone who has lost his way in Arctic glaciers than it is to a wanderer in the Sahara Desert. Economists distinguish value from *cost* or *price* of a commodity incurred to produce or procure the commodity. Obviously, the value of a product must be higher than its cost or price for it to be *cost-effective.*

The concept of *normative value* of information has been developed by economists and statisticians and is derived from decision theory. The basic premise of the theory is that we always have some preliminary knowledge about the occurrence of events that are relevant to our decisions. Additional information might modify our view of the occurrence probabilities and consequently change our decision and the expected payoff from the decision. The value of additional information is, hence, the difference in expected payoff obtained by reduced uncertainty about the future event.

Information supports decisions, decisions trigger actions, and actions affect the achievements or performance of the organization. If we can measure the differences in performance, we can trace the impact of information, provided that the measurements are carefully performed, the relationships among variables are well defined, and possible effects of irrelevant factors are isolated. The measured difference in performance due to informational factors is called the *realistic value* or *revealed value* of information. For most information systems, particularly those supporting middle and top management, the resulting decisions often relate to events that are not strictly defined and involve probabilities that cannot be quantified. The decision-making process often is obscure and the outcomes are scaled by multiple and incomparable dimensions. In such cases, we may either attempt to perform a multiattribute analysis or derive an overall *subjective value.* The *subjective value* reflects people's comprehensive impression of information and the amount they are willing to pay for specific information (Ahituv, Neumann, & Riley, 1994).

Information as an Aid to Decision Making

Simon (1977) describes the process of decision making as comprising four steps: intelligence, design, choice, and review. The *intelligence* stage encompasses collection, classification, processing, and presentation of data relating to the organization and its environment. This is necessary to identify situations calling for decision. During the *decision* stage, the decision maker outlines alternative solutions, each of which involves a set of actions to be taken. The data gathered during the intelligence stage are now used by statistical and other models to forecast possible outcomes for each alternative. Each alternative can also be examined for technological, behavioural, and economic feasibility. In the *choice* stage, the decision maker must select one of the alternatives that will best contribute to the goals of the organization. Past choices can be subjected to *review* during implementation and monitoring to enable the manager to learn from mistakes. Information plays an important role in all four stages of the decision process. Figure 1 indicates the information requirement at each stage, along with the functions performed at each stage and the feedback loops between stages.

CLASSIFICATION OF MANAGEMENT INFORMATION SYSTEMS

There are various types of management information systems. Mason and Swanson (1981) describe four categories of management information systems: (1) databank information system, (2) predictive information system, (3) decision-making information system, and (4) decision-taking information system. The classification is based on the level of support that the information system provides in the process of decision making. Sachdeva (1990) comprehensively presents these four types of systems:

Databank Information System. The responsibility of this information system is to observe, classify, and store any item of data which might be potentially useful to the decision maker. Examples of the kind of data that might be recorded in such a database for a given village, region, or area are as follows:

- Number of farms
- Number of units of arable land (hectares, fedans, acres)

- Average farm size
- Amounts of selected farm inputs applied annually
- Production per year on a unit of land for selected crops

A second example of data that might be recorded in a database (this time involving data internal to the organization) is as follows:

- Number of extension staff by category and assigned to a particular village, region, or area
- Number of work hours devoted by staff to selected concerns for a particular village, region, or area
- Total extension salary costs and other expenses by village, region, or area
- Number of demonstrations conducted for selected farm technologies by village, region, or area
- Number of on-farm trials conducted for selected farm technologies by region or area
- Number of radio, TV, and print media releases regarding selected farm technologies by time period and region or area

Each of these databases can be summarized and converted to single tabular presentations of information of interest to management. When information from two or more time periods is compared, trends can be observed.

Predictive Information System. This system moves beyond pure data collection and the determination of trends over time. Predictive information systems provide for the drawing of inferences and predictions that are relevant to decision making. If data from the above examples were to be used in this way, it is possible to obtain information useful for making predictions or for drawing inferences. For example, tables containing the following information for a given village, region, or area might be produced:

- The ratio between the number of farms and the various categories of extension staff members
- The ratio between the amount of farmland and the various categories of extension staff members

- Amount of extension financial operating resources allocated per year to selected farmer problems or concerns
- Amount of extension financial resources, both salary and operating expenses, allocated per year to selected extension approaches to solving different farmer problems or concerns

Information obtained from these kinds of analyses is normally summarized in a two-way tabular format. And likewise, the information often is compared over time. Managers can then use such information to make predictions, for example to forecast costs of particular undertakings for budgeting purposes or as a basis for predicting results if a given change is made, such as change in the number of demonstrations with a given change in staffing.

Decision-Making Information System. This system goes one step further in the process of decision making and incorporates the value system of the organization or its criteria for choosing among alternatives. An extension organization's values are many and varied. They include concerns for resolving farmer problems, increasing and providing for stability of farmer incomes, and improving the quality of farm life. But they also including and providing for stability of farmer incomes, and improving the quality of farm life. But they also include an intent to provide well for staff members (training, adequate salaries, etc.) and to aid in the process of bringing about rural economic development. Information regarding these various attributes helps managers to make more enlightened decisions. Examples of ways that an extension organization uses information from a decision-making information system are as follows:

- Change in specific farm outputs (yields, practices) following selected extension activities
- Change in staff productivity following selected interventions (in-service training, better transport, etc)
- Comparison of relative costs and relative effectiveness of alternative extension delivery methods
- Analysis of economic returns to farmers who adopt recommended practices as compared to those who do not.

Table : Information Groups in India's Agricultural Extension System.

Levels	Groups	Types of Information Needed
Central	Extension commissioner, joint commissioners, directors, joint directors, etc. of the directorate of extension, ministry of agriculture	(1) Information on human resources, plans, and budgets for various extension services (2) Statewide monitoring and evaluation of activities completed
State	Director of agriculture, additional director, joint directors, etc. of the state department of agriculture	(1) Districtwide information on extension programmes, activities, expenditures, etc (2) Research-extension linkages and coordination with other allied departments such as animal husbandry and horticulture
District	District agricultural officers (DAOs)	(1) Information on extension resources and constraints at subdivision and block levels (2) Training requirements of staff at subdivision and block levels
Subdivision	Subdivisional agricultural officers	(1) Field demonstration programmes, activities planned and implemented by subject-matter specialists (SMSs) (zone) at the block level (2) Technical programme and constraints identified at the block level
Block (county)	Agricultural extension officers	(1) Performance of VEWs in terms of achievements in extension activities (2) Field-level problem of assessment of beneficiaries' response to various extension programmes

Decision-Taking Information System. Examples of decision-taking information systems are not usually found in an extension organization. This is a decision

system in which the information system and the decision maker are one and the same. Management is so confident in the assumptions incorporated in the system that it basically relegates its power to initiate action to the system itself. Airplanes carry automatic pilot systems, which are an example of a decision-taking system.

Once activated, the system itself keeps the plane on course and at the proper speed and altitude (according to parameters determined by the pilot). Another example of decision-taking information systems is found in modem factory production. In automobile production, continuous inventories of parts are maintained by computer as cars move down an assembly line. Orders are placed automatically by the computer when additional parts are needed. This is done without the intervention of a manager.

The choice of an appropriate management information system (MIS) category primarily depends on the nature of the decisions it supports. While unstructured decisions may use MIS-category (I), the highly structured ones, such as production schedules in an industry, may use MIS-category (iv). Further, Banerjee and Sachdeva (1995) observe that "as the deep structure of the decision problem becomes more and more understood, we may move to higher level of MIS i.e., from MIS-category (I) to MIS-category (ii); and MIS-category (ii) to MIS-category (iii); and so on."

ROLE OF MIS IN THE MANAGEMENT OF AGRICULTURAL EXTENSION PROGRAMMES

National agricultural extension systems, especially in developing countries, tend to be very large. For example, in India, the national agricultural extension system employs about 125,000 people. Extension managers at various levels need relevant information in order to make effective decisions. In the absence of such information, they act only on the basis of their intuition and past experience. Data that have been processed, stored, and presented properly will aid them in analysing situations and to make effective decisions.

As suggested above, at every phase of the management process, managers need information in order to make effective decisions. This we call *management information.* It does not include purely functional information or technical information, such as packages of practices for rice or wheat cultivation.

Management information is the information required by managers as they make their decisions, such as the number of extension personnel employed by category, their training requirements, career development plans, job descriptions, budgets, forecasts, benchmark surveys, reports on socioeconomic conditions of people served, and existing facilities (Ramesh Babu & Singh, 1987).

The main purpose of management information systems is to provide management information to decision makers at various levels in the organization. Specifically, in an agricultural extension organization, MIS is needed:

1. To plan the most effective allocation of resources, for example, the allocation of extension personnel under a T & V extension system, the need for communications and training equipment and facilities, mobility, the amounts of required operational resources
2. To choose between alternative courses of action, whether to conduct a study on the impact of the T & V system with the resources on hand or hire an expert to investigate
3. To control day-to-day operations, for example, comparing the actual results achieved and those planned under the T & V system.

DESIGN OF A MIS IN AN AGRICULTURAL EXTENSION ORGANIZATION

The following are suggested steps to follow when designing a MIS for a national agricultural extension system.

Step One: Assessing Information Needs for Planning, Monitoring, and Evaluation

An investigation needs to be conducted into the types of decisions that extension managers have to make. For example, village extension workers (VEWs) seek solutions to their problems from their supervisors. In turn, supervisors need to be in a position to resolve these problems and to document how problems were solved for future reference.

State-level managers also need information to resolve problems. They are concerned with implementing extension programmes district by district. They need information on staffing, transport, research-extension linkages, staff training activities, and successes (or lack of them) in solving technical problems. Feedback is needed from field staff and farmers on farmer problems and on which recommended practices are helpful. State-level managers need to know something about the amounts, kinds, and combinations of media support (i.e., print, radio, television) that have been used for various efforts. They need to know if external factors have limited the success of particular efforts such as supply of credit or farm inputs and they need some assessment of farmers' responses to extension programmes (Raheja & Jai Krishna, 1991, p. 84).

Step Two: Deciding the Levels of Information Groups, Information Frequency, and Content

The number of information groups within an agricultural extension organization has to be decided because each group potentially will require a different type of information. As an example, in India, the reorganized national agricultural extension system can be grouped as shown in Table 1.

Data processing consists of identifying each item of data and systematically placing it within a scheme that categorizes data items on the basis of some common characteristic or feature. Data not organized into a meaningful pattern can serve almost no useful purpose to those who must use them to make decisions. A computer can help in processing the data effectively. Rao (1985) suggested the use of computers in agricultural extension in India. He proposed that computer programmes be focused on district and subdivisional levels. In that way, information collected can be viewed in terms of the crops that are likely to be grown, agroclimatic conditions, soil types, irrigation facilities, resources of the farmers, and availability of various farm inputs.

Documentation (storage and retrieval) involves storing items of information in an orderly manner. Storing information means recording it on storage media from which it can be made available when needed.

Storage media are materials such as ordinary office paper, magnetic tapes, magnetic disks, microfilms, film strips, and a few other devices. Once the information is recorded on these storage media, the system can generate, on demand, information required for making decisions, solving problems, or performing analyses and computations. Information retrieval refers to the ability to take different types of data in the storage media and to array information in some desired and meaningful format. A properly designed storage and retrieval system matches the related variables efficiently and accurately. In some cases, it even suggests alternative courses of action for management to take.

Presentation of information should be in a form and format suitable to the needs of extension managers. Generally, information is presented in reports, statistical summaries, analyses, and so forth in the form of text, figures, charts, tables, and graphs. The presentation of information should be precise, clear, and appealing.

Step Three: Ensuring System Flexibility and Adaptability

Flexibility means the ability to retrieve information from a system in whatever form it may be needed by decision makers. Therefore, data need to be collected in some detail so that they can be rearranged or summarized according to the needs of managers. But system design should not be too complex because it must first serve the needs of the lowest levels of management (i.e., subdistrict) that are likely to be instrumental in collecting important components of the original data. In addition, the system also must serve the needs of the district, regional, state or provincial, and national levels. Therefore, considerable care must be taken in assessing what types of information are required by management at the different levels. At the same time, effort must be made to ensure that the information collected meets acceptable standards of accuracy, timeliness, and coverage for each level.

Need for automation

An automated MIS system contains data just as a manual system does. It receives input, processes input, and delivers the processed input as output. Some input devices allow direct human-machine communication, while others require data to be recorded on an input medium such as a magnetizable material (specially coated plastic flexible or *floppy* disks and magnetic tapes). The keyboard of a workstation connected directly to a computer is an example of a direct input device. Use of automation makes it possible to store immense quantities of information, to avoid many of the errors that find their way into manual records, and to make calculations and comparisons that would be practically impossible in a manual system.

Organization of a database

Data are usually generated at the field level through transaction-processing systems, but once the data are captured, any echelon along the organizational hierarchy may use them, provided that information requirements have been well defined, appropriate programmes have been implemented, and a means has been arranged for the sharing of the data. This would imply that the same data can be used by different sets of programmes; hence we distinguish between the database (a set of data) and the applications (a set of programmes). In a decision support system (DSS), this set of programmes is the *model base* (Keen & Morton, 1978). The term *database* may refer to any collection of data that might serve an organizational unit. A database on a given subject is a collection of data on that subject that observes three criteria: comprehensiveness (completeness), nonredundancy, and appropriate structure. Comprehensiveness means that all the data about the subject are actually present in the database. Nonredundancy means that each individual piece of data exists only once in the database. Appropriate structure means that the data are stored in such a way as to minimize the cost of expected processing and storage (Awad & Gotterer, 1992).

The idea of a large corporate database that can be flexibly shared by several applications or model bases has been realized by means of software packages specially devised to perform such tasks. These packages, called *database management systems* (DBMSs), are available in the market under different trade names such as ORACLE, SYBASE, INGRES, FOXBASE, and dBASE.

Networking and interactive processing

The two principal blocks that facilitate development and use of MIS are DBMS and *telecommunications*. The former makes data integration possible, while the latter brings information closer to the end users, who constitute nodes in a telecommunication network. The notion of telecommunications implies that some geographical distance exists between the computer site and the users' locations and that data are electronically transmitted between them. Remote applications may be executed between two floors in the same building, two offices in the same city, two offices on the same continent, or two places on opposite sides of the globe (Martin, 1990).

System alternatives and evaluation: Centralization versus decentralization

A completely centralized information system handles all processing at a single computer site, maintains a single central database, has centralized development of applications, provides central technical services, sets development priorities centrally, and allocates computer resources centrally. The system's remote users are served by transporting input and output data physically or electronically. A completely decentralized system may have no central control of system development, no communication links among autonomous computing units, and stand-alone processors and databases at various sites. Each unit funds its own information-processing activities and is totally responsible for all development and operation.

An advantage of centralized information systems is that they provide for standardization in the collection of data and the release of information. There also are some *economies of scale. A* centralized system reduces the need for multiple hardware, software, space, personnel, and databases. It may be possible to recruit more qualified personnel in a central facility.

Observations indicate that user motivation and satisfaction are increased under a decentralized environment. This is attained because users feel more involved and more responsible, systems are better customized to their specific needs, and they usually get better response time in routine operations as well as in requests for changes.

It is likely that for national agricultural extension systems, neither a completely centralized nor a completely decentralized system is desirable. While it may be useful to decentralize hardware and software resources at different locations, the development of applications and provision of technical services may better be centralized.

End-user computing

The widespread use of personal computers and computer-based workstations has brought with it the age of end-user computing. End-user computing is a generic term for any information-processing activity performed by direct end users who actually use terminals or microcomputers to access data and programmes. The manager as end user may be provided with powerful software (like DBMS) for accessing data, developing models, and performing information processing directly. This has brought computing directly under the control of the end users and eliminates their dependence on the information systems specialist and the rigidities of predesigned procedures. They may now make ad hoc queries of information and analyse it in various ways. They may write programmes, or may often use ready-made programmes stored in the computer, using the computing power of a local PC or the mainframe to which it is connected.

Illustrative computer-based MIS

A national agricultural extension system is a nationwide system managed by the national government. In India, agriculture is a state subject under the division of powers between the national and the state levels. Nevertheless, the national government supplements the financial resources of the states and provides coordination at the national level.

The state's administrative machinery is divided into districts, districts into subdivisions, subdivisions into blocks. A block is a group of villages and the basic unit for the administration of an agricultural extension programme. Data collected at the block level need to be integrated at higher administrative levels to provide an integrated view at the district and state levels to support planning, monitoring, and decision making.

However, the actual design may vary with the size of the state and other considerations. An integrated database for the entire state may be supported by a mainframe/minicomputer at the state headquarters. Suitable programmes for the analysis of data may be designed to provide an interactive decision support system at the state level. Each district and subdivision may be provided with a mini/micro computer, depending on the volume of data to be handled. The computers in the districts and subdivisions may be networked with the state computer.

The local data may be stored and processed in the district/ subdivision, and the shared data with appropriate level of aggregation may be transmitted to the state headquarters to update the integrated database. The districts and subdivisions would have direct access to the integrated database with proper authorizations assigned to them through their passwords. The blocks may have only the input-output terminals connected to the subdivision computer to feed data to the subdivision and make on-line inquiries as and when necessary.

Summary

In this chapter, we have defined and described the basic concepts of a management information system. The characteristics of good information, namely, relevance, timeliness, accuracy, cost-effectiveness, reliability, usability, exhaustiveness, and aggregation level, have been described. The role of information systems in the process of decision making and the value of information have been explained. Four types of MIS, namely, databank information system, predictive information system, decision-making information system, and decisiontaking information system, have been presented. The role of MIS in management of agricultural extension programmes and the conceptual design of a MIS in an agricultural extension organization have been described.

Basic computer concepts have been explained. The advantages and disadvantages of centralized versus decentralized systems have been examined. The need for organizing databases and their integration and the need for programmes for decision analysis to evolve a decision support system have been explained. An assessment of hardware, software, and networking requirements for a typical computer-based MIS for a national agricultural extension system have been illustrated.

STRATEGIC POSITIONING AND STRATEGIC MANAGEMENT

Strategic positioning is the positioning of an organization (unit) in the future, while taking into account the changing environment, plus the systematic realization of that positioning.

The strategic positioning of an organization includes the devising of the desired future position of the organization on the basis of present and foreseeable developments, and the making of plans to realize that positioning. The strategic positioning method is derived from the business world. The method is aimed at ensuring the continuity of the organization. The strategy determines the contents and the character of the organization's activities.

Terms, such as survival, legitimacy, market positioning, relationship with environment and choice for a certain work area, come up in this context.

Subjects which have been developed reasonably well in literature on strategic management include: information collection techniques, analysis techniques and planning schemes. Not or hardly developed are methods for exploring the future.

Various questions must be asked with strategic positioning:

- How does the future look like?
- How could the organization be roughly positioned in the future?
- How are things in the organization at present?
- How can opportunities be seized and how can threats be met?
- How can this be put into practice in a systematic way?

We will deal with the following aspects:

1. the future;
2. information collection;
3. analysis;
4. choice of strategy;
5. implementation.

The Future

Each futurology is based on the past and present. Whether the future is predicted from the flight of a flock of ducks, or from the way in which coffee grounds spread under a turned cup, or from thoughts of wise men: the waves of the future are always interpreted on the basis of the wavelets which are already visible in the present.

Trend research according to Naisbitt (shifts in the basically closed news circuit) is based on small shifts which announce future developments. If we can get hold of today's trends, we may perhaps extrapolate them into the future.

It is important for everybody to map the non-volatile developments which are relevant to the own organization. A first exploration of the strategic positioning can be constituted by extrapolating the trends and by gearing them to the field in which the own organization operates.

Information Collection

The steps to be taken are internal research and external research.

Internal research

Where does our organization stand? What internal factors are decisive for survival and for failure or success, both in a positive and in a negative sense? It is advisable to draw up a list of own relevant criteria, which are applicable to the branch you are working in.

This will help determine the strong and weak points of the own organization.

External research

What influences from outside can be of decisive importance to the realization of the organization's objectives? Or: what external critical factors are there?

Model lists of such factors are available but the organization should come up with its own relevant criteria, which do not only belong to the sector but also, for instance, to region-specific developments. This will help describe the opportunities and threats of the organization.

Future opportunities and threats are also mapped occasionally by making use of extrapolation (trend curves or mathematical models) or by consulting experts in a systemized way. Or by making one or more empirically founded, plausible constructions of the anticipated developments (scenarios).

Analysis

One can make an analysis of the strategic position by confronting the data of the internal and external researches with each other. An often used method is the SWOT analysis. Four lists of factors are drawn up: Strong Weak Opportunity and Threat. This is usually done in a group meeting of members of the organisation.

Another method is the Product/Market Matrix. Questions raised with this method are: Can you, departing from the existing product range, think of new applications (markets)? And can you supply markets where you are already on firm ground with a variation on your product? (Example: New Zealand sheep farms inventing a new application of wool at times of stiff competition on the wool market: absorption of oil spills at sea, being an existing product on a new market.)

A third method is the Portfolio analysis, which is derived from stock exchange operators wondering: "Which securities must we keep and which must we sell?". A specific portfolio is that of the Boston Consultants Group, which holds the investment or the growth of the branch of industry (Y-axis) against the profit or the market share (X-axis). Four fields then come into being: the stars, the milk cows, the wild cats and the dogs.

Note: for NGO's, the term profit has to be translated in the immaterial yield that should be derived: some distress that is eased; some social interest that is served. The instruments of strategic positioning are derived from business but are fit to serve NGO's as well.

Choice of strategy

On the basis of the analysis of internal and external critical factors - so, on basis of the estimated chances of seizing opportunities and meeting threats - the positioning will be determined. It would be quite nice to make a very specific positioning choice: we aim at becoming an organization which ..... (a description follows, by what the position choice is characterized, in terms of products, customers and image).

Once such a choice has been made, it should be studied what strategy is appropriate to realize that choice of position. In literature rough strategies are indicated, such as stabilization, growth, shrinking and turnaround. The organization can probably indicate much more specifically and accurately what strategy must be opted for. Growth in a certain direction, orientation towards a certain market, etc.

Implementation

The main thing of implementation is that, departing from the future positioning choice, theory is translated into what is to be done in order to realize that positioning.

Example of elements of a strategic plan

Business plan, for instance aimed at:

- internal growth: strengthening of the own position on the existing market;
- market penetration: introduction of products on new market;
- market development: new product on existing market;
- product development or diversification: new product on new market.

Product plan, selection of products or services, determination of their quality, effect of a product (result for customer).

Marketing plan, aimed at marketing mix: product policy, promotion policy, distribution policy and price policy (cost price/ market price/ competition price?).

Production plan, choice of location, choice of equipment and of the production process, production standards, layout. Production planning, production management, stock control, quality control, cost control, maintenance.

Research plan, technological innovation or product modification.

Personnel & Organization plan, positions, recruitment and selection, career development, organizational structure, training and education, organization culture, performance assessment, terms of employment, relationship with the representative advisory committee, organized consultations, trade unions, promotion policy.

Purchase plan, evaluation of suppliers, account management, make-or-buy.

Logistical plan, transport management, stock and handling, run-through times, term of delivery.

Financial plan, registration and evaluation of financial data, responsibility for availability of financing.

Information plan, gathering and processing of data.

Quality plan, consistency, competence, responsibility, accessibility, respect, communication, credibility, understanding, safety, appearance.

Public Relations plan, both internal (mission, propagation of business objectives, motivation of staff) and external.

Strategizing change and implementation of changes

The process of consulting is approaching its finish. Ideas are being transformed to operational plans.

Most of the time the process of change is described as if we are dealing with a fixed procedure and as if consultants are following the path of the theory: intake, dynamic analysis, recommendations, implementation. But life itself is more complex and chaotic.

Implementation of changes in an organisation can be compared with action research in investigation. The moment the consultant makes his or her appearance in the organisation, its reality starts to be influenced.

The mere announcement of change causes already changes.

The art of consulting is to push those changes in the desired direction.

Consulting is not dealing with a scientific determination of the effect of recommendations. The heart of the matter is bringing about feasible and effective changes.

So defined, implementation covers far more than carrying out recommendations in the last phase of a consultancy process. Other topics are also part of the process, like sensitizing the organisation for the problem at hand, strengthening the support for the recommendations and making the organisation susceptible for change. Implementation is an ongoing process, right from the start.

The core question of implementation is: how to use the energy, available in the organisation, in behalf of the realisation of the intended change.

E=KxA, effectivity and acceptation.

The famous formula: E=KxA is applicable: the effectiveness of the recommendation equals the quality of that recommendation multiplied by its acceptation.

The consultant/change agent considers the development of the acceptance as part of the job. Consultant who are blaming the organisation not being fit for their recommendations, those consultants will find the cynics on their hands, but will not manage to put the organisation in motion.

It can happen that an organisation turns out not being able to realize the consultants recommendations. Thinking in terms of action research: in such a case something in the recommendations will be deficient too. Probably the consultant has taken the role of the expert who has not taken into account the possibilities or capacities of the organisation.

Working on acceptation is the part of the process of implementation that always need attention. Because if the right breeding ground is available, the organisation probably had thought itself of a solution. The presence of a consultant indicates the need for help of an organisation in adjusting itself to a changing reality.

Some recommendations can be introduced top down, neglecting the level of acceptance. But such recommendations are rare. When the turning point of the change has to do with (the knowledge, attitude or skills of) people, an active support will be needed for a successful implementation.

Support and Energy

To change an organisation, passive support is not sufficient. What we need is active and dynamic support. Like said before: when the turning point of the change has to do with (the knowledge, attitude or skills of) people, it is not enough that people acquiesce in a new policy, structure or culture. People have to consider the change necessary, and they have to feel the need to support it.

Only then the change has a chance to be integrated in the realm of action. Such a support requires energy.

The energy-scan

Studying the ways an organisation tries to tackle problems (or how it was done in the past) can reveal the employment of energy of an organisation. Sometimes the organisation stresses the possibilities and chances and everyone is mobilised to think about solutions. Such an organisation has forward directed energy. Other organisations are primarily preoccupied with the threats and run the risk to get stuck in that phase. The energy is frozen. Some organisations put their energy in looking for the guilty ones or a scapegoat and keep themselves busy with the question: how could it happen? The energy has a backwards direction. Some organisations only want to be put in the right (I warned several times....)

The ways to cope with problems are not accidental nor incidental. The way an organisation directs its energy is comparable with the current of a river. It is not a choice, it is the resultant of the past. The direction of the stream creates the bed of the river which makes the same direction for the next time more probable. A consultant cannot just order another flow. The art of consulting is to use the common direction of the energy on behalf of the solution of the problem. Not only by placing the problem in the middle of the stream, but by joining the motion of the stream and using its force.

The change itself generates the motion.

Sometimes the intended change itself generates the energy for its realisation. The ideas ignite the enthusiasm of people and all that should be done is to use and direct the ebullition of energy. In some organisation such positive use of energy lies ready to be used. The work of the consultant is to think about ways to employ the energy. Sometimes an extra ignition is needed for a take-off speed to break away. Take-off ignition can be found for example in an opening conference or start-meeting that stimulates the existing energy and offers an approach to the problem, directed to solutions.

Sometimes it is necessary to temporarily evade structural obstacles in order to provide the process of a successful start. For that reason some organisations make use of a temporary infra-structure (a task force with a specific assignment and own channels of communications) by which blockages in the line -or in the communication- no longer are obstacles for the process of change.

How to join the motion.

The intended change not always finds a favourable breeding ground. Maybe the organisation has some energy, but that is being used for other purposes. The consultant could try to apply judo techniques: take advantage of the forces on behalf of the change. The most important activity for implementation in such a case is joining the motion.

The consultant should investigate by what kind of topics people tend to be mobilised. The next step is to join the change-topic to the existing stream of energy: i.e. to the mobilising-topic. This activity can be compared with the smart habits of the small white heron that pokes about in the presence of a cow, making profit of its abundance of food. Use the richness of energy of something else for your own purpose.

A smart energy-seeker always finds streams of energy that can be used.

A disadvantage of this strategy is its inevitable invisibility. If we should make the strategy visible, the change topic becomes visible. But that change topic is not able to generate enough energy under its own steam, otherwise it should be placed in the category above (the change generates the motion).

Joining the motion as a strategy can be used on content and process. For instance: the heron of the gender-approach can make use of for instance the energy of the cow: personnel policy or the quality policy (using another content). Or: the heron gender-approach makes use of the energy of the cow: lunch meetings (using another process).

Using the culture.

The consultant who is invited as a change agent often feels the existing culture as a major obstacle. An example: the organisational culture is procedure driven, while the core of the intended change is to turn the organisation towards an external orientation. Being driven by procedures is a sign of an internal orientation, so at first sight the assignment of the consultant seems to be to fight the existing culture. But organisational culture is never trivial and organisational culture is never composed of only useless elements. It is the task of the consultant to recognise those elements in the existing culture that can be used as materials for improvement.

For instance: we begin to look closer to what we called procedure driven. It turns out to be a summary of a variety of actions (habits): people are used to describe in detail whàt should be done before doing it, hòw it should be done, whò is doing what, in which order and whò will be responsible.

What could the consultant use this culture on behalf of the development of an external orientation??

For instance by organising a series of individual agreements (!) with members of the organisation in order to map out in detail (!) in which networks they participate. Those individual networks will be joined to one external map (!) of the organisation. In a general meeting it will be determined (!) which connections are missing and which should be used better. This common analysis (!) is followed by the precise distribution of tasks (!) and the planning (!) of agreements. To round it off the evaluation (!) is planned.

The consultant uses the existing stream of the culture and makes his or her own preference (for instance to celebrate the start of becoming external orientation with a tremendous party) of minor importance.

Ostentatious challenging the existing culture sometimes brings about admiration, but seldom success.

The impossible culture.

Using the culture (as the heron uses the cow) is not always possible. There are some organisational cultures which make a favourable turn impossible

An example is the organisational culture which is called: popular cynicism. In an organisation suffering from cynicism the people have given up the hope of improvement. In fact they are in a state of collective depression, which is not expressed in the blues. On the contrary, people seem to rejoice that things are rotten. There is a collective ambition to amuse each other with bitter jokes at the expense of the organisation.

An organisation in deep sombreness is a difficult but not impossible challenge for a consultant. Helping an organisation that amuses itself with its misery is well-nigh impossible. The reason for that is because the cynics have committed themselves to a certain attitude and each opening to improvement would strike at the roots of their certainties. People have to reject ideas for improvement because the risk of loosing one's footing is too big.

There are more examples of impossible cultures, but the consultant is not always empty-handed. It is important to explore quietly the spreading of the popular cynicism over the organisation. Is it really uniformly spread, or are there differences in the organisation? The outcome of such an exploration often is that it is only a minority that defines the expressions and the manners and that the majority would like to be hopeful, if they only dared.

The consultant should work with those people in small groups, avoiding for the time being plenary sessions in which the cynics set the tone.

How to make use of people: supporters, opponents and bystanders.

In a lot of change processes the consultant will detect three types of people in the organisation: supporters, opponents and bystanders. It is necessary to begin with the process of change with supporters. Even if the organisation proposes to compose a task force "in which also some critical people who are not in favour of changes" (in a sincere attempt to provide the consultant of a representative group) the consultant should choose for a group that feels like help thinking.

After a while the Help Thinking-group should deal with the question: how to reach the probably biggest group in the organisation, the bystanders, those people who sit on the fence. What could we do to make them enthusiastic?

By displacement of the enthusiasm to the middle group one could try to reach the opponents. In a successful process the opponents have sometimes simply disappeared. Sometimes they wait in the wings in case the project yet happens to fail. Sometimes they develop themselves into people with a positive critical function.

It is important for the consultant to realise that the question of failure or success is not decided by the supporters or the opponents, but that the critical mass is decisive. In a succeeding project the number of people who are joining in swells and at a certain moment it will pass a limit that makes the change inevitable.

Consultants should bear this in mind and should try to recognise this phenomenon, because opponents can have a massive negative effect on their energy and attention. One gruff man who is shaking his head in an audience that is generally enthusiastic, one such a person is able to absorb the energy of the speaker. We call this phenomenon the power of distraction. The consultant in the role as speaker should be aware of this phenomenon. A firm intention to direct the own energy towards the supporters and bystanders may help prevent this unbelievably annoying experience.

The use of necessity.

Generally spoken: the forces in an organisation always tend to continue the once taken direction. Even if the consultant is recruited on behalf of a desired change, even then the energy of an organisation will be directed primarily on continuation of what people were doing. Probably we are dealing here with a pattern of a social psychological nature. Though some experts' starting point is people liking change (as for instance Moss Kanter), the most common point of view is that an organisation is likely to show resistance to change.

The practise of change shows that the most successful changes are realised if a clear necessity for change is apparent. The more tight the link of the necessity is to the survival of the organisation, the more complete and quick will be the change of the organisation.

If the board of an health institution wants to integrate a gender approach in its treatment this will be easier accomplished when the institution has a fast growing number of female patients.

A new policy alone causes no organisational necessity. The change in the group of clients does. That is why consultants speak of a *workable necessity.*

Change and the sense of urgency

Realising changes in organisations requires investment in terms of time and money, but most important in terms of people's attention, reflection and energy to do things differently. Not everybody will accept the intended changes with the same level of willing. People are busy, are more or less content with the way things go or have other priorities. In other words: change is not happening only because someone says it should happen. People change (their habits or working methods) because they believe in the necessity. Because they feel the sense of urgency.

That sense of urgency is not equally clear for everyone in the organisation.

The crucial activity in change is to induce people to do things differently. In most cases this means also a change in organisational culture: in values and norms and in habits and working methods they once developed and agreed to. Culture is a powerful force in the organisation. If the intended change follows naturally the way people are used to do their job, then the characteristics of the organisational culture can be used completely. But if the intended change requires new cultural aspects, then the change will be more difficult to realise. Not because the workers are on beforehand unwilling, but because a change of the organisational culture will fail if it is only based on a declaration of intent. If compelling reasons to change are lacking, then a relapse in old habits is most likely.

Organisational culture can be considered as the personality of the organisation. Like in the case of someone's personality, one can change some aspects of behaviour, but structural changes are far more difficult to obtain and require deep investments. Far reaching changes are only feasible if people feel the urgency to change. (Comparable with psychotherapy: clients can only bear the burden of a therapy if they consider the burden of their suffering heavier.)

An example of a change like that is the change over to market oriented working methods, a process of conversion ıor a lot of institutions in the non-profit sector in Western countries. Being market oriented requires another attitude. Concepts like price quality ratio, measuring output or getting the targets are abominations to those workers in the non-profit sector who work with their clients (or on a topic) from a feeling of solidarity. Such workers can only be motivated to change their working methods if they have a sense of urgency, for instance because the survival of the organisation is at stake.

External necessity.

Far reaching changes need a clear external necessity. The management (or the change agent) has to make visible and perceptible that change is needed in order to survive.

Sometimes such an external necessity is clearly present. For instance because the subsidy is reallocated or finished, because the clientele is changing or because of an increase in complaints.

The making of necessity.

The existence of a necessity to change may be clear for the change agent, but sometimes it has to be made visible and perceptible for other people as well. Sometimes it is needed to look for changes in the outside world that can act as motivators for changes inside the organisation.

One way of doing it is *benchmarking*. Benchmarking is a method of investigation in which products or services are compared with those of another (peer or competitive) organisation. Benchmarking can reveal the (lack of) quality of the own organisation, in comparison to similar organisations. Such results can mean a threat for the future, certainly if competition will play an important role in the future. So benchmarking can help prove that performance should improve (in order to keep joining) and that it can improve (others can do it, so why don't we?)

Sometimes the external necessity is caused by *changes in the outside world*, may it be a threat or an opportunity.

Some institutions are able to change by seizing opportunities. An organisation for instance seizes the opportunities to change its profile thereby promoting the stream of a new segment of the market. Or an organisation develops in a relatively simple way a new supply and puts it on the market that seems ready for it (a training preventing work-stress for example).

Other organisations are more likely to be motivated by rising threats: aggressive competition, decreasing profits, threatening reduction. External threats, like increasing competition or decreasing subsidy are not always experienced as the most powerful motivating stimuli. The first reaction to such threats is rather anger, defence or paralysis. The skill of the change agent is to bend such (understandable) reactions to external threats towards a certain level of enthusiasm. For instance by showing that such a threat can offer new perspectives. For example: a situation of intensified competition offers the opportunity to concentrate more than before on the own core competence.

Finally: the urge for change can be underlined by pointing to relevant *trends and developments*. We mention some examples of trends that can stress the external necessity for the introduction of gender specific health care:

- *Individualisation*: clients increasingly expect care that corresponds to their specific interests and needs.
- *Emancipation nowadays belongs to the mainstream*: the last few years, problems of women and the way to understand those problems are convincingly related by the women movement to gender socialisation. As a result a lot of women came to see their own complaints and problems in a different light. (A Dutch example: before 1980 hardly any woman was seeking help because of sexual abuse. The percentage of women seeking help for that reason increased significantly after 1980, when the women movement brought to light that sexual abuse was a common problem.) Women are liberated and they expect from health care institutions that they have emancipated in a same degree.
- *Women in societal functions and positions*: slowly but surely women get higher positions. This brings new problems, for instance problems of burning out, double burden because of the combination of work and domestic care. Not only men but also women of forty year old land in a midlife crisis. This social upgrading causes gender specific complaints.
- *Increased freedom of choice*: people seem to have more and more choices. The path of life is no longer outlined at the moment of birth. The idea of freedom of choice (apart from the question if such freedom really exists) may intensify feelings of guilt. "It is my own fault, I went with him completely voluntarily.") Most people have indeed more choices, but the wealth of choices held out to them isn't within easy reach. The fact that one cannot realise one's wishes is more and more felt as a personal failure, while the real cause may lie in societal exclusion.

Resistance to Change

Resistance has many faces: open resistance, passive resistance, resistance in disguise. Resistance will bother the change agent, especially as the type of change (change of values or norms which need to be rooted in the behaviour of people) requires participation, active cooperation or even enthusiasm.

Resistance may show up in all phases of the change process. Resistance can be present at the start, when the necessity to change is investigated, if people do not enough accept or experience the necessity. Resistance will be painfully perceptible in the phase of implementation, when the objectives of change have to be translated to actual actions. And again: the more active participation plays a role, the more it will be difficult to deal with resistance. Changes, in which training and coaching of workers are crucial elements, can be fairly well obstructed by resistance. In other words: resistance can lead to a lack of support of those people who are at stake.

Expressions of such a lack of support go from passively waiting and negating the changes, via delay and misunderstandings, via impalpable sabotage to finally open opposition.

An obvious way to break resistance is to launch the intended changes more forcefully. But such a counter pressure leads often to intensified resistance. Something different has to be done.

The change agent has to begin to understand, decode and re-code the resistance.

A positive scheme of thinking about people implies that people want to change. If people in an organisation do not join the changes, then their natural willingness is blocked by something. Such a blockage can be a consequence of a lack of a feeling of urgence, a lack of wanting the change or a lack of capacity to change.

- The feeling of urgence: Someone will be willing to change if he or she really experiences the urge to change and if the people in the workplace have a positive attitude towards the change. Thus if the boss and the colleagues agree with the change or when they show some enthusiasm because of the change. The sense of urgency can be influenced by information on the actual performance of the organisation and the (future) demands.

- The will to change: Someone will be willing to change if (s)he is convinced of the positive results of the change and believes in the positive effects on the work and on the organisation. The will to change can be influenced by motivating.
- The capacity to change: Someone will be willing to change if (s)he is running the process of change her/him-self, as much as possible. Thus if someone can agree with the way the process is directed, if money and time are supplied, if the involvement is as big as possible and if the complexity of the change can be overlooked. Good experiences with previous changes can be helpful.

The capacity to change can be influenced by a high degree of participation.

The change agent will be able, with he help of this decoding key, to investigate the willingness to change and to predict the presence of resistance.

Questions:

- Which consequences for the work do the workers expect of the intended change?
- What kind of emotions are evoked by the intended change?
- Are the workers convinced of the positive effects of the change?
- Are they involved in the process of change?
- What is the attitude of others (management, colleagues) towards the change?
- What is the experience of the workers with previous changes?
- Have the workers enough time and other means to their disposal, in order to realise the change successfully?
- Is the process of change well-directed guided?
- Do the workers consider the change complex?
- Is the process of change at the right moment?

Wanting to (motivation), having to (urge) and being able to (capacity) are three necessary ingredients for a successful implementation.

A combination of presence and absence of those three ingredients can lead to specific problems:

- Motivation OK, but no capacity: frustration. Solution: training.
- Motivation OK, but no urge: delay. Solution: anticipatory experiments.
- Urge OK, but no motivation: reactive attitude of personnel. Solution: motivation.
- Urge OK, but no capacity: paralysis. Solution: capacity building
- Capacity OK, but no motivation: nothing happens. Solution: create take-off energy
- Capacity OK, but no urge: everything waits till the market forces a change. Solution: look for other urge.

The urge (to have to change) is the crucial element at the start and the decision making of the change process. Action: mobilise.

The motivation (wanting to change) is important in the phase of acceptation. Action: negotiate, coach and convince.

The capacity (being able to change) is crucial in the phase of implementation. Action: support, plan and simplify.

Resuming:

- do ask yourself if the resistance can be understood as deficits in the willingness to change
- check in which phase the process of change is
- think if actions are possible that will cover fully the (decoded) diagnosis of the resistance.

Trends

The American author John Naisbitt has developed a method for gaining an impression of future developments. This is based on a content analysis of a large amount of print media. The news segment of the newspaper is a closed system. For economic reasons the relative amount of space for news (relationship between advertising and news) changes little in the course of time. If a topic is added, something else has to be left out.

By keeping careful track of the new and the omitted topics, we can in a certain sense get a picture of the changing market share of competing social aspects.

Naisbitt's content analysis makes use of a monthly evaluation of 6,000 local newspapers. The shifts he reveals in this manner, he refers to as *trends* or *megatrends*.

Trends appear gradually, fads are faster and less long-lasting, they have more to do with fashion. Trends are massive shifts in what is regarded as important by public opinion, regardless of their "objective" importance.

In his book Naisbitt gives impressive examples of the operation of trends. He points out, for instance, that interest in drugs in the news has dropped dramatically in the past ten years, although the problem itself has become progressively greater. In other words, there is no relationship between the attention the topic receives and its objective or "real" importance.

Another example from Naisbitt: in the sixties the "space" for discrimination was filled with worries about racism; in 1969 sexism began to appear in the columns. By 1975 half the space was devoted to racism and half to sexism. From 1977 onwards these topics lost out to increasing concern about discrimination against older people. In the end, two-thirds of the space for discrimination was filled with reports about the problems of "ageism" and the remaining third was shared by racism and sexism. However, as soon as the US Congress raised the age of compulsory retirement in industry from 65 to 70 and abolished the limit for the public sector, stories about age discrimination began to decrease.

Naisbitt wrote *Megatrends* in 1982 and *Megatrends 2000* in 1990. His first book was concerned with the following trends, which, in his view, "shaped the eighties":

1. From an industrial society to an information society
2. From imposed technology to technology processing
3. From a national economy to a world economy
4. From short term to long term
5. From centralisation to decentralisation of power
6. From welfare to self-help
7. From representational democracy to direct democracy
8. From hierarchies to networks
9. From north to south
10. From limited choice to multiple choice

Megatrends 2000 is about the last ten years prior to the 21st century. In that decade, the "most important trends that affect our lives" are, according to Naisbitt:

1. The explosive development of the world economy
2. A renaissance in art
3. The rise of free market socialism
4. Global lifestyles and cultural nationalism
5. The privatisation of the welfare state
6. The rise of the Pacific Rim countries
7. The decade of women at the top
8. The age of biology
9. The religious revival in the third millennium
10. The triumph of the individual

The most all-encompassing trend playing a role in social developments in a large part of the world is Naisbitt's number ten, individualisation. Many "sub-trends" derive from this: quality, success, emancipation of the citizen, etc.

It can be useful for an organisation to research which trends are important to its own field of operation. What are the non-trivial developments which can be derived from trends. And to what extent does a development bring opportunity or danger.

3

Strategic Management in Newspapers

Daily newspapers have become an integral part of our life. On any given weekday, more than 65.6 million newspapers will be printed and read in the United States and Canada. More than 109 million people will read one newspaper and many will read two or more. Seventy percent of all adults read a newspaper "yesterday." Those people who didn't read a newspaper yesterday will most likely see one

before the week is over. In the last five days, 89 percent of adults 18 years and older have read a newspaper.

Newspapers function as a unique and vital force in the daily lives of millions of Americans. They provide the facts and analysis that allow informed citizens to make effective and responsible decisions, not only in coping with the complexities of modern living, but also in protecting the rights and liberties of a free society. Each day more than 100 million people rely on newspaper professionals to provide accurate, timely, and useful information to help them plan their daily lives; to advise, instruct, educate, challenge and entertain.

To fulfill their mandate in a free society, newspapers must remain strong and independent institutions, free to express their views and opinions without political or economic coercion or restraint. Economic strength and constant vigilance are vital to the maintenance of such independence. Newspapers remain economically sound despite the challenges of new technology, changing life styles and the economic evolutions of recent years.

The first newspaper published in the United States was Benjamin Harris ' Publick Occurrences Both Foreign and Domestick. It was printed in Boston on September 25, 1690. This venture was soon suppressed by the governor of Massachusetts and his council because the "paper contained certain reflections of a very high nature and was printed without the required license."

It was unfortunate that this first attempt at newspaper publishing in our country was killed because Harris had lofty ideals and promised that his newspaper's purpose would be, in part, to help people comprehend the "Circumstances of Publique Affairs," so as to assist their businesses and negotiations. Harris also planned to publish his newspaper with businesslike regularity and continuity.

A man far different from Benjamin Harris succeeded in starting a newspaper in April 1704 that was "printed by authority" and continued for 15 years. His name was John Campbell, a cautious promoter who named his newspaper the Boston News-Letter. The eighteenth century was a time of growing maturity, complexity, and more of everything: trade, money, migrants, schools, churches, roads, and books. Such an age could support newspapers: from 1719 to 1783 no fewer than 67 publishers started newspapers, and more than 30 newspapers survived to the time of the Revolution in 1776.

Other newspapers that followed included the New England Courant, begun in 1721 by James Franklin who employed his brother, Benjamin, in his printing shop. The first newspaper outside Boston was Andrew Bradford American Weekly Mercury, founded in Philadelphia in 1719. Andrew's father, William Bradford, started the first New York paper, the Gazette, in 1725. Benjamin Franklin published the Pennsylvania Gazette from 1729 to 1766. The first daily newspaper in America, the Pennsylvania Evening Post and Daily Advertiser, began in 1783 in Philadelphia. At the outbreak of the Revolutionary War, there were 35 newspapers being published in the colonies. The first published west of the Appalachian Mountains was the Pittsburgh Gazette in 1786. The Alexandria Gazette (Virginia), published daily since 1797, is one of the oldest continuously published U.S. dailies. A small, 80-cent classified advertisement appeared in the Chicago Daily News on April 1, 1887. It read: Watch-maker wanted — With references, who can furnish tools. State age, experience and salary required. Address T-39 Daily News. When Richard Sears needed an assistant and Alvah Roebuck answered the ad and was hired, the world's largest retailer, Sears, Roebuck & Company, was born. It all started with a small advertisement in the newspaper and today Sears spends more than $417 million a year in newspaper advertising to perpetuate that small beginning.

Along with the news that binds a community, a nation, or the world together, newspapers have always carried the advertisements that account for the livelihood of individuals and turn the wheels of commerce. In the November 20, 1776 issue of the same Essex Journal which carried the account of Washington's defeat at the battle of White Plains and reported his army as being driven from Manhattan Island, this advertisement appeared: "A pig came to the farm of the subscriber about eight days ago, supposed to be about three months old. The owner may have him again by proving his property, paying the charges and applying to Samuel Emery of Newbury." The Pennsylvania Packet of September 22, 1786 featured an article reporting the recommendation of John Dickinson, Alexander Hamilton, and James Madison that Congress call a federal convention to strengthen the Articles of Confederation leading to a new Constitution. It also contained this advertisement: "Mr. Cenas takes this method to acquaint his friends and the public that he means to be in Philadelphia about the end of September and will open his Dancing School on the 3rd of October, from nine in the morning till one for Ladies and from four till nine for Gentlemen."

Newspaper employment continues to rank among the leaders of the nation's largest manufacturing employers. Revised Department of Labor statistics show an increase of 2,900 newspaper employees, from 421,900 in 1981 to 424,800 in 1982. Daily newspaper circulation increased to 62.4 million, more than 1 million above 1981 totals.

Newspaper advertising climbed to more than $18.3 billion, leading all major media with a 27.3 percent share of total advertising revenues. Daily newspapers totaled 1,710 in number. There were 433 morning, 1,311 evening, and 34 "all day" newspapers. Sunday newspaper totals reached a new high of 768, with circulation of more than 56.1 million.

The number of weekly newspapers was 7,626, with total circulation of 44.3 million. The average weekly newspaper circulation was 5,808. Newsprint consumption as reported by all users was 10.1 million metric tons, with daily newspaper consumption estimated at 7.7 million metric tons, more than 76 percent of the total. Newspapers are good business, too. In recent years in the nation's stock markets, newspaper stocks have outpaced the Dow Jones average consistently. That's why publishers last year alone invested $805 million in new equipment and plants. For the past five years, this amounts to over $3 billion. This involves new printing processes such as offset presses and full- color processing equipment, and satellite transmission of news and advertising matter. The reporter writes the story and the person in the classified phone room actually sets the type that goes in the paper. They type into a video display terminal tied into a computer which hyphenates and regulates column width by driving the typesetting machines. Linotypes and their five column lines a minute of hot type have been replaced by cold type, photographically set at up to 1800 lines a minute.

Because computer typesetting does not have to be rekeyed by a mechanical worker, but goes directly from the writer to the finished typesetting, large numbers of mechanical employees are no longer required and cost savings have been effected. This allows publishers to engage more editorial employees for specialized writing to create a far more interesting product keyed to the local community.

The old "morgue" is now a computer data bank with instantly retrievable information. Offset presses produce higher quality newsprint, on the least expensive of all papers. Newspapers require large numbers of people because of the near round-the-clock deadline nature of the product. They deal with large numbers of news sources, advertisers, and subscribers. Had publishers not been able to replace the plodding high-labor oriented, low-efficiency mechanical hot-type process with the high-speed, computerized cold-type system, the cost of newspapers for both subscriber and advertising would be out of sight. Soon full-page pagination will enable newspapers to make up the entire page including all editorial, illustrations, photographs, and advertisements on a video screen, moving elements by use of a computer. There will not be any actual type either metal or photographic, only characters displayed on a tube. By these huge investments and new techniques, newspapers are and will likely remain the cheapest way to get a large amount of information out to a mass audience.

Many newspapers are producing a weekly section delivered by carrier or mail to nonsubscribers. This is generally referred to as TMC or total market coverage. Thus, virtually every home can be reached in the newspaper's circulation area either by the regular subscriber product and/or a zoned edition going to subscribers, or a nonsubscriber section going to the full-circulation area or specific neighborhood zones within the overall circulation region.

And, newspapers are distributing pre-prints either by full circulation territory or by neighborhood zones. Pre-prints are full advertising sections printed in advance either by the newspaper or an outside printer, sometimes on a nationwide basis for a single store and inserted into the newspaper. They can go to all or part of the newspaper's subscribers or, if the paper has a nonsubscriber product, they can be inserted and distributed with it.

Another current advance in the industry is standardization of sizes. Until recently national advertisers were required to make up an ad in several different sizes to match the many column widths or page lengths. Now advertisers can buy standard advertising units (SAUs). There are at least 57 standard-sized units from which an advertiser can select. Well over 90 percent of the nation's dailies will be able to print it exactly the same size.

THE "BEST" NEWSPAPERS

Adweek, a journalism and telecommunication trade magazine, published a special report in April 1984 listing the best newspapers in the United States as picked by the following diverse panel of specialists:

David Cole, systems editor, San Francisco Examiner and former editor, Feed Back, the Northern California journalism review

Scott M. Cutlip, university professor of journalism and former dean of the School of Journalism, University of Georgia

Osborn Elliott, dean of the Columbia University Graduate School of Journalism and former editor of Newsweek

Everette Dennis, dean, University of Oregon School of Journalism

Jeff Greenfield, political analyst and media critic, ABC News

Daryl Moen, chairman, department of news-editorial, University of Missouri School of Journalism, Columbia

Ron Powers, media critic/commentator, CBS News

George Reedy, Neiman Professor of Journalism, Marquette University, Milwaukee

David Rubin, chairman of the Department of Journalism, New York University

Norman Sandler, White House correspondent, UPI

Paul E. Schindler Jr., Computer Systems News David Shaw, media critic, Los Angeles Times "a prominent industry observer" 8The list they picked in order of preference is as follows:

1. The New York Times
2. The Washington Post
3. Los Angeles Times
4. The Wall Street Journal
5. The Miami Herald
6. The Philadelphia Inquirer
7. The Boston Globe

8. Newsday
9. Chicago Tribune
10. (tie) The Milwaukee Journal
10. (tie) Christian Science Monitor

Not to be outdone, Time magazine published its own list of the "ten best U.S. dailies" also in April 1984. The Time list, it is assumed, was picked by its own panel of editors. Time published its list alphabetically with no order of preference. It is interesting to note that both lists are quite similar. Adweek lists Newsday, The Milwaukee Journal and Christian Science Monitor, which were not found in the Time list, and Time lists the Des Moines Register and St. Petersburg Times, which were not found in the Adweek list. It should be noted that both of the above lists rate newspapers according to editorial excellence and do not take into consideration the business success or failure of any of the newspapers. However, as Mrs. Katharine Graham, chairman of the Washington Post Com-pany has said on several occasions, it is almost impossible for a publication to be editorially excellent without enjoying success on the business side.

John J. Meskil, executive vice-president, media and administration, Warwick Advertising, states that 1984 was a year of golden opportunity for newspapers. Following are his viewpoints in the April 1984 issue of Marketing and Media Decisions: The newspaper industry is making a concerted effort to' obtain more advertising from national accounts.

But the question arises, can newspapers really hope to increase their national business and if so, how can they accomplish this? Currently, newspapers receive about 8 to 10 percent of their business from National Accounts and 90 percent plus from local and classified advertising. Looking at this disparity one might ask, why should the newspapers care if they increase their national business since it represents such a small percentage of their total lineage? The answer to this is that national business is considerably more profitable than retail business. According to a recent 4A study, national advertisers pay 60 percent more than local advertisers for comparable space, so this is the area that newspapers would like to see their growth come from. 1983 was a good year for newspapers. Local ad spending increased with the ending of the recession and should continue this growth to an even greater degree in 1984. National business has been steady or declining but I can't remember a year in the past decade when newspapers were better situated to funnel national advertising dollars into the medium. There are many reasons for my optimism:

- Newspapers have changed their look and their style of editing to appeal to a broader reader target. They can't fight television for instant news and they finally have begun to realize that. Color is being used more widely. USA Today has shown a good many publishers how attractive a newspaper can be by liberal use of color.
- For years, national advertisers have suffered through production problems. Sizes varied considerably from paper to paper, costing the advertiser considerable sums of money to meet each paper's requirements. A few years ago we thought we had finally solved the problem with the introduction of SAUs. But this failed miserably when only 49 percent of the papers cooperated.

Currently, newspapers have some 439 different ad sizes, but in July, this is all supposed to change. Dailies in the top 100 markets are expected to adopt the system of a standard newspaper page and depth measurement of inches rather than lines. This will eliminate lateral "float" and should eliminate production problems in these major market newspapers. This time I believe the newspaper industry will follow through with their decision, thus making the medium easier and less expensive to use. There are several other factors which will enable newspapers to attract the national advertisers that have not heretofore been available:

- New research studies by SMRB and Scarborough which provide extensive demographic data in the top markets. The new studies confirm what we already assumed that newspaper readers are more upscale than television viewers and purchase a higher proportion of goods and services.

- Of perhaps greater importance, the studies show larger readership than even the newspaper industry imagined: approximately 2.7 readers per copy. Previously, if the newspapers were given 2.0 readers per copy by agencies, they considered it generous.
- Newspapers will be easier to compare with other media. The Newspaper Advertising Bureau has published a new booklet that is quite useful which translates newspaper readers into television rating points. If you don't have a copy, I suggest you contact the NAB and they'll be

happy to send you one.

- Television is sold out in almost all dayparts through the first half of the year, and even into the third quarter for news and daytime. Although I don't believe that newspapers can successfully sell against television as a replacement for national advertisers, they cannot help but benefit from this unusual condition. Advertisers will be looking to spend some of their advertising dollars that they could not place on television, and newspapers can be a valuable alternative. Like television, when you advertise in newspapers you get immediate response. Because of their timeliness and daily readership, advertisers can use newspapers to heavy up during critical sales periods for their brands.

If newspapers can prove to these advertisers that their sales were increased by this mix of television and newspapers, they should be able to retain some of this business if and when television returns to a "normal" sales pattern. In my opinion, the remainder of 1984 represents a golden opportunity for newspapers. Finally, I sense a "feeling" among newspaper publishers that they are willing and anxious to change the poor image they have among many agencies and national advertisers. They have a perfect opportunity to sell accounts that they have heretofore not developed. They can broaden the type of accounts that normally might not have considered newspapers; accounts such as computers, new electronics technology and cable. Ironically, I suspect newspapers will get more business over the next few years from cable advertisers hoping to increase audience than cable takes away from newspapers. The key ingredient in newspapers' ability to attract national accounts is "sales." They must make a concerted effort to convince the advertising community that they really want national business and will make concessions to obtain it. They're off to a good start.

CIRCULATION

Nothing can take the place of the intimate local contact enjoyed by a great newspaper. This was eloquently summed up in a piece of writing done by Frank Tripp, former chairman of Gannett Company, Inc.: When any medium other than the newspaper delivers all the world and neighborhood news in detail; ballyhoos local charities and civic endeavors to successful conclusions; borns the babies, graduates them, marries them; and buries them. . . . When it becomes the permanent record of current events; the date book of the community, the housewife's shopping guide; recovers the neighbor's dogs; sells their attics empty; finds them a used refrigerator; tells them who's sick, dead, engaged and married; who's painted his barn or mended his fences . . . then . . . I'll believe that some folks may not have time to read their hometown paper. Circulation in the newspaper business is the distribution of the newspaper to its readers. It is the number of newspapers sold and paid for through various sales methods. The most important are single-copy sales, mail distribution, and home delivery. No matter how excellent the editorial product of the newspaper may be, its advertising revenue will be nonexistent if the newspaper is not sold and read. Circulation departments are becoming more and more vital to a newspaper's operation and are now accounting for 25 to 30 percent of newspapers' total revenue.

4

THE NEWSPAPER INDUSTRY

Newspaper making in the United States is in its third phase. In its first stage, it was carried on by journeymen printers like James and Benjamin Franklin who operated general printing establishments. Next, it became a profession in which editors exercised varying degrees of public influence and power, depending upon their abilities and opportunities. Few of the printer- journalists profited financially from their publications, and the editor-journalist who made money from his venture was, undoubtedly, the exception rather than the rule. As a matter of fact, many of these editors regarded money matters or counting-room affairs, as they called them, as being somehow beneath their dignity.

Greeley made the New York Tribune profitable, but chiefly for others. Raymond and Jones nursed the New York Times into a valuable property, but under their immediate successors its value greatly diminished. The classic example, of course, is that of the elder Bennett who in 40 years ran the aggressive if uncertain Herald from an initial outlay of $500 into a property worth a fortune. In a way, it was not until Pulitzer, Hearst, and Scripps showed what could be done that the business possibilities of newspaper management were widely realized and publishers began to put newspaper properties generally upon a sounder business basis.

In its present phase, newspaper making in America is a billion-dollar industry. As Colonel Frank Knox, publisher of the Chicago Daily News, expressed it, the newspaper has ceased to be literary and has become commercial. This does not mean that it has surrendered or abandoned its editorial function or possibilities. On the contrary, the greater independence made possible by this transition has strengthened the newspaper editorially and made possible the production of better newspapers. This has enhanced the newspaper's influence and enabled it to serve its readers, its advertisers, and the community at large better than ever before.

Big Business. In a very real sense, newspaper making, as it is now conducted, is a manufacturing process. It is, moreover, a complicated one. The raw material consists of two, and frequently three, things: news, including editorial opinion; features; and advertising. The news is gathered and processed by the editorial department. Features are usually bought from syndicates and are intended to build and hold circulation. The advertising, both display and classified, is collected and serviced by the advertising department. The actual production is completed by the mechanical department, and the finished product is the printed newspaper. Its distribution or marketing is handled by the circulation department.

Newspaper making has become an industry requiring a high degree of technical skill as well as a business that calls for a large outlay of capital. News itself is one of the most perishable commodities in the world. Nothing is more stale than yesterday's news, whether it be intelligence or advertising. In few other lines of activity do the minutes count for so much. Few other kinds of enterprise equal the newspaper business in intensity of competition or in the directness of its dependence upon public acceptance. Good will is vital to its success, yet is so fragile and intangible, that bad judgment or unsound or unpopular policies can ruin it almost overnight.

As a result of such conditions, newspaper publishing is a hazardous undertaking. This fact has been recognized by the United States government in its definition of what constitutes a fair return upon capital invested in the industry. As a further result, the newspaper industry in the United States is fairly well stabilized as regards the number of newspapers in operation. In recent years there has been relatively little change in the number of newspapers, and the tendency has been in the direction of fewer and better newspapers. This has been especially marked in the case of mergers and in the development of chain or group newspapers.

Newspapers in Transition. No other nation has witnessed such a swift and startling transition in its newspapers. This may be illustrated in various ways. One hundred twenty-five years ago, for example, not one daily newspaper in the United States had attained a circulation of 1000, and, in fact, few % of them exceeded 600. About the time of the outbreak of the Civil War, there were fewer than 400 daily newspapers for a nation of approximately 31,500,000 people. 1 Yet their combined circulation, despite the current activity, influence, and following of men like Greeley, Bennett, Raymond, and Dana, was less than that of the New York News alone in 1934.

Another phase of the transition is exemplified in the case of Chicago. In 1890, when the city had a population of about 1,100,000 it had 11 newspapers, or one for each 100,000 population. Today, with more than 3,000,000 population, it supports five newspapers of general circulation, two of them morning and three of them afternoon publications, or an average of one for each 600,000 population. Chicago is much better served today by far better newspapers than it was then. Examples of this sort of change can be found in all parts of the country.

As a business medium as well as a social force, the newspaper has outlasted every kind of competition and has strengthened its position in so doing. In point of both circulation and advertising linage, the newspaper has more than held its own against magazines. Under the stress of economic depression, the newspaper, like practically all other media, lost some ground in both directions but not nearly to the extent that magazines did, as will be shown. The newspaper has likewise held its ground against the radio both as an advertising medium and as an agency for the dissemination of news. The growth of the radio as an advertising medium, measured in terms of national advertising, has been chiefly at the expense of media other than the newspaper, such as magazines, car cards, and outdoor forms of advertising.

Americans probably read more newspapers per capita than do the people of any other nationality. Newspaper reading is both a necessity and a habit and as such can be cultivated. The 25 years following 1900 witnessed extensive cultivation of the field with the result that circulations of American newspapers soared. Between 1900 and 1931, the net change in the number of daily newspapers published in the United States was less than 10 per cent, but the total newspaper circulation tripled. Since the increase shown was far out of proportion to the change in population, the conclusion is inescapable that it was due to cultivation of the newspaper habit, which in turn was partly the result of promotion and partly a natural growth. This is supported by the fact, reported by Dr. Alfred McClung Lee in the Golden Jubilee number of Editor & Publisher in 1934, that " while 9.7 per cent of persons 10 years of age and older bought daily papers in 1880, the average has hovered for 10 years well above 40 per cent." This means, in effect, that American consumption of newspapers in terms of the potential number of readers has quadrupled.

CHAINS AND MERGERS

Mergers and the development of news- paper chains have been two of the marked trends in American newspaper ownership and operation in recent years. These have led in turn to fewer newspapers and to an increasing number of cities where one newspaper has a monopoly. Along with other developments these have helped to emphasize the business aspects 'of journalism. These tendencies have been much more marked in the case of daily than of weekly newspapers.

The 1936 Editor & Publisher Yearbook listed 59 newspaper chains in the United States, and 4 in Canada. In the United States, about 350 daily newspapers were owned or operated by these chains. Their numbers are less impressive than their circulation which accounts for about Iralf of the total evening and Sunday newspaper circulation in this country and nearly as large a proportion of the morning circulation. The amazing growth of the chain idea and of the resultant groups is shown by the fact that at the turn of the century there were not more than 10 such groups in the United States, controlling a total of 31 newspapers. The largest were Hearst with 6 newspapers and the Scripps- McRae League with 4, besides 4 other Scripps papers on the West Coast. As late as 1923 there were only 30 chains, comprising some 150 dailies.

In point of the number of newspapers they contain, the present groups include Scripps-Howard with 24 newspapers; Hearst, 25; General Newspapers, Inc., 18; Ira C. Copley Newspapers, 13; and Frank E. Gannett Newspapers, 17. In order of total circulation, the Hearst papers are first; the Chicago Tribune-

New York News, owned principally by the Medill heirs, second; and the Scripps-Howard papers, third. In policies and methods of operation these chains vary greatly, just as they do in size and in value. It would be difficult to estimate the combined value of these groups as going concerns, but just a glance at their combined circulation is enough to show that the total must ran into several hundred million dollars. It is perhaps too early to forecast their ultimate total effect upon the American newspaper industry but they are already making their influence felt with respect to business policies and operating methods.

CRITICISMS AND REBUTTAL

Competitors and other critics have sought to attach a sort of stigma to the chain-newspaper idea.

They argue that there is no essential difference between a chain newspaper and a chain grocery or drugstore or a filling station or any other retail business owned by outsiders and operated as a unit of a group. They contend that such a newspaper can never have local interest really at heart and that the primary motive behind its operation is to make more and still more profits for an absentee owner. They insist that the chain newspaper is inevitably less of a newspaper and more of a common business enterprise.

To all of these objections, the proponents of the chain-newspaper idea have an answer. They admit that occasional owners of groups of newspapers may operate them chiefly or even wholly for profit, but so do at least some individual newspaper owners.

They hold that the chain ownership of a newspaper need make no fundamental difference with the real function of the publication. They point out that the benefits of good management of one newspaper property can be extended to others in the interests of better as well as more profitable newspapers. They cite particularly the economic advantages of group ownership and operation.

The truth is that there is nothing inherently wrong in the chain idea itself. The faults, if any, lie with the human element which utilizes it. There are, unquestionably, good chains, beneficial from the standpoint of enlightened operation as well as profitable in the money sense.

If the ownership is at fault, on the other hand, there is no question but that the evils of vicious or selfish individual operation can be compounded to the detriment of all the cities represented in the group. Sound and wise application of the principles of chain ownership, including large measures of local autonomy and deliberate cultivation of local interests, has been the rule rather than the exception. After more than 50 years, there is no question but that group ownership is a permanent part of the American newspaper picture.

The tendency to mergers has gone hand in hand with the trend toward chain ownership. In Pittsburgh, for example, there were seven dailies not so many years ago. Today there are only three, all of which, curiously, are chain newspapers. And yet there is no serious complaint that the community interests of Pittsburgh are improperly served, nor is there any indication of a movement to establish a home-owned paper.

NEWSPAPER MONOPOLIES

This tendency has left in its wake an increasing number of towns and cities where there is only one newspaper which thus enjoys a local monopoly for all practical purposes. If a newspaper with such a monopoly is operated wisely, more with an eye to the public interest than to maximum profits, it is not likely to be disturbed in the enjoyment of that monopoly. But if a paper loses sight of its primary function, neglects its responsibilities, ignores its opportunities, and squeezes the last dollar out of its customers, it is inviting both competition and disaster.

As in the case of chain ownership, there are two sides to the question of a newspaper monopoly. Again the ultimate answer depends upon how the newspaper is operated and how well it can not only maintain but increase its hold upon its community, particularly as to good will Ohio is one of a number of important newspaper states. It has a population in excess of 6,000,000, to serve which there are nearly 500 daily and weekly newspapers. Dailies are operated in 93 Ohio cities, but the surprising thing is that local daily newspaper monopolies are enjoyed in 81 of the 93 cities Only 12 Ohio cities have local newspaper competition 5 having three dailies each and the remaining 7 two each. In this respect Ohio is doubtless little different from other states of the union. The effect of such monopolies, if properly conserved and operated, has been to strengthen greatly the surviving papers, and to increase their opportunities for both service and profits.

Effects of the Depression

The depression that began in 1929 left its mark upon newspapers, just as it did upon other lines of business and industry. In some ways, however, the consequences were less severe. By way of summary it might be said that, with respect to newspapers, the depression:

1. Emphasized anew the necessity for sound business methods
2. Led to operating economies
3. Intensified competition

4. Diminished advertising revenue
5. Decreased circulation but not in proportion to advertising
6. Gave a new appreciation to the stability of circulation revenue
7. Resulted in slightly higher copy prices in many instances
8. Caused some adjustment of advertising rates
9. Stimulated the development and use of promotion
10. Weeded out the weakest papers, paving the way for more mergers
11. Stepped up mechanical production

Doubtless other results might be cited, and it is not claimed that those listed were felt universally in the newspaper world. It is a healthy commentary upon the fundamental soundness and importance of American newspapers that they weathered the economic storms as well as they did. By contrast with other forms of enterprise!, very few of them went to the wall.

In the face of sharply declining revenues from advertising, many papery were compelled to economize as never before. Staffs were .wiwed.iijL size, tVsage wete trimmed, buying was eWf r "^i^ife4$; w^rjej jpulifeH^J) WffS work was exacted Of or more for his money. In the heyday of advertising, circulation was looked upon as a sort of second cousin when it came to producing revenue. But when both national and local advertising dwindled steadily under the harsh stress of the times, many a newspaper fell back with gratitude upon the solid pillar of sure and stable income from circulation. The post of circulation manager took on a new importance. Many papers adjusted their copy prices upward with slight losses in circulation, most of which were ultimately regained, and with material increase in circulation income.

What doubtless happened in varying degrees with hundreds of newspapers is illustrated by the case of the Chicago Triune. In 1929 its income from advertising was reported to be $32,700,-000 and from circulation about $10,400,000. By 1932 its advertising revenue, despite the best efforts of a superior staff, had fallen to $11,900,000.

Its income from circulation, meanwhile, was $7,000,000, and the circulation itself at the same time had dropped from 880,995 in 1929 to 771,190 in 1933. Like many another circulation director, Louis Rose of the Tribune emerged from the depression years with far more authority, importance, and prestige than at the beginning. In this period the dollar volume of a Florida daily shrank 80 per cent, yet it continued to serve its customers and showed a profit.

Data compiled and issued by the U. S. Department of Commerce tell better and more concretely than anything else what happened to the American newspaper industry during the onset of the depression. Neither the employment nor the payroll indexes fell off to anywhere near the extent that occurred in other lines of industry, while the average hourly rate of union labor declined only slightly.

The progress and effects of the depression, following the so-called Coolidge boom, can also be seen in another table pre- pared by the U. S. Department of Commerce. The first effects of the depression are revealed by a comparison of the figures for the years 1929 and 1931. In the latter year as against two years before, there were 1313 fewer publishing establishments and 10,157 fewer employees, while wages were down some $27,700,000. The cost of materials, fuel, and electric current had shrunk by some $92,000,000, and the value of products was reduced by $330,000,000. Yet these establishments employed more numbers at higher wages in 1931 than they had in 1925 during the Coolidge era, and the value of their products was within less than 3 per cent of the total in 1925. A considerable further shrinkage was recorded for 1933.

Newspaper Expansion

In the eighties total annual newspaper revenues were about $135,000,000, and the amount was about equally divided between advertising and circulation. At the time the depression began in 1929, total newspaper revenues were in excess of $1,000,000,000 annually, of which advertising accounted for more than 70 per cent. In the 50 years down to 1884, the number of daily newspapers in the United States grew from 80 to 1200 and their combined circulations from a total of 240,000 to 6,000,000. But in the succeeding half century, the number of newspapers in this country increased to 1911 and their combined circulation to 36,700,000, or slightly more than 1>’5 papers daily for each of the 30,000,000 American families.

What explanation is there for this vast change? What has made the American public the largest per capita consumer of newspapers in the world? The answer lies in a number of things. These include a high standard of literacy, unsurpassed means of communication over long distances, a quality product at a low price, vastly improved mechanical facilities, greater professional skill on the part of newspaper men, the growth of the press associations, and the development of advertising both as a source of reader interest and of revenue. To these Lee adds cheapening means of manufacture, lowering paper costs, and improving news distribution and feature syndication. The invention of the Linotype, the development and simplification of the stereotyping process, and the improvement of high-speed presses revolutionized the mechanical aspects of printing. In the matter of presses alone, Lee estimates that a single plant today could turn out within a few hours a mass of 4-, 8-, 10-, and 12-page newspapers equivalent in size and number to the total output of all American daily newspaper plants in 1884.

Despite the appeal of the vastly improved metropolitan papers and their insistent circulation promotion, the home-town paper has more than held its own. This is partly because there is no real substitute for it, but more especially because of the great improvement in communication facilities including particularly the press association and feature services. These agencies have made it possible for the small city daily to compete on its own ground with the large city paper. It is now able to offer its leaders the same last-minute wire news and the same comics and other features, in addition to local and personal news which the large city paper cannot hope to supply adequately. This has been made possible by the spread, improvement, and relatively low cost of the press association and feature services. This has the disadvantage of stamping too many papers with the same pattern, but by the same token it has helped to revolutionize the small-town newspaper.

Improved Transportation

Going outside the newspaper plant the joint advance in motor transport and hard-surfaced highways has likewise greatly extended the radius and possibilities of the daily newspaper. The publication which a few years ago was more or less dependent upon trains and interurbans now operates its own trucks and airplanes to handle out-of-town circulation to surprising distances. As a result, it has expanded its circulation territory so that it is not uncommon for it to distribute direct to subscribers 100 miles or more distant. The rural customer who a few years ago received his paper by mail a day late gets today's paper within a few hours after it is printed. But for these major developments, the newspaper could not begin to produce or distribute the large circulations which are everywhere manifest and the end is not yet. They have made possible mass production of newspapers on a scale that was undreamed of by the previous generation of publishers. They have enabled the small-town daily to be largely self-sufficient and together have helped to lift the newspaper business into the class of a major industry.

A Factor in Distribution. Not less amazing than these other influences was the sudden growth of newspaper advertising as a recognized factor in distribution. Up to 1913, according to William A. Thomson, director of the bureau of advertising of the American Newspaper Publishers' Association, the total outlay for national advertising in newspapers did not exceed $50,000,000 in any one year. 1 In 1929, by contrast, it had risen to $260,000,- 000, and, even in the depression year of 1934, it was back to $163,- 000,000 after slipping to $145,000,000 in 1933.

The national advertising possibilities of newspapers were not only unappreciated, but many advertisers who were using other media were definitely prejudiced against them. Automobile manufacturers, for example, who are now one of the largest users of newspaper space, shared this prejudice.

It remained for the World War and particularly the spectacular use of the newspapers in the sale of $24,000,000,000 worth of United States war bonds to convince the skeptics. By 1928 Thomson cites the fact that 33 automobile manufacturers alone were spending about $50,000,000 annually for newspaper space, or an amount equal to the outlay of all national advertisers for newspaper space only 15 years earlier.

The amount grew steadily year by year, the peak being reached in 1929, after which there was a decline until 1934 when the advance was resumed. But even during the depression the newspapers strengthened their position as a national advertising medium and enlarged slightly their share of the national advertiser's dollar. They held this position despite the redoubled efforts of the older competing media and in the face of competition from radio, a new and aggressive rival.

The growth of newspapers into a billion-dollar industry paralleled the development of advertising into the billion-dollar class and of circulation in unprecedented volume. According to U. S. Department of Commerce statistics, 1 the combined value of newspaper advertising and subscription sales in 1923 was $803,497,000, while the combined daily circulation of American newspapers was 35,733,107 and the total Sunday circulation was 24,511,693. By 1927 the newspaper revenues from circulation and advertising rose to $977,467,000, the daily circulation to 42,343,210 and the Sunday circulation to 27,695,859. The peak was reached 1929 when sales totaled $1,073,119,000, daily circulation swotted to

42,947,824, and Sunday circulation was 29,011,648. In the first two years of the depression, daily circulation held its own fairly well, but Sunday circulation was off more than 1,500,000, and revenues were down more than $185,000,000, most of which was advertising loss.

The government figures as to products and receipts for the newspaper and periodical industry covering the 10 years just prior to, and immediately following, the start of the depression.

A-B.C.'s of Newspaper Economics

From the standpoint of its sales problem, the economy of the newspaper is relatively simple. It has only two things to sell: white space (advertising) and circulation.

The task of the management is to sell advertising and circulation in such volume and at such a price as will spread the publication's business fairly equitably over the year, enable it to meet its bills as they become due, retire its indebtedness, if any, replace equipment as it wears out or becomes obsolete, set aside a reserve fund for any emergency that may arise, and pay a fair profit. The newspaper business is seasonal to some extent with respect to both advertising and circulation but not to an extreme degree.

Advertising and circulation are highly interdependent. In the ordinary newspaper the one cannot exist without the other. After 1910 only two newspapers of general circulation managed to exist without advertising and both of these succumbed under the rise of wartime prices.

These were the two experimental Scripps papers in Chicago and Philadelphia. Important as it is, a newspaper's circulation, no matter how extensive, is insufficient, alone, to support it financially. Conversely, a newspaper cannot get advertising in volume unless it can show a solid and substantial circulation.

The principal operating expenditures of the newspaper fall into four groups: labor, raw material, equipment, and news and other services. To these must be added the overhead expense. The cost of newspaper labor depends largely upon the size of the city and the wage scales in effect. On the whole, the mechanical force is a favored class with respect to wages, thanks to the influence of the union.

Pay scales in the business office are apt to be higher than in the editorial. Newsprint constitutes a heavy item of expense. Plant equipment, such as typesetting machinery and presses, is likewise costly. On the larger papers in particular, it is less apt to wear out than to become obsolete in the face of mounting competition and mechanical improvements adopted by rival newspapers. The cost of news and feature services is remarkably small, considering the value received, and is determined, in general, by the quantity bought, by the size of the paper in terms of its circulation, by the size of the town, and by competition both of newspapers for desirable features and of syndicates for the business of the newspaper.

Financial Objects

In respect to its finances, then, the task of the newspaper is three-fold: to meet its operating expenses, to pay a fair profit, and to establish itself so firmly that it can be independent of whatever pressure might be brought to bear against it.

The perishability of its principal commodity news, the intensity of the competition, "and its dependence upon the confidence and good will of the public combine, as has been said, to make the newspaper business highly hazardous. It is incumbent upon the newspaper, therefore, as a matter of self-preservation to build wisely and firmly.

The strong newspaper must be in a position to preserve its freedom. A newspaper that is in debt or that is dependent upon a small group of advertisers or that can be bent to financial pressure is a newspaper that is likely to be a community liability rather than an asset.

If a newspaper is to fulfill its entire function, courageously, honestly, and unselfishly, it must be able to do so without fear or favor. A newspaper that can be influenced by outside financial or business pressure is hardly in a position to render its full measure of community service.

Fortunately, most newspapers are on a solid financial footing. A publication that is not a going concern does not last long. Under economic stress, it is apt to suspend publication or to be swallowed up in a merger. It is a striking commentary upon the solidity of the American newspaper industry that, in the face of the depression that began in 1929, it weathered the storm with very few casualties by contrast with other lines of activity. This is further proof that the newspaper in this country has been put upon a sound business basis, a policy which enhances rather than detracts from the news and editorial functions of the paper.

It is this fact that spells opportunity for the newspaper publisher and for the worker in the newspaper business office. It is more and more evident that the publishers of newspapers of tomorrow will come from the business ranks rather than from the editorial side. Financial opportunities and rewards in the business office, too, are limited only by what the employee or executive can produce. By contrast, the average editorial employee moves in a narrow orbit.

5

Newspaper Organization

GENERAL PRINCIPLES

When the press was in its infancy, personal ownership of newspapers was the rule. As has been described, the first newspapers were published by journeymen printers and their successors. Later the editor was usually the publisher also, and frequently the owner of the newspaper as well. In many cases newspapers were owned and operated jointly by two or more partners or by small groups of individuals. One partner gave his chief attention to the editorial department, and the other took care of the business office.

Individual ownership continued through the period of personal journalism, but, as newspapers grew in size and in number and as competition increased, this gave way almost entirely to the corporate form of organization. Like other forms of business and industry, newspapers took advantage of the benefits made possible by incorporation: longer life, larger capital, limited personal financial liability, and greater flexibility. The advent and development of so-called newspaper chains expanded the financial and industrial organization of newspapers still further with the result that in some ways they resemble the large corporations in other lines of activity and are similarly nationwide in their scope.

There are limitations, however, to the resemblance between the incorporated newspaper and other incorporated businesses. While the organization of all newspapers breaks down into two main subdivisions the editorial and the business departments the newspaper conforms less to fixed rules of organization than almost any other business of similar size and importance.

A comparison of almost any two daily newspapers, under different ownerships, will show that executives or employees holding the same or similar titles often perform widely different functions or have different responsibilities. From the functional standpoint, in other words, newspapers are still organized along individual or personal rather than uniform lines.

Newspapers Different. Other differences are to be found between the newspaper corporations and other corporations. Despite exceptions that can be cited, these may be summarized as follows :

1. In the actual production of the newspaper some corporate officers play lesser roles than operating executives who are usually salaried employees.
2.- Similarly, certain corporate officers, like the vice-president and the secretary, are found less often in newspaper corporations. Where they exist, they are apt to have less responsibility than hired operating executives.
3. Unlike that of many other corporations, the common stock of newspapers is rarely offered to the public, although preferred stocks and bonds of newspaper properties are sometimes available.

Control of the common stock carries with it, of course, control of the corporation. In their study of newspaper organization, covering more than 200 daily newspapers, Miller and Hornberger found certain other tendencies, including these:

1. Personal factors tend more to determine newspaper organization than in ordinary business practice.
2. Save for the overhead organization, there is little difference between chain and nonchain newspapers.
3. Of all the departments of the newspaper, the mechanical department is the most standardized.

4. The type of newspaper organization usually depends upon whether the editorial or the business office is predominant or whether they are on a par.

In the main these tendencies have grown stronger since 1930, while others have appeared. The pressure of necessity has compelled more attention to the business and the production departments of the newspaper. In most newspapers, the former had to redouble its efforts in the face of declining advertising revenues between 1930 and 1934. The latter had to improve the finished product and step up production despite composing-room and pressroom economies. The circulation department has been elevated to a new importance on a par with, and in some cases even above, that of the news and advertising departments. Promotion has taken a permanent place in the setup of the newspaper. It is now a full-fledged, well-developed department on the larger dailies, while its importance and necessity are recognized on even the smallest papers.

KINDS OF ORGANIZATION

Differences among the various types of organization relating to newspaper management will now be examined in some detail. In order of complexity and outreach, they can be classified as follows :

1. Weeklies and semiweeklies
2. Independent dailies in
    a. Towns or small cities
    b. Cities of medium size
    c. Large cities
3. Chain or group newspapers
    a. Hearst
    b. Scripps-Howard
    c. Paul Block
    d. Brush-Moore
    e. Other

4. Cooperative organizations
   a. General
   b. National
   c. State and regional
5. Special
   a. Advertising
   b. Circulation
   c. Promotion
   d. Production

DIVISIONS AND SUBDIVISIONS

In general, any newspaper still has two main divisions, the editorial and the business departments. For many years the former overshadowed the latter, but more recently the business department has been placed on a par with the editorial. While it would be misleading and untrue to say that the American newspaper has been commercialized, the fact remains that the business and economic aspects of publishing have been revolutionized since 1900. With this change, the .business department has taken on a new importance on the principle that sound business practices are as necessary to the newspaper as sound editorial policies.

On even the smallest newspapers, the business department has at least three principal subdivisions, and on the largest newspapers there are six or more, depending upon circumstances. Besides the general business office, these subdivisions are the advertising, the circulation, and the mechanical departments. In recent years many newspapers have developed promotion departments as a means of selling and servicing the paper more effectively for both readers and advertisers. On the largest papers, also, the management and maintenance of the building and the physical plant are of sufficient importance to call for a separate department. Each of the subdivisions described can be broken down in turn into smaller subdivisions. Newspaper advertising is of two principal kinds, display and classified, both of which can be further subdivided. Circulation is handled as city and suburban, state and mail, depending upon its classification. The mechanical or production department is made up of the composing room, where the type is set; the stereotyping department, which makes printing plates from the type forms; the pressroom, where the printed page becomes a reality; and, in the case of the largernewspapers, the engraving room, where various kinds of illustrations, such as cartoons, sketches, diagrams, and photographs are translated into engravings. The promotion department is sometimes a separate division, although various types of promotion may be handled directly by the editorial, advertising, and circulation departments. Each of these functions will be treated later in detail.

The type of organization of a newspaper depends to a large degree upon its size. In the smallest newspapers there is a fairly simple operating setup, and, while there is some overlapping of functions, the division of labor is both simple and natural. The larger the paper, however, the more complex is its organization, particularly on the business side. As a paper grows, the number of its business and mechanical employees far exceeds that of the editorial department. Simplest Type. On the smallest newspapers the editor himself may solicit advertising while gathering news, a girl employee may divide her time as society editor and bookkeeper, or the advertising man may collect news items along with the advertising copy.

Small City Daily

On the smaller dailies, the division of labor remains fairly simple. Yet even here the superior numbers of the business department are revealed.

Complex Type

On a newspaper like the New York Times, on the other hand, the organization of a single department is exceedingly complex. As the size of the paper increases there is a greater trend toward specialization and nearly every worker tends to become an expert or specialist in some line.

Editorial Department

As the editorial department is concerned here only incidentally, it will suffice to describe it in general terms. This department is responsible for the news and editorial contents of the paper. As a rule the editor, or some one designated by him, also has charge of the makeup of the paper, i.e., the placing of the type in the forms and the general arrangement of what goes into the paper. In some cases, as with the Scripps-Howard newspapers, the editor for special reasons may also have charge of the composing room. There is apt to be a greater diversity of organization in the editorial department than anywhere else on the paper. But even here the division of labor naturally falls into several groupings, such as local or city news, outside or telegraph news, the editorial page, and the various news departments such as sports, society, financial, markets, music, the drama, and aviation. The arrangement depends upon a variety of factors: the size of the paper in terms of circulation and outreach, its personnel, and the preferences and policies of its owners and executives.

Physical Arrangement

Gravity has much to do with the physical arrangement of a newspaper plant. Because of its weight and bulk as well as to facilitate the handling of the printed papers, the pressroom equipment is generally found on the ground floor. This makes it possible to give the heavy presses a solid foundation and expedites the distribution of the papers.

The composing room and stereotyping department may be adjacent to the pressroom or above it. In smaller plants the entire business office may also be found on the ground floor or first floor or, where all departments are on one floor, at the front. A common arrangement is for a counter or railing where the public may be met and where classified advertisements are taken. Behind this are desks for other business, advertising, and circulation employees. Where the mechanical, business, and editorial departments are on separate floors, the arrangement varies. The only uniform practice is for the production department to occupy space on or close to the ground level for the reasons given. If three floors are used, part of the business department may be on the second floor and the editorial on the third, or the reverse may be true. In a way there is a similarity to the production line of an automobile plant: the tendency is usually for the work to be carried on in a straight line and from the top floors down to the assembly which, in the case of the newspaper, is the pressroom.

In many shops, the composing room will be found on the same level and back of the editorial department. In economy of time and effort, the advantages of such an arrangement are obvious.

TYPES OF MANAGEMENT

From the standpoint of management, newspapers may be classified in several ways. The type of management that is followed depends usually upon such factors as local custom, the size of the newspaper, the kind of ownership, and the personal preference of the owners. The principal classifications are:

1. *Owner-operator.* To be found most frequently in small papers where the owner gives direct personal attention to the conduct and operation of the paper.
2. *Publisher.* In which the principal owner or his agent, bearing this title, has direct and general charge of all the departments of the newspaper.
3. *Dual Management.* Best exemplified perhaps in most of the Scripps-Howard newspapers and where, for all ordinary purposes, the editor and business manager share the responsibility for the operation of the paper.
4. *General Manager.* In which an executive with this title has general charge of all the departments of the newspaper. He is in turn directly responsible to the publisher, if the latter is an individual, or to the board of directors, if the latter is a corporation. To be found on larger newspapers but less frequently than the publisher type.

In the case of chain or group newspapers, the type of management likewise depends upon the kind of ownership and the policies or preferences of the owners. Mr. Hearst, for example, exercises close supervision over all of his publications. For ordinary purposes, he operates through general and regional managers as well as the immediate heads of individual newspapers. As a result, the Hearst newspapers are under a highly centralized control The Scripps-Howard newspapers, by contrast, exemplify the decentralized operation and management of a large group of newspapers. While there is an imposing general superstructure in the case of the Scripps-Howard newspapers, with an editor-in chief and general business executives, the individual editors and business managers enjoy a large measure of local autonomy. Such a policy is also followed by the owners and operators of other groups of newspapers in the belief that such practice yields the best results. The Brush-Moore newspapers in Ohio are another example of this type of management, as are the Paul Block newspapers.

Scripps-Howard Papers. The Scripps-Howard newspapers, for the most part, also typify dual management. As long as the general policies laid down from time to time are followed, the general management believes in giving the local editor and business manager a free hand in operating the Scripps-Howard newspaper for which they are responsible. As a rule these newspapers over the years have been well managed, profitable, progressive, and economical.

They do not go in for showy buildings or expensive locations. They have been operated on the basis of paying their way as they went, of plowing a sizable share of the profits back into the business, and of laying aside an appreciable reserve fund against a rainy day. Another phase of organization and management for which the Scripps-Howard papers are conspicuous lies in the editorial control over the composing room. In all other respects, the organisation of the mechanical or production department of these newspapers is like that of any other newspaper, the stereotyping and engraving departments and the pressroom being under the business manager.

The Scripps-Howard practice with respect to the composing room is due to the belief of E. W. Scripps, the founder, that the editors of Kis papers should have control of their contents. In case of any question arising between the editor and the business manager of a Scripps-Howard newspaper as to what shall be permitted in its news and advertising columns, the final decision, as far as local authority goes, lies with the editor. The Scripps policy is explained by Negley G. Cochran, one of the publisher's biographers, as follows:

1 With Scripps the success of a newspaper depended upon the editor. Advertising and the business office were subordinate. To make sure of editorial supremacy, he made the composing room subordinate to the editor. When the editor OK'd the composing room payroll that settled it and the business manager had to pay it. The point was this by controlling the composing room the editor controlled every line of type that went into the paper, whether news or advertising. Scripps started this system of control when he and Sweeney founded the Cleveland Press.

After the editor, through his composing room, set all the type and locked the forms, the forms were turned over to the business manager, who controlled the stereotype foundry and press room. All the business manager had to do was to stereotype the forms the editor gave him, put the plates on the press, print the paper, sell it, and sell advertising space. It was none of the editor's business whether advertising space was sold or not that was something for the business manager to worry about. Of course, the editor could hope secretly for profits, but Scripps wanted to keep his mind off of advertising as much as possible which generally wasn't much.

General-manager Type

The general-manager type of organization is represented by the Cleveland Plain Dealer, which also typifies an inland metropolitan morning newspaper. The business manager is responsible to the vicepresident and general manager over whom are the president and the board of directors.

Multiple Type

A rarer form of organization is limited to the great chains or to several of the largest and financially most powerful individual newspapers. This might be called a multiple type, in which one newspaper property is pyramided upon another or is appended to the first or strongest. The details differ with the individual properties, depending upon their nature and scope. The Scripps-Howard and the Hearst groups might be taken loosely as representing one such form, with varying degrees of control of properties worth many millions of dollars. Both of these groups also have subsidiaries of various kinds.

Vertical Type

Still another type of business organization is represented by the New York Times or by the Chicago Tribune, which are not only vastly successful and profitable newspapers themselves, but operate other large TRIBUNE c o

Most of the states have their own state and other local associations, societies, and agencies more or less similar in nature to those listed above but on a smaller scale. Such organizations are usually cooperative and are maintained for the discussion and solution of mutual problems, the development, and, if need be, the defense of mutual interests. Their headquarters or offices are located in various state capitals, in Washington, and in such business centers as New York, Atlanta, Chicago, and San Francisco.

6

CIRCULATION PRINCIPLES

Circulation is the life blood of the newspaper. In its way circulation is an index not only of the influence of a newspaper but of its value as a going concern. As such it is not the only yardstick but it is perhaps the most important one. Newspapers and other publications manage to exist with little advertising, and a few in modern times have survived without any advertising, but none can hope to last unless it has the vital element of circulation.

The problem of circulation is primarily one of sales and distribution. The depression years have placed a new emphasis on the importance of circulation, the circulation manager, and circulation revenue. In a sense the pendulum has swung part way back to the days when newspapers survived or perished on the strength of their respective circulations and advertising was still in the embryo stage. Certain it is, at any rate, that the years since 1929 have witnessed not only a new recognition of circulation as a vital element in newspaper publishing but, more especially, have stressed the importance of quality circulation as against mere bulk circulation.

THE CIRCULATION MANAGER

In similar fashion, the circulation manager attained unprecedented importance in the newspaper organization after 1929. It used to be that he was a person of no special training and, seemingly, of no particular importance in the office. On most newspapers, he was a necessary functionary who did a more or less routine job in a more or less routine way. He saw that the papers were distributed and that was about all. He was rarely, if ever, consulted and, in general, was a person of no great consequence.

The rest of the picture was something as follows:

Most city circulation was carrier delivered; the routes, as a rule, were office owned; there was little promotion; most country circulation went by mail; the carriers folded their own papers, sometimes even "stuffing" the different sections; they also built their own routes about as they pleased and carried rival papers; outlying carriers and newsstands were served by bundles thrown off streetcars; edition times were irregular and papers were often late, especially on days when more than one section was published or the presses broke down.

Today all of this is changed. Not only has circulation itself been re-evaluated, but the circulation manager or director, as he is known on some of the larger papers, is an important personage in the newspaper setup. He is a specialist in his line just as the advertising manager, the promotion man, the chief editorial writer, and the mechanical superintendent are in theirs. He is listened to not only about the things that immediately concern his department but about the general policies of the publication. On some newspapers, it is not far from the truth to assert that he is the most important figure in the organization next to the publisher. Louis Rose, of the Chicago Tribune, and M. L. Annenberg, the publisher, formerly of the Hearst organization, typify the current trend.

In an address before the Inland Daily Press Association in 1934, Frank S. Newell, circulation director of the Toledo Blade and former president of the International Circulation Managers' Association, listed the qualifications of the present-day circulation manager. Among other things, he said that the circulation executive must enjoy the complete confidence of the executives and owner of the newspaper and must himself be interested, loyal, and share the responsibility for the profitable operation of the paper. It is his duty, he added, "to produce circulation of such quantity and quality that it will, in turn, produce the best possible results for the advertiser . . , ," the circulation manager being, in short, "the sales manager of a product sold by a tremendous volume in highly competitive fields."

In similar vein, an editorial in the September, 1935, issue of Circulation Management pointed out that the circulation manager of today is a four-ply executive. He is at once sales manager, delivery superintendent, office manager, and an executive department head. "Today's circulation manager is no longer responsible for circulation alone," the editorial went on. "He holds in his hands much of the responsibility for the success or failure of the entire publication. He, therefore, must counsel with every other department, he must give his help in all matters of policy, no matter what department they may directly affect. He must consider carefully every change in plans or procedure in the light of how they will increase or lose circulation, and thereby affect the entire business. There is nothing strange in all this belated recognition except the fact that it took newspaper publishers and executives so long to come to it. What they finally came to realize was that the circulation chief, more than any other person on the newspaper, has his ear to the ground. He knows what readers want. He knows what sells papers and, conversely, what will not. As a result he is now consulted as to the play of news, the issuance of extras, the purchase or use of features, the addition of mechanical equipment, and other matters which the publishers of a generation ago could not see had anything to do with circulation. What has occurred, in short, has been the recognition of circulation or distribution as the hub of the newspaper. To expect a circulation manager to sell a newspaper that is out of step with its competitors in news and advertising facilities, feature service, and mechanical equipment is to ask the impossible. It was a recognition of this simple yet fundamental fact that led one middle western publisher to use his circulation department as a training and proving ground for his personnel. If he takes on an embryo reporter, it is via the circulation district. The beginner stays there an indefinite length of time until he learns something of the readers' likes and dislikes. He gets these through the reports of carriers under him and by personal calls upon subscribers in following up stops, starts, and complaints. This publisher also routes beginners in the advertising department via circulation and classified advertising before they are actually apprenticed to display advertising.

He testifies that in his own long experience on both sides of the newspaper editorial and advertising he really got down to the grass roots of newspaper publishing for the first time when, as a reporter, he was given what was at first the distasteful task of calling upon subscribers and nonsubscribers to find out what they liked and disliked about the particular newspaper for which he was working at the time. He emphasizes that he learned more about what the newspaper consumer wants and does not want than he had learned in years of previous newspaper work.

While not many publishers are ready to adopt his personnel training methods, there is a growing recognition of the fact that the judgment of the circulation manager is apt to be based on cold facts while that of editors and other newspaper executives is likely to be purely theoretical as to what readers want. There is no question but that by the very nature of his work he is much closer to the reader than any other person connected with the newspaper. This being the case, the publisher who does not capitalize upon the experience, the wisdom, and the contacts which his circulation department must have is pursuing a shortsighted policy which will act inevitably as a brake upon the progress and possibilities of his newspaper.

Circulation Revenue

In like manner, circulation revenue has taken on a new importance. During its first 70 years or so in America, the daily newspaper was almost wholly dependent upon the proceeds of circulation. Few of the early publishers actually made much money from their publications because of the high copy price, because of the limited circulation possible at that price, because of the tardiness of subscribers in paying for their papers, and because of the lack of advertising revenue. It was common to charge 6 cents for a four-page daily, and even then many publishers were dependent upon commercial printing or some form of subsidy to make both ends meet. This picture began to change with the growth of the penny press a century ago bringing in its wake, more especially after the Civil War, the development of advertising. The situation was reversed for a third of a century or more down to 1930 when it seemed that, for most well-established newspapers, circulation revenue was more or less incidental, i.e., it was overshadowed by the growing income from advertising. As far as the records show, only the Chicago Daybook and the Philadelphia News-Post were solely dependent for a time upon circulation revenue, carrying no advertising. But these were two experimental newspapers, established by E. W. Scripps to prove his belief that newspapers could exist without advertising. Both were necessarily limited as to circulation, and both quickly gave up the ghost under the pressure of wartime conditions.

Since 1930, newspaper publishers everywhere have not only reappraised circulation as a whole but they have definitely embarked upon a policy of asking the reader to share more of the cost of the newspaper. In other words, many newspapers have made subscription price adjustments, either wholesale or retail or both, which now appear to be firmly established as a matter of permanent practice. These changes grew out of both necessity and conviction.

Under the lash of the depression, advertising revenue fell off alarmingly. Publishers trimmed their sails to meet the storm in various ways, but this was not enough. Something had to be done to offset, at least partially, not only the loss of advertising income but of unavoidably increased publishing costs. Fortunately, circulation had fairly well held its own during the first years of the depression, and many publishers turned to their readers as a source of legitimate additional income. This was a perfectly logical and proper step. In fact it would have been quite in order, even without a depression. For one thing, considering its unit price, the newspaper was unquestionably the lowest priced commodity in general use. For another, the reader was the chief beneficiary of many improvements such as the extension of the teletype, the spread of wire photo, the greater bulk of high-class features, the development of color printing, and the greater radius of circulation distribution. It was no more than fair, therefore, to ask him to foot the bill. Further, the price adjustments that were made were so small as to work no hardships upon anyone. The newspaper, considering its importance, represents the least drain upon the consumer's purse of anything of consequence that affects his daily life.

More Uniform Prices

As a sort of byproduct to all of this, one other tendency grew out of the depression years. This was a greater standardization of newspaper prices. Frank S. Newell, circulation director of the Toledo Blade, found in 1933 that the wholesale prices of daily newspapers in the United States ranged from 1 to 4 cents, while the retail prices were from 1 to 5 cents. Moreover, the price of the newspaper was no index of its real worth or merit as a newspaper. The Kansas City Star or the Columbus Dispatch at 1 cent, for example, was as good or better than another newspaper selling for 2, 3, or even 5 cents. Many newspapers whose price for home delivery by carrier had been 12 cents a week went to 15 cents a week and from 2 cents per copy on the street to 3 cents. There are signs that 15 cents a week for home delivery and 3 cents per single copy will be the standard price for most American dailies.

By the end of March, 1936, Editor & Publisher reported that the total Sunday circulation of American newspapers was at a new peak of more than 28,000,000 after a dip to 24,000,000 three years earlier. In the same manner, the circulation of afternoon papers had risen to 24,000,000 after dropping to just below 22,000,000 in 1933, and morning papers had attained a new all-time high of more than 14,000,000. This relative stability of circulation as compared with advertising was both a convincing demonstration of public dependence upon the newspaper and of the intrinsic merits of the newspaper as an advertising medium. It unquestionably saved many a newspaper from serious financial difficulty. Taking 1929 as the base, the relatively slight decline and the prompt recovery of newspaper circulations are shown graphically by the following table prepared by Editor & Publisher:

With this kind of a showing, it is small wonder that newspapers emerged from the first effects of the depression more firmly entrenched in the public confidence and stronger financially on the circulation side than ever before. But there were other changes than those mentioned. Publishers and advertisers alike have become much more interested in the quality of circulation than in its mere quantity. Both were to blame for the previous emphasis on volume and the relative ignorance or indifference as to whether the circulation was either economical or effective in terms of the advertiser's dollar. The advertisers, as O. C. Harn, managing director of the Audit Bureau of Circulations, commented, insisted upon more volume, and circulation managers went out and accommodated them without inquiring too much into its cost or efficacy.

This has now been remedied to a considerable extent, the culls being weeded out and waste or unprofitable circulation from the standpoint of both the newspaper and the advertiser being largely eliminated on most daily newspapers. The publisher really has had no choice for he has had to do it both in self-defense and in justice to the advertiser.

Function of Circulation Revenue

Besides so much inequality in copy prices among individual newspapers, there is perhaps equally great diversity as to the part circulation revenue plays in financing the newspaper. There seems to be only theory as to what it should cover and different publishers operate on different bases in this respect. A canvass of this situation made by Editor & Publisher based on the records of a dozen representative newspapers showed that their average revenue from circulation was 20.6 per cent of their total income, but, in the case of individual publications, this ranged from 13.3 to 28.9 per cent. A previous similar survey showed many newspapers to be netting less than 15 per cent of their revenue from circulation.

Some publishers are satisfied if circulation produces sufficient revenue to cover the cost of maintaining that department, including circulation promotion. Others have a rule that circulation revenue should cover the cost of the newsprint used or that the income from the sale of papers be enough to operate the circulation department and pay for part of the newsprint. Most publishers probably would be well off if their circulation produced enough revenue to maintain the department arid pay for the newsprint used, leaving the income from advertising to cover all other costs and provide a reasonable profit. A safe rule is that, in setting up an operating budget, the copy price should be fixed to bring what the product is reasonably worth and to cover a definite part of the expense of producing the newspaper, including at least the cost of operating the circulation department.

CIRCULATION FACTORS

It appears simple to take population and other statistics and work out some of the more evident circulation characteristics of a typical daily newspaper in the United States. For example, daily newspapers are relatively rare in towns of less than 2500 population. The number of Sunday newspapers, too, is rather small. At first thought one might conclude that a certain minimum population with average community activities is required to support a daily newspaper or a Sunday newspaper. Ohio, for example has a population of 6,600,000 which supports 107 afternoon, 9 morning, and 20 Sunday newspapers. Does this mean, on the average, that a population of some 60,000 is required to sustain an afternoon newspaper, with 740,000 for a morning publication, and 330,000 for one on Sunday? Not at all, for circumstances greatly alter cases. In general, the circulation of the average Sunday newspaper is greater than that of either the afternoon or the morning newspaper, and the latter, though fewer in number, has a larger average circulation than its afternoon competitor. Yet the state of Texas, fifth in population, and California, which is sixth, rank first and second in the number of Sunday newspapers. The explanation lies chiefly in the vast size of those states. One other example might be mentioned. At the close of the World War, New York City seemed to have all the daily newspapers of general circulation it could support. Indeed, the general tendency as exemplified by Pittsburgh and Chicago, to name only two cities, was definitely in the direction of fewer newspapers. This was brought about through mergers of existing newspapers, the abandonment of some, and the demise of others. Yet in 1921, the News was launched in New York in the belief not only that there was a place in that city's journalism for a new kind of newspaper but that a large and profitable market for such a publication lay in a previously untapped element of the population the great middle class. The rest is history. The New York News, starting from scratch under highly competitive postwar conditions, has not only set the pace for American journalism in a number of important respects but has far outstripped all other American newspapers, daily or Sunday, in circulation.

The opposite tendency is illustrated to some extent by what occurred in Youngstown where until mid-1936 there were two dailies. The Vindicator was founded in 1869 and the Telegram in 1885. The latter was purchased in 1922 by Scripps-Howard, but its situation became more and more difficult after 1929 when it became evident that the Youngstown market was less and less able to support two such newspapers. Finding that they were unable to buy out the Vindicator, the Scripps-Howard interests sold the Telegram to the owners of the other newspaper. This was somewhat similar to what occurred previously in Baltimore where Scripps-Howard sold the Post to the Hearst interests.

In announcing the Youngstown merger, W. W. Hawkins, Scripps-Howard chairman, made the following pertinent comment: Having convinced ourselves over the period of the last five years that it was impossible for us to acquire the Youngstown Vindicator, the Youngstown Telegram was consolidated today with the Vindicator in response to economic demands. Decreased revenues, following the depression, mounting production costs, together with increased taxes made the continued operation of two newspapers in

Youngstown journalistically as well as economically unsound. Therefore it was the belief of the Telegram that one paper would better serve the public so far as news enterprise is concerned with a smaller aggregate cost to the community as a whole. Particularly during the last two years we have indicated our willingness to correct this unhealthy condition. . . . The steadily increasing tax burden is in our opinion bound to compel a realistic view of situations of this kind wherever they exist. What, then, are the factors that affect newspaper circulation?

There are at least six major ones. In their relative order of importance these are: (1) economic, (2) social, (3) geographic, (4) policy, (5) mechanical, and (6) promotional. Each of these will be considered in some detail.

Economic

From the editorial standpoint, the function of a newspaper is essentially social, but from that of the business office, it is necessarily economic. In publishing circles, more and more emphasis is being placed, therefore, upon the market of a newspaper. This may vary widely for two newspapers published in the same city. From the standpoint of circulation, the kind of clientele a given newspaper has to some extent is optional with the publisher, but each newspaper must have an adequate market or it cannot survive, much less prosper. If it is a new publication, the newspaper must be able to get subscribers and keep adding to its circulation. If it is one already established, it must be able both to keep its old readers satisfied and to attract new ones. The law of newspaper survival, in fact, has its roots in circulation. To put it briefly, there must be enough potential readers to take the newspaper, and they must represent enough potential purchasing power not only to subscribe to or buy the newspaper but to patronize the potential advertisers. There must be sufficient population 'and enough wealth and business activity, in other words, to constitute a market. Bulk population, however, does not necessarily mean bulk purchasing power. There are areas of the United States, for example, which are fairly well populated, but the population is of such a nature and its subsistence level is so low that it is an unprofitable market. This is true, for example, in some portions of the South because of the large negro population. It pertains likewise to other parts of the country, particularly in some of the larger cities, where a considerable proportion of the populace has been on relief.

A newspaper market, then, must consist, in part, of a population with fairly good and steady income or wages, and of relatively high purchasing power.

It needs sufficient diversity of business, professional, and other kinds of activity to keep it from stagnation or, worse, ruination in the event that one or more major industries go on the rocks or something else affects it. Unless most unusual circumstances attend it, a one-industry town Hometimes wakens to find the props knocked from under it. It is like putting all the eggs in one basket. Many examples of this could be cited. From the economic point of view, then, a newspaper must be able to count upon a steady and sizable group of readers who not only can but will patronize its advertisers with a reasonable profit to all concerned.

Social

A newspaper's market is defined not only by the credit rating of the people who make up the community but by their social characteristics. These include such things as literacy, education, politics, religion, and cultural advantages. If the population has few illiterates, sets considerable store by its schools, prides itself on its churches, takes an active and intelligent interest in politics, reads a great deal, and reckons its accomplishments not only in material but in social things, it comprises a potential market which any newspaper publisher might envy.

Taken as a whole, the United States is a nation of newspaper readers, but some sections of the country are better than others in this respect, either through the excellence of their newspapers or through habit, education, or other factors.

Geographical

. The physical as well as the economic and social characteristics of a community help to determine the market of the newspaper. This is geography in the broad sense of the term. A section much of which is desert is obviously a poor market unless there are compensating factors. Nor are the publishing prospects good where the population is Sparse and the few towns are widely separated. As a rule, the more dense the population the better the market, although this will not always hold. Conversely, the sparser the population the less promising the market. Plains or prairie regions are apt to be better than mountainous areas. This is reflected not only in the number and kind of population but in distributing costs. A newspaper published in a town or city which serves a fairly compact and populous region easily reached by good and numerous roads is much superior as a market to one which is more or less isolated or which calls for long circulation hauls.

Policy

The kinds of policies a newspaper follows have some bearing upon its market from the standpoint of circulation. A newspaper which has a strong following in the community as a result of sound policy and a long record of public service is in an enviable position. It can be independent and still keep public opinion on its side unless it goes to extremes. It is unlikely, for instance, that a strong Republican newspaper could hope to succeed in the deep South. The editorial tone of the newspaper, its policies as to news, its typographic makeup, and its interest and activity in public service, all help to shape its circulation market.

Mechanical

To an increasing degree the mechanical facilities of a newspaper have a direct bearing upon the size of its circulation market. These have to do, for example, with such things a press speed, color and engraving facilities, and motor delivery. A newspaper whose presses are unequal to a growing circulation or to emergency demands upon them or which are slower and of smaller capacity than those of a competitor necessarily limit the radius of the circulation market of a newspaper. To some extent reader interest is apt to follow that newspaper which keeps abreast of such improvements as color printing and pictures. It appears to be definitely true that smaller newspapers which have added the so-called one-man engraving plants have literally compelled their local competitors to follow suit in some fashion or to risk material circulation losses.

By the same token, changing transportation conditions have altered the distribution problem for newspapers. The abandonment of many railroad trains, the disappearance of interurban lines, the development of bus systems, and, in particular, the emphasis upon a greatly extended home delivery by the newspaper itself as a result of much improved highways have all contributed to this end. Many newspapers now cover much more territory on the day of publication than they would have dreamed of doing a dozen years ago, and the end is not yet. This particular problem will be discussed more in detail later, but it is only one of a number which help to make the publishing picture of today far different and vastly more complex than it was at the close of the World War.

Promotional

To the more or less obvious factors affecting circulation there are added those of newspaper promotion in general and of circulation promotion in particular. It has been said many times that there is no such thing as natural circulation it must be built, unit by unit, it must be cultivated faithfully and energetically, and it must be increased within proper limits. All of this is brought about by the kind of particular effort which, for want of a better name so far, is called promotion. Within limits also, the circulation of a newspaper can be defined according to the purposes and policies of the publisher. These are partly a matter of choice and partly of the proper kind of promotion to attain the ends sought. Newspaper promotion is just beginning to come into its own, with circulation as one of its major objectives.

KINDS OF CIRCULATION

By circulation is meant, in general, the number of readers a given publication has. It is somewhat comparable to the radio audience, although it is usually much more definite and concrete than the latter.

But there are many kinds of circulation each having to do with a special phase or aspect. To some extent, these may be grouped in pairs. These include gross and net circulation, forced and natural circulation, numerical and merchandise circulation, duplicating and overlapping circulation, A.B.C. and government statement, and waste. These may be defined as follows :

Gross Circulation

The total number of copies distributed on a given day, all editions included, regardless of later returns from dealers, copies to advertisers, exchange copies, free copies, and those for office use.

Net Circulation

The number of copies actually sold on a given day, all editions included, after deducting all file, return, free, exchange, and other copies printed but not sold.

Natural Circulation

That circulation which a newspaper might expect to get and hold in a given market by intelligent sustained effort, taking into account the nature and size of the reading public in that area.

Forced Circulation

That circulation which some newspapers get by high-pressure salesmanship, extreme and sensational editorial policies, lurid typography, excessive use of premiums, and other unsound and unstable promotion methods.

The difficulty with forced circulation is that it is costly, unstable, and uncertain for both the publisher and the advertiser.

Numerical Circulation

Similar to gross circulation; generally, the circulation figure without reference to the kinds or effectiveness of the circulation it represents.

Merchandise Circulation

Circulation in terms of its effectiveness to the advertiser. Circulation that is highly effective will show a high proportion of merchandise circulation, while in circulation that is slow or uncertain in this respect the proportion will be low.

Duplicating Circulation

That portion of the .circulation which represents purchases of more than one copy by the same individual or members of his family on the same day, as for example, the purchase of a noon edition or stock final on the street with the delivery of the home edition by the carrier at the residence. As a rule this proportion is small.

Overlapping Circulation

That portion of the circulation of a given publication which overlaps that of a competitor.

This, too, varies with individual newspapers as well as with different cities. If there is considerable overlapping, it must be taken into account by the advertiser in shaping his advertising policies with respect to the publications. If repetition and reiteration serve his purpose, well and good. If not, he must key his advertising copy according to the medium used.

A.B.C. Circulation

Net paid circulation as defined by the rather strict rules of the Audit Bureau of Circulations as distinguished from either the so-called Government Statement or the Publisher's Statement. (For details, see the chapter on the Audit Bureau of Circulations.)

Government Statement

Net paid circulation as defined by the postal regulations and as required of daily newspapers at least once a year in a sworn statement to the government.

Waste Circulation

Circulation which is either unproductive to the advertiser or so expensive to the publisher as to be unprofitable.

It is evident from the foregoing that many things enter into circulation. The type of circulation that will suit the needs of the general or national advertiser may be quite ineffective and unsatisfactory for the purposes of the retail or local advertiser and vice versa.

The type of steady reader which comprises the bulk of circulation of one newspaper may be exactly suited to the requirements of one kind of advertiser and of little use to another. Specialty and quality shops catering to a limited but wealthy clientele, for example, would hardly be served by a publication which circulated largely among readers of low purchasing power. What the advertiser is usually interested in with respect to circulation is steady if not immediate returns.

The kind of circulation most likely to produce such returns is that which goes into the home. In smaller cities this circulation is represented by home-delivered circulation, but, in large metropolitan centers like New York where traffic and other physical conditions make home delivery impossible, it is represented by circulation which enters the home by other means, chiefly street and newsstand sales of papers which are taken home by the reader.

With most newspapers the emphasis, then, is upon concentrated circulation. This is dense circulation or readers living within a relatively short distance of the city of publication. Next to this is what is sometimes called the area of delayed returns. It is made up of readers living at a somewhat greater distance but still within the trade area served by the newspaper. Its population density, too, is less than that of the first group. Still beyond this class of readers are those who come under the head of waste circulation readers who live at such a distance that they are virtually useless from the standpoint of advertising returns. The three groups may be represented by concentric circles as shown here:

Ordinarily, a newspaper with the largest proportion of circulation giving direct advertising returns will be the best buy for the advertiser. For his purposes, a paper with 45,000 circulation classed as direct returns out of a total of 54,000 is more valuable, for example, than one in which the proportion is only 50,000 out of 80,000. On the basis of total circulation, the proportions will vary with different communities.

They will also vary according to the kind of publication. The Chicago Daily News prides itself upon the concentration as well as the relatively high purchasing power of its readers. By deliberate choice, it puts its emphasis upon local circulation or circulation within a relatively short radius of Chicago.

The Chicago Tribune, on the other hand, not only has a strong following in Chicago but has found it feasible and profitable to extend its circulation effectively over all or portions of five states. The debate between these two leading newspapers as to their respective merits is well known. The general principle has been advanced that newspaper circulation should be built on the theory that its value decreases rapidly as the distance from the city of publication increases. There is no final answer. As far as circulation is concerned, the advertiser, like the reader, must make a choice and cut his advertising cloth to fit the medium used.

The Scripps-Howard newspapers, too, aim at concentrated circulation while the Hearst publications go in more for bulk circulation. Indeed, Mr. Hearst's emphasis has always been on mass circulation.

If he had left no other mark on American journalism, he would still be remembered for his spectacular feats in building circulation. Different publishing methods yield different kinds of circulation which the advertiser must take into account to get the most out of his purchase of space in the various publications.

In general, the theory is that, if a newspaper can command a circulation totaling 20 per cent of the population of a given territory or in the ratio of 1:5, it has about reached the saturation point. This is on the basis that the average family consists of about five persons. This ratio does not necessarily follow, however, because of the many factors described that may affect circulation. If a relatively large number of newspapers are published in the community, it may be that none of them will attain the proportion indicated. Again, there are instances where individual newspapers exceed the theoretical figure and actually sell more copies daily than there are families in the community.

This is true in the case of the Columbus Dispatch which in 1935 had the unusually high figure of 113 copies sold daily in Columbus for each 100 families. This was explained not only by an active and aggressive publishing policy but by the important fact that it sold locally for 1 cent a copy. This is one reason why Dispatch promotion for a long time was built around the theme, "The Dispatch ALONE is all you need/' It had a total A.B.C. circulation in 1935 of 147,000 as against 80,000 for the Citizen, its afternoon competitor, owned by Scripps-Howard. Yet there is an answer to even such an impressive showing. The Citizen in an advertisement later in Editor & Publisher countered with these points:

1. CONCENTRATION. . . . Circulation concentrated 87% in 35-mile ABC Retail Trading Zone where 96% of Columbus, Ohio, Retail Volume originates.
2. ECONOMY. ... A rate in line with the size and sales potential of the Columbus market.
3. READER INTEREST. ... The Citizen is sold on the street and delivered by carrier at double the price of the other evening paper, yet reaches 67% of all homes, is 78% carrier delivered truly a preferred newspaper reaching an able-to-buy audience.

To sum it up, circulation ideas and principles have changed with the years. The laissez-faire policies of 25 years ago have given way to more accurate principles as to the factors affecting circulation and the best methods of building and holding it. The circulation department has come to full flower in the publishing business, and it is recognized that whatever the editorial and advertising merits of a newspaper may be they are worth little unless the circulation department has adequate opportunity to effect the optimum distribution.

It is further recognized that there is no known short cut to circulation supremacy but that to attain it there must be foresight, intelligent planning, sound execution, and unremitting effort. Above all it is seen that there is no substitute for quality in circulation and that, at least for the average daily newspaper, a concentrated circulation is next in importance to quality.

7

Circulation Practice

In some ways circulation practice has changed even more than the principles underlying circulation. The transition and the trends have already been suggested to some extent. This change was epitomized by John L. Meyer, secretary-treasurer of the Inland Daily Press Association, in an interview in Editor & Publisher'.

Describing old times, he said, " When I was a circulation manager we sold spoons and dishes, and sometimes actually threw in the paper as an added premium. Well, we made many new readers. Today, however, circulation managers sell the newspapers and are interested in adding net revenue to the papers income. They are getting down to the net of things, not merely the quantity."

The days described by Mr. Meyer are gone forever. It is now recognized that it is impossible to run a circulation department "by guess and by gosh." The successful operation of such a department calls for as much skill and brains as the conduct of any other selling agency, if not more, for the newspaper is one of the most perishable commodities in the world. As has been said so often, nothing is more stale than yesterday's newspaper, and to prevent its being stale is the task of the circulation manager and his department.

The first requisite of an effective newspaper distribution is a competent circulation executive. Given a circulation head who knows his business and is alert and aggressive, the next requirement is for a well-organized circulation department geared to the needs of a particular newspaper in terms of circulation volume, competition, and the potential as well as the actual circulation. The type and size of the departmental organization naturally depend upon the circulation factors already described. What will be effective in one set of conditions may be quite inadequate in another.

In general, however, a daily newspaper of any size is organized to serve three distinct groups of readers: (1) those who reside in the town or city of publication, (2) those who live in the near-by trade basin, and (3) those who live at a distance. These correspond roughly to home, suburban or state, and mail circulation.

They also produce to some extent, in the order named, the three types of advertising results described in the last chapter: (1) direct or immediate, (2) indirect or delayed, and (3) waste. In the main also, the first group represents the bulk of readers of the average newspaper, the second is next largest, and the third the smallest. The proportions vary with individual newspapers, but these generalizations will hold for the average daily. The smaller the newspaper in terms of circulation the simpler its circulation department. As the newspaper extends its field, its distributing machinery becomes more intricate and complicated and it requires high efficiency in a far-flung organization to get the necessary results. A newspaper of 100,000 circulation may easily have 2000 persons connected with its circulation organization, each of whom is a vital link in the chain between the publication and its most distant subscriber. The maintenance of good will and reader confidence hinges upon the spirit and effectiveness of the entire circulation personnel from the circulation manager to the last carrier or street seller. All of this calls for good organization and effective management plus intelligence and a keen sense of public relations.

On a newspaper like the New York Times or the Christian Science Monitor the circulation department is literally a farflung empire for whose well being the circulation manager is directly responsible. On such newspapers, the organization is necessarily complex and there are numerous subdivisions, each with its own specialties. Somewhat different methods of salesmanship and distribution are needed as between home delivered or local circulation and the other types on practically all classes of newspapers.

With respect to the details of organization, allowance must be made for essential differences between individual newspapers. The general scheme or arrangement of the circulation department is suggested, however, by the outline on page 53, besides those given in the chapter on Newspaper Organization, Each major subdivision will be discussed in turn.

CITY CIRCULATION

Since it is the largest and in many respects the most important, city circulation will be dealt with first. As the outline suggests, the local distribution falls under three headings : home delivery, street sales, newsstand sales. As stated previously, home-delivered circulation is the most important of these. If the newspaper is a sizable one, it may have a city manager in charge of all phases of local circulation and responsible directly to the general circulation manager.

There are three methods of home delivery, two of them involving boy carriers and a third utilizing adult carriers. The last is to be found in only a few cities. The two juvenile systems are the so-called Little Merchant or Junior Merchant plan and the Office Collect method.

Until a century ago, it will be recalled, there was practically no such thing as home delivery. Unless he received his paper by mail, the subscriber was expected to call at the publication office for his copy. It was not until the advent of the penny press and the adoption of the so-called London plan of retailing newspapers that circulation began to assume its present characteristics. Under the London plan, as adapted from its English counterpart, newspapers were sold at wholesale to newsboys who in turn sold or delivered the copies to customers and paid the publisher for them. This helped to solve the double problem of delivery and of collections.

But as recently as 1910, circulation methods were more or less haphazard. In the last two years of grammar school and all through high school, the writer carried papers in a city of more than 200,000. In the beginning, he had a small morning-paper route, but for five years had an afternoon route of between 150 and 200 customers. The latter consisted of subscribers of two competing newspapers. He owned the route outright and, like other carriers, was permitted to buy, sell, or trade customers without let or hindrance as far as the circulation departments of the two competing newspapers were concerned. No restrictions were placed upon the size of the route which, for a brief time, numbered more than 300 customers.

The carrier was nominally responsible to a confectioner who ran a branch agency as a sideline and, incidentally, did a land-office business in candy, sodas, hot dogs, and other delicacies. Yet he got his draw at the mailing room downtown, three miles distant, because he could make better time by bicycle than to depend upon the horse-drawn delivery wagon then in use. A customer sold for 50 or 60 cents as a rule, but a particularly desirable one might bring as much as $1. When he gave up his business, the carrier might pass his route on to a younger brother or sell it to another boy.

All the main office was interested in was that the papers be delivered and paid for promptly. All of this has changed. The haphazard, laissez-faire methods of yesterday have given way to system and salesmanship. With few exceptions, the customer is owned by the newspaper itself, the carrier serves an apprenticeship and, on most newspapers, is taught the fundamentals of selling along with other basic business principles. As a result, nothing is left to chance, and the customer gets better service and the boy receives higher rewards than did his predecessor of two decades ago.

OFFICE COLLECT SYSTEM

Under this arrangement, the routes and the customers are the property of the newspaper which hires boys merely to deliver the papers. Each boy gets a fixed stipend per week, the amount depending generally upon the copy price of the paper and the size of the route. The collecting is done by full-time employees of the circulation department who work from the office. The collections are made monthly or weekly according to the policy of the newspaper.

While this arrangement has had a certain vogue, it is open to serious objections. It is more expensive and less productive to the newspaper in that it requires the services of additional employees to make collections and it gives the carrier relatively little incentive to do anything except to deliver the papers issued to him. It does not fit in with any effective scheme of building circulation. It is not surprising that it appears to be giving way steadily to the less expensive, more effective Junior Merchant plan.

Junior Merchant Plan

The basis of the Little Merchant or Junior Merchant plan is that the carrier is, in effect, an independent retailer and not a salaried employee. He is far from being wholly independent, but the progress he makes and, particularly, the financial and other rewards he achieves hinge almost entirely upon his own ability and efforts, backed by sound training and spurred by proper incentives. He is under close and constant supervision. His pay is in almost direct proportion to the satisfactory service he gives and the business he produces. First of all, the boy is carefully chosen. It is not too much to say that the present generation of newspaper carriers is a handpicked group and will stand comparison with a like number of boys of the same age anywhere. In former days there was a lot of maudlin sentiment about " the poor newsie " which would be distinctly out of place today. In most instances, the boys are chosen only after making formal application and after a careful investigation of their records. They must come within certain age limits, they must attain satisfactory grades in school, they must come well recommended, and many newspapers require that they furnish a bond. This last is not only to insure their honesty and to safeguard the publication against losses from unpaid papers, but in the interests of the boy's own business training. Once the boy's application is approved, he generally serves an apprenticeship. Depending upon the size of the city and the policies of the newspaper he is to represent, this may be either as a substitute carrier or in street selling. This is done to give him some experience and to test his earnestness as well as his ability. The boy who is a good street salesman does not always make a good carrier and vice versa. The apprentice system nevertheless insures adequate representation and enough carriers to meet the ordinary needs of the newspaper.

When a regular route becomes available, it is turned over to the boy who by this time has passed the preliminary tests. As a rule his route covers a fixed territory for which he is held responsible. He must not only give good service to the customers on that route but he is accountable for nonsubscribers in his sector. That is, he is under constant pressure and is given continual incentive to go out and build up his route within the limits defined. This means soliciting nonsubscribers, and it calls in particular for watching new families who move into the neighborhood.

The Junior Merchant pays for his papers at the wholesale rate and collects for them at the retail rate. He is thus literally engaged in merchandising. He is required to make his collections at regular times, and, in particular, he must pay for them once a week, usually either Saturday or Monday. In order to do this he must make his own collections promptly. In this way the newspaper itself is saved the trouble and expense, which it has under the Office Collect system, of making collections, and the boy gets a varied business training in dealing with his customers, in handling money, in making collections, and, generally, in doing business in a businesslike way. The effectiveness of this method of collecting is shown by the testimony of a newspaper with more than 125,000 circulation that in any given week there is not more than $10 or $15 outstanding for the entire city.

Against this is the experience of a paper of much smaller circulation which showed that besides the extra collection expense involved it lost from $1800 to $2000 a year in bad circulation accounts. By changing to the Little Merchant plan in this case, collection economies were effected, the average carrier earned $7 weekly as against $4 formerly, the circulation was increased with correspondingly greater revenue for the newspaper, the collection losses were eliminated, and its promotion problems were simplified.

This experience has been duplicated many times. That of two other newspapers, the Fort Smith, Ark., South Western American and Times-Record, will suffice to emphasize the point. They changed from the Office Collect to the Junior Merchant plan July 1, 1934, with stress being laid on collections. Of their 72 carriers under the old method, all but three qualified under the new. According to G. C. Gardner, the circulation manager, the change resulted in more business and higher profits. Carrier circulation increased 34 per cent, revenue was about $150 a week more, expenses decreased, the office detail was less, the delivery service was improved, the work of the boys was dignified, they received better training, and the cost of getting new starts was less than before.

The emphasis on better training for the carriers is an essential part of the Little Merchant system. Under it, the boys are given sound coaching in the fundamentals of the business. They get not only the theory but the practice, and they have added incentive to apply what they are taught in the continuous and special selling campaigns that are carried on by the newspapers. Indeed, largely as a result of the development and expansion of the Junior Merchant idea, the major emphasis in circulation building has been centered on the carrier, who benefits accordingly.

One not familiar with the application of the idea might wonder whether the plan does not lend itself to undue exploitation of the boys. While it is true that the carriers are under continual pressure to produce results, there is no real ground for any fear that the newspapers take undue advantage of their carriers. In this connection, certain insinuations by advocates of the proposed Child Labor Amendment to the federal Constitution that it is necessary, in part, because of conditions among newsboys are distinctly without foundation. As a matter of fact, the great majority of newspapers take a highly beneficent attitude toward their carriers and street sellers.

They not only look after their business conduct and training but they take a definite interest in their personal welfare and wellbeing. Various kinds of rewards and incentives are offered not only for additional business and efficient collections but for the best service to customers. Many newspapers publish special papers in the interests of their carriers. Some maintain carrier bands and other kinds of activities. These will be discussed more in detail in the following chapter on Circulation Promotion.

Adult Carriers

In a few cities, such as Cincinnati, Pittsburgh, New York, and Chicago, adult carriers are used for home delivery in whole or in part. With them it is a full-time job and, owing to their age, experience, strength, and special working conditions, they are enabled to deliver enough papers to yield a reasonable wage. Such practice is the exception rather than the rule and in all probability would not be feasible except under special circumstances. The general practice in such cases is for the carriers to deliver all the papers on a given street or in a given territory, including competing publications. They pay for their draw at the wholesale rate and make collections at the retail rate. This type of delivery is perhaps more dependable and efficient in some ways but is open at least to the objection that it does not give the opportunity or incentive to produce new business that the Little Merchant plan does.

Legal Status of Carriers

It is more than an academic question whether the newsboy is the agent or employee of the newspaper or whether he is, in the legal sense of the term, an independent contractor. Not only personal but property rights are involved. If the carrier is an employee of the publication, he is likely to come under workman's compensation laws and the newspaper is also, to some extent at least, responsible for his acts. If he is an independent contractor, however, he must stand on his own feet in the event that he is injured or that he commits a tort while engaged in delivering his papers. There is also the question of the ownership of the routes. The test seems to lie in the degree of control exercised over him and the answer is not wholly clear. To the extent that most newspapers own the customers and the routes into which they are grouped and from the fact that the boy takes instructions from the publication as to the method of serving those customers, he seems to be an employee. But from the fact that he buys his papers wholesale, delivers them, and collects for them at the retail rate and is otherwise free to do as he pleases, he is an independent contractor. As a matter of fact, the courts of most states where the question has arisen have ruled practically unanimously that the carrier is, in effect, an independent contractor.

Further, the workmen's compensation acts of some states, specifically New Jersey and California, are so written that newspaper carriers are definitely excluded from their provisions. The question has now been raised as to whether they will come under the new federal Social Security Act and the first opinion seems to be in the negative unless they are on salary. In an opinion cited in Circulation Management, it was pointed out that "where the control is to the result only of the work, the person employed is an independent contractor." This applies, of course, to most carriers. In engaging a boy as a carrier, moreover, a newspaper can stipulate the terms of such limited employment, including control over the route assigned to him, its ownership, the basis on which he is to be paid, and other pertinent matters.

Newsboy Regulation

Various legal measures to safeguard the employment of persons under age apply to newspaper carriers and sellers. These take the form of local ordinances, state laws, and some federal regulation. The newspaper industry itself has also had the wisdom and foresight to take steps to protect those in its employ. Under the National Industrial Recovery Act, in the early days of the New Deal, certain restrictions were agreed upon between the federal Department of Labor and the American Newspaper Publishers' Association for incorporation in the newspaper code. Not long before the U. S.

Supreme Court held the N.I.R.A. unconstitutional, the code authority for the daily newspaper business submitted an amendment to the code which provided, among other things, (1) that boys under twelve years of age should not be engaged in the delivery of newspapers on routes, (2) that boys under fourteen years of age should not be engaged in the sale of newspapers in cities of 50,000 population or over, and (3) that no boy under twelve years of age should be engaged in the sale of newspapers in a city of less than 50,000 population.

This proposal received the almost unanimous approval of the more than 1200 publishers who had given their assent to the code. After the N.I.R.A. was thrown out, most newspapers continued to live up to the provisions, and in 1936 the A.N.P.A. committee on the newspaper boy issued a plea that all newspapers adhere to these minimum-age limits.

A number of cities have ordinances that limit or prohibit the hawking of newspapers at night. These have the double purpose and merit of keeping youths off the streets at unreasonable hours and of reducing unnecessary noises at night so that the good burghers can sleep. Among the cities that have adopted such regulations are Port Chester, N. Y., and Girard, Ohio, while in Charleston, W. Va., the publishers and the civil authorities agreed in 1936 upon rules to keep small boys from selling newspapers on the streets after regular hours as an excuse for violating the local curfew law.

Newsboy Trends

In general, signs point to fewer but older newsboys with somewhat higher earnings. In all, there are some 500,000 newspaper carriers and street salesmen in the United States whose earnings from the sale of newspapers run probably between $90,000,000 and $100,000,000 a year.

A report made at the International Circulation Managers Association convention in 1934 showed a total of 497,352 carriers and street sales boys with average weekly earnings of $1,691,871.77.

This was a decrease from the previous year of 90,935 boys and $258,783.66 in weekly earnings, but the earnings of the average boy rose from $3.32 weekly to $3.40, those of carriers being slightly higher than those of street sellers. The survey covered 1489 newspapers. It showed only 2530 girls engaged in carrying or selling and only 3 per cent of the boys under twelve years of age. Those over sixteen comprised the largest age group with 35 per cent, while those between fourteen and sixteen made up 24 per cent. Carriers worked, on the average, 72 minutes a day as against 198 minutes for street newsboys. This was a distinct increase for both groups. A U. S. Department of Labor report in 1935 pointed out a striking tendency on the part of newspapers to employ older boys for this work, the proportion of boys between fourteen and fifteen having doubled and that of boys under ten years of age dropping from 17 to 4 per cent from the corresponding groups as disclosed in studies made in 1922 and 1926.[5] The report was based upon a study of the data on about 3100 newsboys and 1200 magazine sellers in 17 cities.

SUBURBAN CIRCULATION

Just how the circulation outside of the town or city of publication is handled will depend upon the special conditions in individual cases. If the suburbs or near-by towns are close enough and the number of copies involved is large enough, branches or districts similar to those in the city are frequently set up, and the work of carriers is supervised much as in the city. This is particularly true of big city newspapers with a large outlying circulation in contiguous territory. If the number of carriers involved is small, they may be handled through special dealers or distributors and, of course, there are many independent carriers.

The Columbus Dispatch, for example, has dealers or distributors in some 35 outlying towns who act in the same capacity as the district managers in Columbus with the local carriers responsible to them. Many of these dealers or distributors are located in county seats, where they work on a commission basis. Some of them are on a full-time basis and some occasionally handle other out-of-town papers but never another competing Columbus 'paper.

MOTOR ROUTES

Competition, the spread of improved roads, reader demands for later news and better newspapers, and changing transportation conditions have all contributed to the development of extensive motor delivery of newspapers. Here again the methods in use are shaped according to the needs and facilities of individual publications. In some cases trucks, owned by the newspaper, are used to deliver papers quickly over a large territory extending in all directions from the place of publication. In others, cars owned and operated by the drivers but maintained by the newspaper are used. Bus lines are used sometimes to supplement these methods and, of course, various combinations will be found.

The efficient and effective operation of motor routes calls for good organization and management. They must be so arranged as to give prompt yet profitable delivery. A route must be long enough to justify itself and yet not so long as to be burdensome or to delay the delivery of papers to the last customers. A car may carry bundles of papers for distribution by carriers in outlying towns or it may give "slinger" service or both. "Slinger" service is the delivery of individual papers to subscribers along the way.

Many newspapers follow the practice of providing metal tubes on posts into which the papers are inserted, or they may be tossed onto the porch if the farmhouse is close enough to the road; hence the name " slinger." The tubes are generally supplied free to rural subscribers and bear the name of the newspaper. The route man is held responsible for their being kept in condition and for their removal if the subscriber moves or discontinues the paper. Because the use of mail boxes is limited by postal rule to matter carried in the mails, it is illegal to use them for papers delivered by carrier.

Motor routes are expensive, the costs varying with local conditions. When they are justified and when they are not are questions that must be decided on their merits. In an article in Circulation Management on "Motor Routes on Smaller Papers," C. J. Copeland, circulation manager of the Johnson City, Tenn., Press, gave these answers: (1) if the newspaper, has no real competition and does not need the additional circulation, the answer is probably "No"; (2) but if the competition is strong, if more circulation is needed, if additional circulation will permit an advertising rate increase, if other transportation facilities are limited, if the newspaper is an afternoon publication with morning-paper competition, and if the rural area is partially industrialized, the answer is probably "Yes."

In the case of this particular newspaper, the development of motor routes and the additional subscribers they afforded, resulted in a material increase in circulation. Of a total of 11,000 circulation, 3500 copies were hauled in bundles to outlying carriers and 3000 were delivered to subscribers en route. In laying out the routes the Press followed only two general rules: make each one a complete circuit and get the papers delivered before dark.

They averaged about 70 miles in length and two plus subscribers per mile. Unprofitable portions of routes were eliminated by continuous checks. The drivers owned the cars, were required to carry liability insurance on them, and were paid about 3 cents a mile and from 5 to 7 cents a week per paper as commissions. The Press maintained 22 routes. The Spencer, Iowa, Daily Reporter, published in a rich farming section, has 27 small towns within a radius of 30 miles, only two of which had railroad or bus service suitable for the delivery of an afternoon paper. Four cars were put on to deliver the Reporter to these towns, yielding enough circulation to pay expenses and "a nice profit."

Expenses were reduced by effecting a combination with two big city newspapers serving the same territory, the Reporter's cars hauling their bundles as well as its own. The revenue from the two outside newspapers paid more than two-thirds of the expense. To make motor delivery possible and profitable, newspapers have properly increased the copy price to subscribers thus served. For many years it has been the custom to give rural readers a subscription rate much lower than those in the city. About the only justifications for this practice were (1) that others did it; (2) that the country reader as a rule received his paper the day after publication; and (3) that such circulation did not cost much. Newspapers soon found, however, that they were losing money on mail subscriptions priced at $3 or $4 a year that were taken over on motor routes. The present practice is to charge customers on motor routes substantially the same as city readers. As to the necessity and propriety for this change there can be no argument.

AIRPLANE ROUTES

A growing number of newspapers have purchased airplanes which are used for combination purposes. In time there is no question but that the airplane will be adapted to limited circulation use. The Oakland, Calif., Tribune was one of the first to do so. By contract with an aviation line, it arranged for air delivery to seven near-by cities from which the papers were picked up by buses and trains. Street and Newsstand Sales. In larger cities, teen-age girls have practically disappeared from the street selling of newspapers and such sales are confined to men or to boys who are out of school or who, at least, are not in day school.

The men may be of any age, depending upon the policy of the newspaper. Such salesmen are supplied from trucks which make the rounds of downtown or other strategic street corners. The salesmen may have fixed stations or may be permitted to roam, again depending upon the policy of the publication, although the former is the more prevalent. In some cases both types of selling are used. Newsboys who have no fixed corner or station are known in some cities as "bootjacks."

Newsstands, too, are supplied by newspaper trucks with definite routes. The papers in such cases are not usually made up into bundles, but the "draw" is supplied by count from the supply on the truck. In the case of street-corner salesmen, the trucks may make the rounds several times to replenish their supply.

Returns

One serious question confronting newspapers is the problem of returns. In order to reduce expenses, to cut down the losses from unsold papers, and in some degree to keep sales at a maximum, most newspapers have a fixed policy as to the number of papers returnable by a dealer unsold. If a newspaper is too lenient in this respect, it can easily let the number of unsold copies run to many thousand a year as simple arithmetic will show. For example, a newspaper that has four city editions daily and serves 200 newsstands of all sorts will have unsold returns of half a million copies a year from this one source if it permits each dealer to return only two copies of each of the four editions daily. One way to reduce the returns is to limit the draw or the number of papers issued to each newsstand. Where returns are permitted some newspapers require that the entire paper be returned, while others will accept the signature from the top of page one. This is especially true for out-of-town dealers.

Copy Prices

As has been explained, the copy prices charged for a newspaper are important. They must be low enough to be within steady reach of the customer, and yet they must be high enough to yield the publisher a proper and proportionate share of the revenue of the newspaper. In individual cases, the determination of copy prices will depend upon the various factors involved, such as costs, competition, and quality of the product sold. Habit is also something of a factor for it has been demonstrated time and again that readers are willing to pay anything within reason if they feel that they are getting their money's worth. The range of copy prices of dailies in the United States is from 1 to 5 cents. It has been said that there is no economic justification for a 1-cent price on the part of any daily.

Yet the Columbus Dispatch for some years has sold at that price locally and 2 cents elsewhere, while the example of the Kansas City Star at 17 cents a week for the morning, afternoon, and Sunday issues is well known. Such cases, however, are the exceptions that prove the rule. For the great majority of newspapers, the standard price has been 2 cents a copy and 10 or 12 cents a week. More recently this seems to have shifted in the direction of 3 cents a copy or 15 cents a week by carrier.

It would not be surprising if this became the standard price in the future. Comparable rates are given for the month or by the year, although most subscribers served by carrier pay by the week or, less frequently, by the month. The mail subscriber, on the other hand, generally pays by the year in advance although as a special inducement to rural readers during times of depression and drought, some newspapers have arranged to accommodate them for much shorter periods.

Price Adjustments

In the face of conditions caused by the depression, newspapers generally found it necessary to readjust their scale of prices. Many of them, as noted, increased the price to the reader and adjusted their wholesale rates accordingly. A few changed only their wholesale rates a fraction of a cent. Another fairly common step, taken either by groups or by individual action, was to raise the price to the mail subscriber who, on the average, was paying a little more than half of the rate charged the city reader. Many newspapers, too, boosted their circulation income by changing from the Office Collect to the Junior Merchant plan of distribution.

Where newspapers raised their copy price after giving due notice, three results were common in practically every case: (1) an immediate gain in circulation revenue, (2) an immediate loss in circulation, (3) an early recouping of most if not all of the circulation loss. The changes demonstrated that such action, if taken at the right time and in the right way, can be made to the definite improvement of the position of the newspaper.

When the St. Louis newspapers made the change, for example, the Post Dispatch ran full-page advertisements showing the prevalence of retail newspaper prices elsewhere ranging from 3 to 5 cents, and its public was convinced. The same device was used effectively in other localities. In many cases, too, newspapers added new features or additional services such as wire photo so as to give their readers a better product in return for the increase.

In making such a change, it has been pointed out that the fall or early winter is the best time because then the normal seasonal gain will be more than likely to offset the immediate loss. It has been shown also that the change can be made regardless of competitors, but there is a distinct advantage if several or all the local newspapers involved take similar action at the same time. After the change has been made, experience indicates that the loss in home-delivered circulation is apt to be made up more quickly than that from street sales because of the price differential of half a cent, and also that the bulk of the loss is recouped within three months either from new subscribers or from old ones who find that they cannot do without the paper. In taking such an action the newspaper also weeds out the least desirable readers from the standpoint of the advertiser. In any event, it seems evident from what has occurred since 1930 that the day of extremely low rates is gone forever.

Commissions

As with so many other things, there are no fixed standards as to circulation commissions paid by newspapers. There are signs of some cooperation, especially as to mail rates, but the individual newspaper is free to fix its own tariffs. Where copy price increases have been put into effect in recent years, publishers have properly shared the additional revenue with carriers and solicitors. A fraction of a cent difference in the rate will add thousands of dollars to circulation revenue on large newspapers.

Mail Circulation

The handling of mail circulation is something of both an art and a science. It requires special office machinery and has a technique all its own. In mail circulation the newspaper is dealing with the subscriber at long range, although the distance may vary from five miles to half way around the earth. In any event, direct contact with such readers is largely limited to correspondence and to the publication itself. This calls for a special variety of promotion, salesmanship, and service. It also requires close cooperation between the mailing room and the post office to insure that such subscribers get their papers promptly and regularly. Mail subscriptions differ from other kinds of circulation in several ways. With most daily newspapers, they comprise the smallest proportion of total sales. They are required to be paid for in advance, either quarterly, semiannually, or by the year. Much of such circulation comes voluntarily from former residents and others who have a special interest in the community or in that particular newspaper. What soliciting is done is usually carried on by direct mail or in some instances through other subscribers and, more rarely, by personal solicitation. It is important that a definite routine be established for the handling of circulation-department mail. This is especially true both as to the dispatch of papers and as to incoming correspondence relating to mail circulation. This is to insure that orders, changes, complaints, and requests are handled expeditiously and to guard against errors. Such mail generally falls under the five headings of (1) new orders, (2) renewals, (3) changes in addresses, (4) stops, and (5) miscellaneous.

New orders and renewals, in particular, should be handled as promptly as possible. The amount received should be credited in the proper place to the subscriber, the proper records made out promptly and the correspondence filed so that it is readily accessible if needed. In regard to these as well as to changes in addresses, promptness and accuracy are the marks of effective management and anything less only breeds trouble. The use of a fixed method for handling such mail not only protects the interests of the subscriber but insures a more even flow of work in the circulation department.

The alert mail division of the circulation department also keeps a calendar of starts and stops which should be entered when the paper is first ordered. This consists of making an index of all mail subscriptions expiring on a given date. As the time approaches, it is only a routine matter to send the reader notice that his subscription is about to expire and enclose the first promotion literature to get him to renew it. This is anywhere from a month to ten days prior to the expiration. If the first notice does not bring the desired results, successive means are used for a reasonable length of time.

It has been said that non-renewals fall into three classes : those who do not want it, those who put it off, and those who cannot make up their minds. If those in the first group really mean it, the newspaper is wasting its time on them when the first two or three notices are of no avail. The satisfied reader and those who can be persuaded to renew after some hesitation are the principal sources of renewals. A renewed subscription is generally more valuable than a new one to both the newspaper and its advertisers for the simple reason that it costs less to get and represents a satisfied customer who is dependent upon and has confidence in the publication.

Complaints

Regardless of their source or even their merit, complaints must be handled promptly and tactfully. The customer is not always right; in fact, he is often unreasonable with carriers but he must have an opportunity to think that he is right. If papers are missed, or are late, or are thrown in the wrong place, the deficiency must be corrected as soon as it is reported. Most newspapers have found it good practice to encourage subscribers to report bad service at once.

They generally follow it up with a return postal card or a personal call from the substation manager or some other "trouble shooter" to make certain that the difficulty has been ironed out and the customer is now satisfied. A system of rewards and penalties applicable to the carriers is also in vogue in many cities, A boy who carries a route for three months without a complaint, for example, gets one form of reward. If he goes for another three months, he gets a still better one, and so on. Conversely, if complaints are made about him by customers he is subject to penalties. One newspaper, for example, has a system of fines, starting at 25 cents. Of course, if a boy is chronically the subject of complaints the only thing to do is to replace him.

Turnover and Seasonally

Even if carrier service were perfect and ordinary renewals were 100 per cent, there would still be an appreciable turnover in circulation. Deaths and removals alone would account for a large number of losses in the course of a year. For this reason, circulation is always dynamic and never static, and the circulation picture is changing constantly. There is always a marginal group of city readers, too, who are more or less on the move, and, unless the changes in address are followed up promptly, they are apt to be lost to competitors. In addition to outright losses in circulation due to causes beyond the control of the newspaper, there are seasonal fluctuations. It is practically the universal experience that circulation is heavier in the fall and winter than it is in the summer. Street sales may be up in the summer but home delivery is generally down. For one thing, many families go away on vacation for part or all of the summer, and even the stay-at-homes have other interests and activities such as golf which tend to reduce sales. Extremes of weather likewise affect circulation, particularly street sales. Morning newspapers are perhaps less likely to be affected than afternoons because of sports and because business houses and professional men take the paper throughout the year.

The efficient circulation department tries both to anticipate and to overcome such fluctuations. The vacation losses can be offset in part by a campaign to encourage readers to have the home-town newspaper sent where they are going. Other types of promotion can be used to bring in new subscribers to help compensate for seasonal losses. Both methods have been successfully used separately or in combination. This takes no account, of course, of losses caused by objectionable editorial or news policies. Such defections must be remedied in other ways.

Number of Editions

How many editions a newspaper publishes will depend generally upon the nature and extent of its circulation and the competition it has to meet. Of late the tendency has been to reduce the number of editions rather than to increase them. Many of those that are retained consist of little more than a page one makeover or perhaps one additional inside page replated. In a number of fairly large cities the sale of noon, baseball, and other special editions has fallen off to such an extent that they are no longer profitable. The radio has been responsible for this to some extent.

In a number of cities, too, publishers have come to realize that they face common problems in such matters and that the solution lies in the direction of cooperation rather than futile competition. The result has been in agreements to abandon certain editions and to divide the sales time as between morning and afternoon papers. Such agreements have been worked out, for example, in New York and in Cleveland. In the former, seven newspapers took joint steps to reduce production and circulation costs. Strict standards were set up for the closing of first and last editions of the cooperating publications. Previously the first editions of morning newspapers appeared as early as 6 P.M. Under the terms of the agreement, this was moved back to 8 P.M., while the press 'time for the final edition of the cooperating afternoon papers was fixed at 6 P.M. and their first edition between 10 :30 and 11 A.M.

This arrangement makes possible the publication of an afternoon paper completely within the 8-hour day of the mechanical departments and the consequent elimination of overtime. The participating morning newspapers lost some circulation as a result but this was small when weighed against the savings. The newspapers cooperating were the Newst the Mirror, the American, the Post, the World-Telegram, the Journal, and the Sun. Unfair Practices. In the same manner, ethical and progressive newspapers have been working toward a code of fair practices in circulation management. Before such a code could be put into effect, it was necessary to define what constituted unfair practices. A list of such practices as reported to the Inland Daily Press Association covered newspapers which :

- Lowered subscription prices in the outlying territory of competitors.

- Gave full rebates to Sunday motor dealers.
- Paid bonuses to country carriers and dealers.
- Sold at less than published rates.
- Offered insurance policies at cut rates.
- Used premiums without adding the cost.
- Enabled solicitors to cut prices by giving excessive commissions.
- Permitted extra time- for payment on subscriptions obtained by carriers.
- Conducted certain types of subscription contests.
- Continued sending papers indefinitely after the expiration of the subscription.
- Entered clubs with magazines.
- Delivered by truck beyond the retail-trading area.
- Distributed papers free by carrier in the city of publication.

The postal regulations and the rules of the Audit Bureau of Circulations have helped to curb the excessive zeal of some circulation departments. So have the general and special trade associations in the publishing field. About the fairness or unfairness of some of the practices cited, there is still some debate. It is a good sign, however, that the newspapers themselves are setting their house in order in these respects. Forms, Filing, and Records, Good management of an effective circulation department calls for accurate, adequate, and quickly accessible records and reports. These must cover: (1) the subscriber; (2) the carrier, salesman, or agent; and (3) circulation income and expense. Against the danger of insufficient or poorly organized records there is the counter danger of setting up too much office red tape. Simplicity is, therefore, desirable as a safeguard against error and in the interests of speed and efficiency. The number and kinds of records and forms will vary with the volume and character of the circulation of individual newspapers. Some newspapers will find it possible to operate with a minimum system. Others, because of the sheer volume of business, the extent of the territory covered, and the number of individuals involved, will require complicated methods. The Topeka, Kans. , State Journal for example, has devised a card for carriers which replaces half a dozen forms previously used. Printed in duplicate, it not only provides for starts, stops, changes in addresses, and complaints but for payments made by the carrier and other information. All this is accommodated on a card by 5 inches. The Warren, Ohio, Tribune makes use of a monthly report to the parents of each carrier as to his progress in "business training" during the previous month. The Colorado Springs Gazette and Telegraph has a monthly grade card for its Junior Merchants, the reverse side of which shows their school standing as well. A number of newspapers also use merit certificates of one sort or another in connection with the Little Merchant carrier system.

Other forms in use include those for cashbooks and for traveling representatives. A fairly simple, yet effective, type of the former is one used by the Elyria, Ohio, Chronicle-Telegram. 4 It gives a ready reckoning of circulation income and at the same time affords a check against the A.B.C. book and the cash register.

COLLECTION AND OTHER FORM LETTERS

These, too, can be more or less standardized. A series of collection letters can be devised to deal with most delinquent subscribers. Such letters, in general, should be tactful, original, simple, and direct. Above all, they should have a personal appeal, even if they are only multigraphed. Form letters can also be used, under some circumstances, to handle routine complaints concerning nondelivery of papers through the mails and other similar matters. Experience is the best teacher in such matters.

Twine vs. Wire

A volume might be written about the details of circulation practice and problems. One further example will suffice here. It has to do with the relative merits of twine and wire for tying newspaper bundles. To the uninitiated, this might seen like a simple matter.

Most newspapers, in fact, have long used twine and will probably continue to do so. Yet some, like the Chicago Daily News, have abandoned twine for wire with highly satisfactory results. The experience of this paper has been that it ties much more rapidly than twine and is better insurance against thefts and broken bundles. The saving of time permits later deadlines which in itself is an important item. The task of buying twine for newspaper circulation department use becomes more complex when it is learned that there are some 5000 sizes and kinds in current use of which perhaps 10 per cent are suitable for newspapers. Twine for newspaper bundles must neither break nor stretch, it must have adequate working strength, it must not cost too much, and, when stored, it must retain its natural moisture. Working strength is resistance against the cutting or chafing action of twine in a tied bundle. It is different from tensile strength. In general, that twine is best which has strength, adaptability, and economy. Some newspapers employ metal fasteners with twine which they are thus enabled to use as much as 75 times.

From the foregoing, it will be evident that circulation management is in itself both a business and an industry that call for effective selling, efficient distribution, and a high degree of skill, energy, and experience. If the newspaper's eggs are in any one basket, it is the circulation basket. The best editorial product in the world is worthless if the sales and circulation machinery is faulty. On the other hand, one has only to look around to see publications of limited editorial merit marketed in large volume by skillful merchandising on the part of the circulation department.

8

Circulation Promotion

It is the primary purpose of circulation promotion to strengthen the circulation of a publication. This may take the direction of greater reader interest or additional subscribers, or both. Anything that contributes to these ends, therefore, comes within the definition of circulation promotion. Yet it is sometimes difficult to draw a sharp dividing line between circulation promotion and other types of newspaper promotion.

This is for several reasons. One is that promotion that achieves a primary purpose may also accomplish a secondary result as a byproduct. Another is that on most newspapers the promotion function is perhaps less standardized and less well organized than almost any other phase of publishing activity. In consequence, circulation promotion is sometimes handled within the circulation department and sometimes by the general promotion department. On backward newspapers there is no definite or regular provision for such promotion.

In general, however, it may be said that the building of circulation through promotional effort takes one of two forms: (1) that aimed at the reader; (2) that directed at the sales personnel of the newspaper. Circulation promotion is at least as old as the penny press, but it is only in recent years that the term has come into general use. Allowing for special adaptation, the principles of general promotion may be applied to newspaper circulation. They are partly a matter of psychology and partly a matter of economics.

Capitalizing upon fundamental human qualities such as curiosity or the lure of a bargain will bring results in newspaper merchandising just as surely as it did for P. T. Barnum or for any commercial enterprise. The only limits to the form promotion takes are those of common honesty and human ingenuity. It runs the entire gamut from quota and other forms of pressure selling to many types of contests. Even the use of premiums and cut rates has not been entirely outmoded.

SALES PROMOTION

Because the newspaper must first capture the subscriber before it can undertake to keep him, various types of circulation sales promotion will be dealt with first. For a long time the emphasis in subscription campaigns was upon the use of premiums and the employment of adult solicitors who worked on a commission basis. Currently the use of premiums has fallen into some disrepute as being unsound, uneconomical, and undignified, and most daily newspapers now put their chief dependence upon their carriers to maintain and to increase their circulation. For the most part there has been a return to sanity here, but some newspapers still rely upon high-pressure methods. The services of professional circulation promoters are still used to a limited extent by small publications, but this is chiefly in the weekly rather than in the daily field. Such agencies are usually companies which make a business of building circulation for publications which lack the facilities or the experience for helping themselves. The customary arrangement is for them to work on a percentage basis, the publisher paying most if not all of the expenses, including any prizes and premiums that may be offered. This method has the advantage of enlisting professional experience, but is also open to the serious objection that additional circulation so obtained may be too temporary or expensive to be of any real or lasting benefit to the newspaper.

The basic requirements of any newspaper selling campaign are few and simple: (1) it must be effective; (2) it must not be too complicated; (3) it must be reasonably economical; and (4) it must produce quality circulation, i.e., circulation that is really valuable and useful to the publication and to the advertiser. In addition, experience has shown that circulation campaigns must be not only productive but cumulative. A newspaper derives no real benefit from circulation obtained through great effort and expense if it cannot keep most of the subscribers thus added. Examples are numerous of expensive circulation campaigns that yielded legions of new readers who dropped by the wayside within 90 days when the contest ended or the sales pressure was relaxed. Just two will suffice. In one, a reader promotion contest added 14,000 subscribers in January. These were gone, besides some 2000 others, by June. Two other newspapers spent $150,000 each in similar promotion, and the resulting gains did not last eight months. These emphasize the need, too, for holding circulation as well as getting it.

For these reasons, many newspapers have abandoned spectacular high-pressure campaigns which produce temporary results in favor of continuing promotion which has the dual advantage of sustained incentive for the sales force and lasting interest for the reader. In most instances, such a policy is more logical, less expensive, more productive, and certainly more lasting in its results. The discovery, or rather the realization of this fact, has given added impetus to the importance of, and necessity for, an adequate and permanent promotion program.

Carrier Promotion

The whole scheme of present-day newspaper sales promotion fits right in with the Junior Merchant plan. As noted in the preceding chapter, circulation salesmanship is at the root of this idea. The boy who cannot produce results, not only in terms of good service to the customers entrusted to him but in new subscribers, is quickly weeded out, while the boy who is a producer is rewarded in direct proportion to what he is able to produce, particularly in the way of new starts. There are two types of campaigns which may be likened, respectively, to the use of the rifle and the shotgun. The one has as its purpose the attainment of a definite objective, such as a given number of new subscribers, or the building up of circulation in a new sector or in a weak area. The second represents an effort with scattering effect which, under the law of averages if for no other reason, is bound to produce some results. A newspaper may use either or both, depending upon its needs. In the case of the carrier, the incentive or reward must be keyed to the boy. Many newspapers give cash prizes and others offer merchandise, such as sports or recreational equipment in season. Capitalizing upon the natural desire of almost every one to travel, an increasing number of publications are using attractive trips as the main awards to their best carriers. Some of these are day trips to points of interest, while others are all-expense tours lasting the better part of a week and even longer. This type of promotion has been shown to produce large dividends.

The prevalence of the practice of requiring or expecting carriers to solicit new business is shown by the survey of 1489 newspapers already referred to. Boys were compelled to solicit new business by 434 of the papers reporting, while 431 expected them to do so, and 542 encouraged them to do it. Only 51 said they had no policy in this respect. Experience seems to show that in any circulation contest, regardless of the nature of the rewards or prizes to the carriers, the smaller the number of new subscriptions required and the shorter the term of such subscriptions, the greater will be the results. For example, it is easier to sign up new subscribers for a three-month trial than it is for six months. Likewise, a boy is more apt to produce results if 10 new starts will bring him a prize than if he is required to get 15 or 20. It has also been shown that contests are distinctly more difficult for the boy if the required number of new starts exceeds a dozen. The problem then is to make contests hard enough to produce substantial results and yet not so difficult as to discourage the boy.

The Charleston, W. Va., Gazette has an interesting plan of rewards and incentives which illustrates what can be done. When a boy is first accepted by the Gazette, he is rated as a Newspaper Boy. After he has made certain accomplishments, he becomes a

Junior Merchant, and, when he produces 100 per cent in sales and in service, he is promoted to Master Salesman ; about 20 per cent of the boys qualify for this status. In addition, there is a group of supersalesmen, limited to 30 and known as the "30 Club." When a boy gets his first promotion as a carrier he is given a belt and a buckle bearing the name of the paper and the insignia of the degree in color as well as a cap with the same insignia. The Junior Merchant and Master Salesman degrees likewise carry caps with their respective colors and insignia. All Master Salesmen are sent to a free camp for a week, while the 30 Club boys get a special cash bonus of 50 per cent of their paper bill the week before Christmas, the amount running from $1 to $15. After a boy has been in service for a month he may apply for his first merit chevron," providing his record has been up to standard and he has shown some sales ability. It is entirely optional whether he applies, but most of them do, according to Chester H. Roberts, assistant circulation manager of the Gazette, because promotion brings higher rates for starts. Thus, a new boy who has not been promoted gets only about 7 cents an order as against 20 cents for the Master Salesman. A boy is required, however, to pay into a savings account, the payment amounting to 10 per cent of his paper bill each week for ten weeks.

A sales meeting is held each Thursday evening when each boy must fill out a sales report. The only way he can do this is to canvass his own route, and he is given credit or penalized according to his sales report. On Friday evenings the same report is given to him at another sales meeting, and he can fill it out only after canvassing anywhere he cares to, on other routes as well as his own. The results of these efforts and duties are recorded at his substation, and, at the end of the month, he receives certificates on the basis of the points he has made. He may redeem these either in cash or in prizes.

The boy becomes eligible for his second merit chevron after he has been in service at least 2^j months, has paid his savings deposit quota, and has won at least 10 gold certificates denoting a gain of 10 subscribers on his route. If he meets these qualifications he gets an official Gazette Junior Merchant sports jacket and his rate on start orders is raised to about 10 cents. Similarly, the boy can attain the Master Salesman's status only after at least six-months' service and not less than two months after he has won the Junior Merchant's degree. Master Salesmen are eligible to the free camping trip, to a Christmas bonus and membership in the 30 Club. Boys may be suspended from any of the degrees, however, for failure to maintain their records and each boy is made to feel his responsibility. The program not only teaches the boy to stand on his own feet but it produces circulation results, and it yields favorable publicity for the newspaper.

The Atlanta Georgian-American conducts a carrier Honor Roll which has proved to be very helpful in promoting better service, increased circulation, and prompt collections. These incentives are offered to boys on the Honor Roll: weekly theater tickets, a special party for those on the roll 4 weeks in succession, a cash bonus of $5 for those on the list for 26 successive weeks. The Honor Roll is printed each Sunday. The plan worked so well that it was extended to include the district managers. To win a place on the roll the boy must have observed these requirements:

1. Reported to regular and special meetings at appointed times.
2. Worked his route faithfully for new business on nights as required by District Manager and checked in to him at appointed place and time.
3. Did not have a complaint for the past seven days.
4. Followed all instructions, as given by District Manager, to the letter.
5. Recommended by District Manager as having put forth every effort to increase Bulldog sales and to secure regular subscribers from Bulldog customers.
6. Paid account in full on time as required by District Manager.
7. Route book in perfect order and neat and turned in to District Manager on time for checking.
8. Conduct was above reproach and appearance neat and satisfactory at all times.

9. Service record at office denotes strict attention to details, such as Insurance, Magazines, and transfers; also shows progress on route.
10. Sales Manual was carefully studied and used to improve sales ability. Sales Manual was used on solicitation.
11. Made quota as set by District Manager.

The Columbus Dispatch uses a system of honor buttons for carriers. To be successful, the carrier must deliver his papers without misses or complaints, he must complete his collections on time, he must make a profit from his route and must develop sales ability. For a satisfactory record for three months he is entitled to a celluloid honor button, for six months a bronze button, and for nine months a gold button. He is graded monthly by his district manager. He is provided with a sales manual and he receives the Dispatch Hustler, a tabloid newspaper issued monthly in the interests of carriers. The names and standings of leading carriers are printed together with accounts and descriptions of outstanding accomplishments, information about contests in progress or impending, and other matters of interest to the boys. Merchandise Prizes. A list of things the average boy wants would fill a small book. In offering prizes, therefore, the circulation manager has only to capitalize upon this natural desire to spur his carriers to productive effort. Tangible prizes generally take one of three forms: cash, merchandise, or trips. The range of merchandise awards runs all the way from things in common use and demand by boys to novelties. There are any number of novelty manufacturers in the United States whose wares can be so used. A newspaper can usually buy merchandise at wholesale rates for this purpose.

Merchandise prizes frequently take the form of seasonal goods or things which the boy would be unlikely or unable to get for himself. With the return of the bicycle to popular favor, quite a number of newspapers have provided this useful prize as a sales incentive. The St. Paul Daily News and the Chicago Tribune are two leading newspapers which have used this type of award with highly satisfactory results.

The former organized a Daily News Bicycle Club which was open to any boy or girl in the St. Paul city circulation area except carrier boys and members of their families. The bicycles were displayed at school playgrounds and carriers urged boys and girls on their routes to join the club. The Daily News gave bicycles for quotas of from 18 to 24 six-month subscription orders while the Tribune awarded bicycles for 12 six-month subscriptions. The quota in each case will depend upon how much the circulation department can afford to pay for new subscriptions.

Trips and Tours

This form of reward has become increasingly popular in recent years. The urge to travel is universal not only with boys but for adult solicitors and readers as well. The restoration of reduced fares has given added stimulus to travel prizes. To cite only a few examples, the Worcester, Mass., Evening Post for some years has conducted a six-day tour of Washington, New York, and Annapolis; the Hartford Courant promoted a trip to Europe; the Boston Herald-Traveler ran a tour to Washington for 75 boys; the Columbus Citizen took 300 carriers on a four-day trip to Washington, the Nashville Tennessean has used not only trips to Washington and Chicago but Central American cruises.

The testimony of H. H. Swan, circulation manager of the Worcester Evening Post is interesting in this connection. Five ordinary circulation campaigns, he reports, netted 4129 new subscriptions. Six contests using tours as the incentive, however, yielded 12,371 new subscriptions plus long-time good will. The matter of expense is also one to be considered. Costs are somewhat less for a large party than for smaller ones. Further, Mr. Swan points out, subscription orders obtained by the Evening Post by the use of tours cost an average of 49 cents in 1934 as against 51 cents for other prize offers, while in 1935 the costs were 60 and 62 cents, respectively. The advantages claimed for the use of tours and trips are that they get good results, they cost less for each new subscription than other methods, they offer a wide variety of promotion angles, they arouse public interest, and they help the morale of the staff and circulation organization. The Long Island Daily Star has used a cumulative sales campaign which, it is claimed, can be adapted to newspapers of almost any size. 1 It applies also either to tours or to other kinds of prizes. The plan, briefly, is to divide the carriers into groups of 15 or 20, determine the minimum number of subscriptions necessary to win the award, pit the groups against each other, award the prize, which may be a trip, a bicycle, a motorcycle, or an outboard motor, each time the quota is obtained, then carry the contest forward by successive steps. This last is done as each prize is awarded by carrying forward the standing of all the boys except the winner toward the attainment of the next quota. As Charles M. Schofield, circulation manager of the Daily Star, explains it: If the prize was won by Carrier No. 1 with 10 subscriptions, and Carrier No. 2 produced seven subs but did not win, then Carrier No. 2 and every other nonwinner would start on the next drive with his present standing to his credit. Carrier No. 1, however, would have to start all over. In other words, all the subscription orders a boy secures during the entire length of the contest always remain to his credit until such time as he gets a prize. Therefore, the more orders he piles up in each "drive" the closer he becomes toward being the next winner. We call it a "hit" each time the stated number [quota] of subs is sold and a prize is awarded. . , . Nonwinners are rewarded with smaller prizes. The plan can also be extended to include district managers and it can be carried on simultaneously with other contests. For example, while the Daily Star was running a trip to Florida as the major prize on the basis of 50 subscriptions, it gave a zipper melton coat as an added incentive each time a group produced 15 new subscriptions, the orders counting toward both the garment and the trip. The success of the idea can be judged from the fact that in an organization of 225 carrier-salesmen 40 trips were awarded.

Country Circulation

Many of the methods and ideas used to build city circulation can also be applied or adapted to country circulation. Individual newspapers follow different policies in paying country circulation agents. Some pay a straight salary, others pay solely on a commission basis, and still others combine salary and commission. Various bonus schemes can be extended to include such salesmen if desired.

The Flint, Mich., Journal uses satisfactorily what is called the zone system of R.F.D. solicitation with the surprising record of 94.9 per cent renewals for a six-month period. It obtained a list of the number of active rural-delivery mailboxes on each route in its territory. The routes were divided into groups, each of which a solicitor can cover every two weeks, working on a commission basis. The Journal uses a complete card index of these subscribers, keeping a dated list of call-backs and expiration dates by towns. The lists are made up on the first and fifteenth of each month 15 days ahead so as to give the agent an opportunity to make the call before the subscription expires. The solicitors also contact the carriers in each town in their area at least once a month, thus doing away with country agencies. The Journal has also found that it helps to permit farmers to pay once a month since most of them are much more willing and able to do this than to pay for a year in advance. The Johnson City, Tenn., Press has already been cited for its development of profitable motor routes in rural territory.

Starting from scratch, this newspaper canvassed its territory as to rural circulation possibilities and set half the houses within sight of the roads as its goal. It delivered sample copies of the paper free for two weeks without any obligation and then solicited the rural residents thus served. By good follow-up and close attention, 3000 circulation was added in this manner.

Mail Circulation

Since mail subscriptions are payable in advance, usually for longer periods than the city reader signs up, and since the opportunity for personal contact varies considerably, the mechanics of this type of selling are somewhat different than for others. Such circulation may be obtained through personal solicitation, through local agents, or direct by mail. Once obtained, it is still another problem to hold such circulation. The Des Moines Register and Tribune, with 100,000 paid in advance circulation, have an impressive record in this respect.

To get renewals by mail, they use five types of notices as follows :

(1) a circular letter three weeks in advance of the expiration date;

(2) another circular letter a week in advance; (3) a postal card mailed early in the week of the stop; and (4) and (5), postal-card notices one and two weeks, respectively, after expiration. The number of notices to send in such cases will be determined largely by experience as there is no point in sending circulation appeals indefinitely after it has been shown that they do not produce results.

It has been proved time and again that letters are more effective than other kinds of notices for the simple reason that they are more personal. Cards, however, make good reminders and can be used for supplemental notices. It has also been shown that for some psychological reason the color of the envelope used has some bearing on the percentage of replies. The enclosure of an addressed return envelope also helps although it is not necessary to affix a stamp. In general, that circulation appeal will produce the most results which gets the most attention, is simplest to read and understand, has a personal appeal, and is easiest to answer.

Club Methods

Clubbing is commonly understood to apply to joint subscriptions for more than one publication such as a newspaper and a magazine, or a newspaper and a farm weekly. Still another type was used by an Ohio newspaper which engaged an organizer to get five or more friends to subscribe at one time. The inducement was that each of the five got a 50-cent reduction in the price of the paper and the organizer of the "club" received a merchandise prize. This was conducted on a sliding scale with added prizes for more clubs and more expensive prizes for larger groups. The advantages claimed for it are that it gets better year after year, costs less than selling by mail or solicitor, gives subscribers the benefit of a legitimate reduction on the rate, builds good will, and gets readers active in urging others to subscribe.

Carrier Newspapers

Many of the larger newspapers and quite a few of the smaller ones for that matter publish a house organ for carriers. The details vary as to its nature and frequency, but the purpose is the same everywhere: to stimulate the interest and pride of the carriers and to help swell circulation. In this guise it becomes a piece of circulation promotion. Some of these publications are printed, and some are multigraphed or mimeographed.

Most of them are issued monthly to all carriers. Some of them are published with the editorial help of the boys themselves, thus adding to their interest since the editorial staff can be rotated among the different circulation districts. The publication gives a fine opportunity to record the standings of various boys and to compare the different districts. It provides a medium for announcements of new contests and awards and a multitude of matters concerning the carriers. Newspapers which use this form of promotion generally find it well worth the modest effort and expense it involves. The advantages of such a publication are thus summarized by P. F. Johnson, circulation manager of the Lincoln, Neb., Star, writing in Circulation Management:

1. It helps to get carriers to conduct a continuous campaign for starts and keeps them all on their toes.
2. It helps to hold present subscribers by stressing the importance of good service.
3. It helps collections by reducing the loss from poor pay carriers and by prompt payment of bills.
4. It helps exert a good influence on the carriers.

He also points out that the little newspaper fits in with the Star's boy-welfare program, and by having teams of carriers edit the Junior Star, as it is called, their interest and activity are insured. It features such things as an Early Payers list and a High Increasers' list together with a special honor roll of the five ranking boys each month. It helps to develop a spirit of unity among the boys as well as a healthy rivalry.

Newsboy Bands

A number of newspapers have found the promotion of newsboy bands useful and profitable. The Fort Wayne, Ind., News-Sentinel, for example, has sponsored such a band since 1924. It has grown so that it is now necessary to operate two bands. W. G. Andrews, circulation manager of the News-Sentinel, is authority for the statement that "it has performed a public good will service and has been of immeasurable value to the newspaper." In the first dozen years of its existence this band gave some four hundred public concerts in Fort Wayne and near-by towns, including a series of summer concerts. Once organized and with a competent director, such a band supplies its own incentive and energy. It need not cost much most of the instruments and the uniforms can be given as circulation prizes and the expense can be charged to promotion.

Carriers' Convention

Many papers find it highly profitable in strengthening their relations with their carriers to promote special events for the entire group once a year or oftener. This may take the form of a picnic or some other outing. The Des Moines Register and Tribune have perhaps gone as far or further in this direction than any other newspaper of like circulation.

The sixth annual convention and frolic of Register and Tribune carriers in 1935, for example, was attended by some 13,000 carrier-salesmen and members of their families from all parts of Iowa. It included a special performance of a three-ring circus, a downtown parade two miles long with many floats and 14 bands and 4 drum and bugle corps in line, and a Western League baseball game. Also on the program were brief talks by executives of the newspaper.

READER PROMOTION

As distinguished from carrier promotion, reader promotion may be defined as that type in which the reader is the immediate or direct target. It may be a separate campaign or it may be auxiliary to a subscription campaign. It may be intended to produce some specific result or it may have as its object the building of good will for the newspaper. In a way, this last variety belongs under the heading of institutional promotion and will, therefore, be discussed in the chapter on General Promotion.

Reader promotion has two principal objectives: to add new readers and to keep readers interested and satisfied. The former, as suggested, is tied up with circulation sales campaigns. The latter is designed to hold the subscriber once he has signed on the dotted line. As pointed out in the discussion of circulation principles, it is increasingly recognized that satisfied customers are the best asset of a newspaper and that it is quite as important to retain circulation as it is to add to it.

Premiums

The use of premiums fell into disuse because of the fact that much of the merchandise was shoddy or the practice was overdone. In some highly competitive circulation campaigns, individual newspapers exceeded all the bounds of reason. The feeling grew that this means of getting circulation was unsound economically and beneath the dignity of reputable and responsible newspapers. Of late years, however, there have been some signs of the return of the premium to favor but on a somewhat more dignified basis. The advantages of premium offers are: (1) they are spectacular and thus attract quick attention, and (2) they appeal either to the possessive or bargain instincts of the customer. The disadvantages are: (1) the premium tends to cheapen the newspaper which, after all, ought to be sold on its merits; (2) circulation so obtained is likely to be unstable and transient; (3) for this reason, it is apt to be too costly in terms of lasting results; and (4) it lends itself to abuses and competes to some extent with local merchants.

Combination offers of merchandise in return for coupons clipped from the newspaper plus a small cash payment are common devices. The genuineness of the bargain is sometimes open to question but such offers usually evoke a ready response. For example, a California newspaper offered new subscribers signing up for the paper for six months a 7-pieee water set in return for a coupon and 65 cents. 1 The coupon had to be presented at the newspaper plant, however, where the subscriber was shown personal attention and taken on a tour of the plant to impress him.

An example of circulation building by high-pressure methods, including premiums, that exceeded all bounds was the contest in which London, England, newspapers engaged some years ago. Lord Beaverbrook, in a page one announcement, admitted that between Mar. 1 and June 30 his London Daily Express spent more than $1,000,000 in gifts and prizes to get new readers or about $2 per new subscriber. 2 It did succeed in pushing the total circulation to 2,054,348 in June, but, of this, some 88,000 was lost by August, and the proprietor admitted that crossing the 2,000,- 000 mark by such methods, which included the giving away of free sets of Dickens, was futile.

Contests

There are perhaps more kinds of contests than there are newspapers. Further, there is a vogue in types of contest just as in other things, and circulation and promotion managers are forever looking for something new. Some kinds of reader-contests have been junked as too expensive, too dangerous, or too unproductive. Some years ago, for example, the ' 'Miss America" contest in which local beauties were chosen under the sponsorship of individual newspapers for competition in a grand finale at Atlantic City attracted wide attention. Imitations sprang up until it reached the point where every firemen's and grocers' picnic elected a beauty queen and interest in the spectacle lagged. Reader contests may be sponsored by newspapers individually or in groups. The former vastly outnumber the latter. They also differ in that the former are usually part of a continuing promotion program while the latter are apt to be seasonal or periodical. Examples of joint-promotion stunts are the Soap Box Derby and the Golden Gloves boxing tournaments. Experience has shown that in general those reader contests are best which keep up the interest of the reader over the longest period at the least expense. It has been proved, too, that contests need not be expensive in order to produce results. Top prizes of as little as $5 or $10 frequently draw a surprising number of entries in a contest. This is particularly true of prizes for such things as original limericks, Little Audrey stories, amateur snapshots, and letters or slogans on a special subject. There is danger, however, that a newspaper may overdo itself in a reader contest. This is particularly true where a publication grows reckless in its zeal not to be outdone by a rival. In Toronto, for example, the Evening Telegram announced a trade name and slogan contest based on 50 cartoon pictures with cash and merchandise prizes totaling $4500. The Daily Star countered with a proverb contest built around 48 cartoon pictures in which prizes valued at more than $8300 were offered, including three automobiles. Not to be outdone, the Mail & Empire then put up 15 free trips to the king's Silver Jubilee for persons turning in the largest number of votes based on subscriptions within a given period.

Several months later, K. A. McMillan, of the Star, was quoted as saying that a recent contest had increased its circulation from 240,000 to 290,000 within 10 days. It held the gain throughout the three months of the contest but a month later the circulation had shrunk to 246,000, indicating a net gain of between 3000 and 6000. He conceded that such kinds of promotion were "just a little undignified, and the increases from them largely illusory," but argued that under certain conditions they were a necessary evil.

Reader contests designed to produce added circulation as well as to hold circulation usually run for a longer period than those intended merely to sustain interest. They also carry more and larger prizes. The psychology of this is obvious for the greater the rewards and the larger the number eligible to them the more persons will be attracted. And by the time a contest has run 60 or 90 days, the chances are favorable that the reader has acquired the habit or at any rate his sales resistance has been broken down so that he is a good prospect for a renewal. There is no reason why a newspaper should not run more than one contest at a time provided they do not conflict. It might conduct a contest with a fairly general appeal, for example, at the same time it has one for an editorial department, such as sports or the woman's pages. As a matter of fact, some variety is essential to give spice to promotion although occasionally a certain kind of contest proves to be so popular that there is considerable reader demand for another like it.

Editorial Promotion

The cooperation of all departments concerned is essential to the success of any promotion. If the editorial department adds an important feature but the circulation department does not capitalize upon it, much of the value is lost. Instead of putting up circulation bait in the form of gaudy prizes, many newspapers have found it to their lasting advantage to improve or expand their editorial contents and facilities and to impress the reader accordingly. As a matter of fact, if readers cannot be "sold" on the newspaper as a product, no amount of promotion will retain their interest or confidence. After all, it is the job of the circulation manager to sell what is in his newspaper. Lou J. Hoffmann, circulation manager of the St. Louis Star-Times, found that it pays to dramatize editorial features as a means of attracting attention and building circulation. If a new serial or a new comic strip, for example, is about to begin, the principal characters in it can be depicted in appropriate costume and paraded about the city. The purpose, of course, is to get everyone talking. This calls for the use of such devices as announcements in the news and advertising columns, brass bands, men on stilts, sandwich men, movie shorts, a tie-up with local dramatic clubs, billboard space, car cards, three sheets on circulation delivery trucks and so on. The possibilities are limited only by the imagination and ingenuity of the circulation and promotion managers. It is always a good thing to weave such promotion into local activities as far as possible, and it pays to experiment all the time. If one thing does not work, another will. Carriers and solicitors, too, should be utilized in talking up the new feature or added facilities. The Chicago American ran a novel and extensive promotion campaign on a new serial entitled "Anastasia," the theme of which was built around a beauty parlor.

It broke the ice in its preliminary campaign with one-word ads with only the name "Anastasia." Its delivery trucks bore posters with the same word. At street corners and in beauty shops it gave away 250,- 000 bars of soap with wrappers urging people to read " Anastasia." It placed thousands of cards in telephone booths and in paper napkins at drugstores and ice-cream parlors besides 500,000 rotogravure broadsides that were distributed in its territory, It used full-page promotion advertisements in the paper and backed them up with a radio program. To cap the climax it even persuaded local beauty shops to advertise "Anastasia" waves and manicures! As another example of promotion novelty, the Cynthiana, Ky., Democrat offered $4 to the person who could prove that he had "the most-read Democrat" i.e., read by the most persons. One-year subscriptions were given as second and third prizes.

Insurance

A favorite circulation-promotion idea in recent years has been to offer low-cost life or accident insurance to subscribers. The bait of a $500 policy for as little as 50 cents a year is too much for most readers to resist. This is especially true when the insurance is made available to all members of the subscriber's family from school age up. Most newspapers which have adopted the insurance idea have found that it not only produces reader interest and good will, but is profitable.

The Schenectady Union-Star offers a case in point. This paper with a circulation of 21,000 offers a full-coverage policy and has 10,000 policies in force. The policy sells for 4 cents a week, pays for itself and part of the cost of building circulation, and nets the newspaper 58 cents a year profit. In the language of K. L. Butler, circulation manager of the Union-Star, it " works without effort."

The policy of insuring readers was commented on in an editorial in Editor & Publisher which read as follows:

More than ten years' continuous experience with insurance as a circulation premium has convinced both publishers and underwriters that the most effective policy is one which pays reasonable claims promptly and fully. The trick agate clauses which in the early days gave the reader only the cheap coverage that he paid for, and not always that, are definitely of the past.

The broad coverage afforded by some newspaper insurance is exemplified by two claims recently paid by the Chicago Daily News. One claim was paid to the widow of a man shot by gangsters who mistook him for his son, a labor leader. And another $250 went to the widow of a reader who was asphyxiated in his garage while changing a tire. Either of these might have been among the freak accidents which some early policies covered to the exclusion of more usual casualties. They are unusual, but the underwriters can afford to cover almost any hazard of modem life for the premium collected above the circulation price. Newspapers have found that they cannot afford to give less if they want their insurance to create circulation and hold friendships. Like other forms of promotion, reader insurance can be used in a number of ways. It can be made available to all readers and members of their immediate families, or it can be used with only part of the circulation. One morning newspaper, for example, uses insurance as a means of promotion with rural and mail subscribers but not with its city readers. The former is the more common practice, however. A partial list of the various kinds of reader and good-will promotion recorded in Editor & Publisher for a period totaling only eight months in 1935-1936 disclosed more than 100 varieties. They ranged from relatively simple contests such as those for amateur photographs to novelties like "whopper" contests for the biggest lies, "bore" or "pain-in-the-neck" contests for persons or things irritating readers most. The crossword puzzle remains a perennial favorite as does the contest for identifying 'quotations from the Bible or from well-known books or poetry as depicted in drawings or cartoons with cash prizes totaling as much as $15,000. Contests based upon votes sometimes result in ill will instead of good will. This is one reason the old-fashioned popularity contest has largely given way to newer, more novel, and safer types of promotion.

Varieties of "teaser" contests or guessing or memory games can be run without any prizes for that matter and used to promote reader interest in the newspaper. One such stunt is to run a brief series of questions daily or weekly based on news in the issue of the paper in which it appears. The questions are printed on one page and the correct answers on another. Teaser notices or questions can also be used preliminary to the appearance of a new serial, a new comic strip, or some other editorial feature. To dramatize the speed of its delivery service to its readers and to show the vast improvement over pioneer days, the Birmingham, Ala., News and Age-Herald staged a race between a pony express and a modern truck carrying papers. The truck covered the route of 147 miles in 3 hours and 17 minutes while the pony express, even with fresh horses every 5 miles all afternoon and night, required a total of 18 hours, 34 minutes, and 45 seconds to complete the distance. Reader interest was stimulated further by the offer of cash prizes for the closest guesses as to the difference in time between the two. The examples cited only begin to suggest the endless possibilities of circulation promotion.

9

The Hallmark of Circulation

Publishers have changed their attitude greatly as to revealing the details of their circulation figures. Not only do most of them willingly supply accurate totals to advertisers and others interested, but they go still further and provide an authentic breakdown as to the distribution of their circulation in the city of publication, in the adjacent territory, and elsewhere. This is just the opposite of the policy originally followed. Most publishers either concealed their circulation figures or, in answer to inquiries, supplied "claimed" or "estimated" totals. Beyond this they were apt to hold the view that the details of their circulation were their private business and to be held as a closely guarded secret. The advertiser, in consequence, rarely knew what he was getting for his money, and space buying in terms of circulation was more or less of a gamble, particularly at distant points.

There was something of an analogy here between the early bank situation and the newspaper business. Businessmen and private individuals in one part of the country had little opportunity to verify bank notes issued in distant parts of the country. Some effort was made to publish lists of reputable banks and a table of the relative values of their notes of issue, but this was uncertain, incomplete, and largely a private venture. So with the newspapers. Not even authentic lists of newspapers were available, and circulation was a highly speculative quality which for the most part was a matter of guess.

Eventually it came to be recognized that the advertiser as well as the publisher had a stake in the newspaper. This was true of both the retail and the general advertiser. The realization of the soundness of this view grew as the annual outlay for advertising space mounted in publications of all kinds. Doubtless it would have come, anyway, but it was stimulated by the growing intensity of competition between different media and within the field of each medium. Involved in the process was a long struggle for the impartial verification of circulation so that advertisers would know definitely what they were getting for their money, so that individual publications at distant points could be compared in authentic, uniform terms, and so that different kinds of media might be similarly compared by advertisers, by agencies, and by publishers. This development had its fruition in the present Audit Bureau of Circulations.

First Stage

The first stage which led to this development might loosely be defined as the period down to 1870. 1 In those days the aim was to compile mere lists of publications, but even this was difficult because advertisers and agents alike were poorly organized, publishers were secretive, and means of communication were only partially developed. Except for the larger cities, therefore, advertising agents were able to supply little information about publications, and a list of publications for a distant state or region was expensive to compile and comprised rare and valuable information to be guarded closely. The possession of such a list gave an advertiser or an advertising agent a considerable advantage over his competitors. Out of this situation grew the space broker who was the predecessor of the present-day advertising agency. His stock in trade, in the language of Editor & Publisher, was his lists of publications and that agency was considered most successful or the most profitable with which to do business which had accumulated the most extensive lists of media. It was not a matter of quality or extent of circulation among these, it was simply the location and name that counted with the advertiser. He had not yet thought of circulation investigation.

Second Stage

George P. Rowell, of Boston, one of these early agents, was responsible for the transition to the second stage. In 1870 he decided to issue a newspaper directory. Not only was such a thing unheard of but an uproar followed from the advertising agencies in New York and elsewhere. They argued that his proposal meant giving away their chief stock in trade, and that if advertisers had free access to such information, it meant the ruination of the advertising agencies through the loss of their business. The outcome was that the agencies were compelled to be something more than mere space brokers. The summary sketched here is based chiefly on the account in the Golden Jubilee issue of Editor & Publisher, July 21, 1934, p. 310.

Various items of information were given concerning the publications listed in this first American Newspaper Directory. The circulation figures it contained were those given by the publisher. Other facts made available included data as to the rates, the location, the population served, and the politics of the publication. Besides the opposition of the advertising agencies, the directory at first got little real cooperation from the publishers in the matter of accurate circulation figures. The publishers were generally antagonistic on this point, and they were slow to realize the value of authentic information to themselves as well as to the advertiser. To encourage them to take a different view, Rowell originated the so-called Gold Mark system which consisted of a circle and dot placed opposite the name of the publication which supplied a sworn statement of its circulation. Rowell himself made no attempt to verify the figures given but to prove his own confidence in their correctness he had a standing offer of $100 to anyone who could disprove them. Meanwhile advertisers began to show a livelier interest in the whole matter of circulation. They were no longer satisfied with total figures even where they were authentic. They wanted to know the details of circulation where it went, who paid for it, how stable it was, how much of it was productive, and any other facts which would enable them to make their advertising more effective. This led to the organization in 1899 of the Association of American Advertisers which sought to take advantage of the frequent statement of publishers by this time that their circulation records were open to inspection and audit by the advertiser.

The association was made up of national advertisers. It was the national advertisers, consequently, who took the first steps to verify circulations. But their facilities were limited both as to funds and personnel, and the results were inadequate and unsatisfactory. When a publisher submitted his books for examination by the Association, he paid for a certificate, and the entire matter was purely optional with him. If he was unwilling to cooperate, there was no way whereby he could be compelled to lay his circulation cards on the table.

Third Stage

The Association dragged on somehow until 1913 when matters became so bad that its sponsors concluded that it must be abandoned, Advertisers failed to appreciate its benefits and possibilities, and the cost of maintenance became prohibitive for those who were members. Two new movements, one in the East and the other in the Midwest, were gathering force at the time with objectives similar to those of the Association of American Advertisers. One of these, the forerunner of the present Association of National Advertisers, was begun in the East. The other, further advanced, had sprung up in Chicago, and, within a short time after they discovered their objectives were largely identical, the two joined hands.

The plan proposed by the advertising agents was to form a bureau, based on the personnel and organization of the Association of American Advertisers, in which mutual interests of the advertiser, the advertising agent, and the publisher would be recognized. There was considerable skepticism over the practicability of such a program, but the sponsors were confident enough of its soundness to raise $5000 among themselves to promote it among those who might be interested in it. The final test lay in whether pledges which would yield $100,000 a year could be obtained to carry out the proposal.

AUDIT BUREAU OF CIRCULATIONS

Enough funds and pledges had been received by December, 1913, to make it possible for the backers of the plan to proceed. The first step was to incorporate the Audit Bureau of Circulations under the laws of Illinois; The A.B.C., as it is generally known, has a number of things in common with the Associated Press. Each is a purely cooperative organization, run for the' benefit of its members. Both are nonprofit making, the members of both are elected upon application, each is under the control of its board of directors, and in both cases the operating executive is a general manager who is chosen by and is responsible to the directors. The A.B.C. really got under way early in 1914 when its first convention was held at which its bylaws, rules, and regulations were adopted. At this meeting a detailed plan of operation was submitted. In August of that year the incorporation was completed and the charter issued. The original plan called for a bureau to be made up of advertisers, advertising agents, and publishers interested. All were to be represented on the board of directors but the advertisers were to be dominant. Funds to operate the bureau wore to come from dues to be assessed against publishers on the basis of the circulation of their publications and against advertisers and their agents on the basis of the service rendered to them. First task before the newly organized bureau was to define just what "net paid circulation" meant, and the next was to standardize the information the publisher was to supply. Previously a "subscriber" meant whatever the publisher cared to make it. It might be just a name, or a person who had ordered the publication but never paid for it, or a bona fide customer, who not only received the publication but paid for it promptly.

Under the United States Postal Regulations, publishers of daily newspapers were required to publish twice a year sworn figures as to their daily average of paid circulation. But this particular regulation did not apply to other publications, and, in particular, the information it supplied was not detailed enough for the purpose of the advertisers. Further, the government requirements were not rigid enough in other respects. Some other answer to the perennial question of circulation was needed. The first A.B.C. definition of a subscriber was one who had paid at least half the advertised subscription price for the publication and who was not in arrears more than a year. This was regarded as a long step forward, for up to that time no uniform definition had been proposed to which all of the interested parties could agree. This was at least partly because there was no authoritative agency to adopt and support such a definition.

Its Objects

As defined by Article I of its bylaws, the objects of the A.B.C. "shall be to issue standardized statements of the circulation of publisher members; to verify the figures shown in these statements by auditors examinations of any and all records considered by the Bureau to be necessary; and to disseminate circulation data only for the benefit of advertising agencies and publishers." Reports issued to members include verified facts and figures having to do with "the quantity, quality, distribution of circulation and circulation methods; thereby enabling quality as well as quantity to be established." The Bureau also reports "facts, without opinion."

Definitions, etc., for By-Laws and Rules, with Glossary of Terms, from Structure.

Membership

There are six classes of membership. These are: advertisers, local advertisers, advertising agencies, associate advertising agencies, publishers, and miscellaneous members. Those eligible to membership, according to the bylaws, include "any advertiser, advertising agency, or publisher of a publication with paid circulation as defined by these bylaws, or any individual, firm, or corporation desiring circulation information."

Applying for Membership

Applicants for membership must agree to observe the bylaws and rules of the Bureau. A favorable vote of at least 13 directors is required for election to membership. In addition, applicants for publisher membership must deposit a year's dues, submit their books and records for an audit, and bear the cost of the preliminary examinations and initial audit. The books and records of the applicant must, of course, be adequate to the purposes of the Bureau or, if inadequate, must be changed accordingly. The release of the Bureau's audit constitutes both the qualification and acceptance of membership by the applicant but until such time no announcement may be made that the application is pending.

Paid Circulation

According to the A.B.C. definition, a publication with paid circulation is "one of which 50 per cent or more of its distribution qualifies as paid under the standards of the Bureau and of which the total net paid circulation, according to such standards, plus bulk sales, advertisers' copies (one copy only to each advertiser), advertising agency copies and correspondents' copies, equals or exceeds 60 per cent of total distribution."

Statements

Publisher members are required to make and file with the Bureau, on forms supplied by it, sworn statements of circulation for semiannual or such other periods as the Bureau may determine. The circulation manager and the business manager or publisher must sign and swear to such statements which are audited by the Bureau according to its rules.

Access to Records

To accomplish any of the objects described, the Bureau has the right of access to all such books and records of publisher members that it deems necessary in making an audit. This right is not limited to the investigation of a statement filed by the publisher, but may be exercised at any time.

Dues and Service

Dues vary according to the type of membership and the service rendered, as the case may be, 'For advertisers, the annual dues are

$40, and such members are entitled to Publisher's Statements and Audit Reports up to 100 publications. For service in excess of this, the directors fix the charge which shall not total more than $240 a year. Local advertisers receive reports based on the city where they are located. Their dues range from $5 to $15 a year according to the number of reports furnished. Advertising agencies pay dues of from $150 to $700 a year depending upon their gross space billings during the previous year. Associate advertising agencies pay for each service annual dues of from $50 to $230, likewise based upon their 50 cents for each additional 100 distribution, to $789 a year for those with 1,000,000 distribution, plus M cent for each additional 100. For an independent weekly, semiweekly, or triweekly the charge is $52 a year for 2000 distribution, plus 30 cents for each additional 100. The weekly newspaper with 1,000,000 distribution would pay $551 a year, with 1 cent for each additional 100. The magazine rates are slightly different but start also at $1 a week.

Control of the Bureau

The management and control of the Bureau are vested in a board of 27 directors who serve without salary for two-year terms. The board is apportioned as follows: 12 advertiser members, 3 advertising-agency members, 6 daily newspaper publisher members, 2 magazine publishers, 2 farm paper publisher members, and 2 business-paper publishers. The directors name the managing director of the A.B.C., though he is not one of their own number. The officers of the Bureau include a president, three vice-presidents, a secretary, and a treasurer, elected by and from the board of directors. The presidency is limited to advertiser members.

Penalties

The directors have the power to censure, suspend, or expel a member for various offenses. These include: (1) false or fraudulent Publisher's Statements to the Bureau; (2) refusal to allow auditors of the Bureau full access at any time to all records deemed necessary for a complete audit; (3) violation of any of the publicity rules of the Bureau; (4) failure to pay dues or other indebtedness as required by the bylaws or rules; (5) failure to make and file the Publisher's Statement as required by the bylaws and rules; (6) failure or refusal to sign the Bureau suspension of service agreement in case of absence, incompleteness, or inadequacy of records.

Charges

Provision is made whereby any member may file charges with the board of directors against any other member. Such charges must be in writing, must specify the offenses in reasonable detail, and must be signed by those making the charges. A copy of the charges must then be served upon the accused member who has 10 days in which to make a reply or longer if the board deems proper. His answer, too, must be in writing, must be filed with the managing director, and must be signed by the accused member. When the reply is filed or if the accused member refuses or fails to make an answer, the board proceeds to consider the charges. The accused member is notified of the meeting which he is entitled to attend, and, at which, he may examine and cross-examine witnesses and present such evidence or explanation as he may desire. The board then decides the guilt or innocence of the accused member, and, if it finds him guilty, it may censure, suspend, or expel him. Its findings are final except that he has the right to appeal to the membership at the next regular meeting. A suspended member is required to perform all the duties expected of other members but is entitled to no service from the Bureau during the period of suspension.

Standards

As the basis for making the audits required by the bylaws, the A.B.C. has in force a number of detailed regulations establishing definite standards of circulation. These relate to a variety of subjects and include such matters as net paid circulation, bulk sales, gift subscriptions, premiums, contests, merchandise offers, credit and installment subscriptions, renewals, extensions and transfers, and subscriptions and accounts in arrears.

Net Paid Circulation

Basic prices are defined as the "prices at which the publication may be purchased by any one, at any time, for a definite duration." Special or reduced prices are specifically excluded from the definition. Net paid circulation is defined as "copies of publications which have been paid for by the purchasers, not for resale," under these conditions: (1) if the sale be a single copy sale, it shall be paid for at not less than 50 per cent of the basic single copy price; (2) on term order for a year, the subscription must be paid for at not less than 50 per cent of the basic annual price; for more than a year at not less than a pro rata of the basic price for the period offered; for less than a year at not less than 50 per cent of the basic price for the period offered; (3) a term subscription for one year or more paid in accordance with this rule may be included in net paid circulation, if the publisher so desires, for not more for clarifying amendment relative to the detailed definition of "basic price." More than six months after the expiration of the period; (4) a term subscription for less than one year may not be included in net paid circulation after its expiration unless the amount actually paid equals at least 50 per cent of the full basic annual subscription price. Lost, missed, damaged, or other unsold copies must be classed as returns and so deducted. For sales of an extra to be included in net paid circulation, it must carry all national advertising scheduled for that day.

Copies Paid for by Others

All copies sold in quantity except those to public libraries must be reported as bulk sales and are counted as such only when at least 50 per cent of the single copy price is paid for single copy sales and not less than 50 per cent of the basic mail subscription price for term subscriptions. Copies bought by hotels and restaurants for free distribution to their guests count as bulk sales if they yield the paper at least half of the single copy price, either in cash or in accommodations. Under the heading of "Mail Subscriptions Special are included subscriptions sold in quantity to corporations, institutions, or individuals for employees, subsidiaries, or branch offices, as well as subscriptions received in connection with an advertising contract, provided they yield the paper not less than 50 per cent net of the basic subscription price. Similarly, gift subscriptions are classed as individual" mail subscriptions and counted as paid circulation, provided they bring at least half of the basic annual subscription price or the newsstand price.

Premiums

Anything offered to a subscriber in addition to the regular issues of the publication itself must be shown in the Bureau reports as a premium. This rule applies whether the premium is given with or without additional payment above the subscription price and regardless of whether it is given only to new subscribers or to all subscribers. This applies also even to back copies unless the subscription is retroactive.

Premium with Subscription

Where there is a premium in connection with a subscription offer at least 50 per cent of the basic subscription price for the period offered, plus the full value of the premium, must be collected to make the subscription valid. Where the value of the premium is not given, or where the value stated is less than its cost to the publisher, the A. B.C. requires that 25 per cent be added to its cost to the publisher. If the premium is merchandise or service whose value cannot be determined by this method, it is fixed by a comparison with the price at which other similar merchandise or service is available to the subscriber through commercial channels.

Combination Subscriptions

Where subscriptions for two or more publications are sold in combination, the A.B.C. rule is that the minimum price for such combination shall be the full basic price of the highest priced publication, plus not less than 30 per cent of the combined full basic subscription prices of the other publications in the combination.

But in no case shall the price be less than half of the combined basic subscription prices. The saving effected "may be expressed in monetary terms or percentage," but the offer must mean a saving spread over the various publications in the combination.

Contests

New provisions covering subscription contests were adopted in an amendment approved in 1936. Under them when a contest for a prize is promoted or a publication uses a feature with which a prize or reward is connected, the Publisher's Statement for that period must contain a complete description of the contest or feature. This applies whether single copies or term subscriptions must be purchased by the contestant. Average daily sales for the period of the contest must also be included with the Statement. If the number of copies sold to obtain from the paper a coupon or some feature essential to a contest can be computed, the number of such sales must be deducted from the paid circulation for the period. The rule does not apply to contests of skill in which there is no direct return to the publication publishing them.

Credit, Deferred, and Installment Subscriptions

A credit subscription is one based upon an agreement to pay, or acceptance of a note in payment, for a subscription. It is regarded as being in arrears until at least half of the basic annual price has been paid, and the term of such a note or agreement is limited to three months if such annual subscription is to be counted as paid circulation. A deferred subscription is one in which the subscribers receive the publication a month or more late, the subscribers being served from returns. To be counted as paid circulation, they must yield at least half of the basic price but are shown separately. On a subscription payable in installments or payable on delivery, only those copies are carried in paid circulation which are actually paid for, until at least half of the basic annual price is paid. An issue of a publication becomes a back copy immediately upon the appearance for sale of the next succeeding issue. Back copies sold for export to foreign countries may not be reported as either paid circulation or free distribution, effective June 30, 1937.

Renewals and Extensions

A subscription is regarded as a renewal if it is received and paid for within six months after it expires. If the basic subscription price of a publication is reduced, the unexpired portion of the subscription paid for at the higher price may be extended in proportion. Subscriptions more than three months in arrears are not included in paid circulation but must be reported as unpaid.

Analyses and Classifications

In order to give those interested a more detailed and more exact picture of the circulation of a particular publication, various analyses and classifications are provided. One is by states or provinces and another by population groups. In the case of business papers an occupational breakdown is called for.

Newspaper Rules

In this connection, certain regulations are in force which apply exclusively to newspapers. Some of the more important of these rules and definitions follow: Carrier circulation is that kind of circulation whereby a paper is "delivered regularly by carrier into the home, office or other place of business, and paid for on a weekly, monthly or other term arrangement." Independent carriers are those who buy papers and deliver them as just described, keeping their own accounts and making their own collections. City mail subscribers are those who call for their papers at the local post office or who receive them by mail in the city zone.

Zones

For the purposes of the A.B.C., all circulation territory is divided into three zones. The "city zone" is roughly the city of publication, but it may be more than that, and it is defined by agreement of the publishers concerned, with the approval of the A.B.C. managing director, or may be established by him in case the publishers are unable to agree. The "retail trading zone" is the area beyond the city zone which produces retail trade for a given community, its boundaries to be fixed also by the publishers concerned or, if they cannot agree, by the managing director. Its boundaries are determined by radius, by county lines, or some other distinguishing factor. Usually county or township lines are followed for this purpose. Circulation outside of the city and retail trading zones is designated as "all other."

Miscellaneous

If, in a given period, the average circulation of a daily paper on a certain day of the week is 15 per cent in excess of, or below, the average for the other days of the week, the circulation for such a day is shown separately, and the average for the other five days is shown as the daily average. One copy sent to an advertiser for checking purposes is classed as "Advertisers," but all additional copies so used are classed as "Complimentary." Copies may be sent to prospective advertisers and classed as "Samples to Prospective Advertisers." Three classes of firms, corporations, and individuals regularly engaged in the business of soliciting subscriptions are recognized. They are, respectively, "catalogue subscription agencies," "field selling subscription agencies," and "independent individual subscription salesmen." Subscriptions so obtained must be reported accordingly. If two or more publishers are joint owners of a field selling subscription agency, subscriptions so obtained are accounted for on that basis in the reports.

Publisher's Statements

The semiannual newspaper statements required by the A.B.C. cover the periods from Oct. 1 to Mar. 31, and from Apr. 1 to Sept. 30. For other varieties of publications, the periods are from Jan. 1 to June 30, and from July 1 to Dec. 31. The rules also require that a Publisher's Statement must be made to the Bureau within one month after the close of the period covered by the statement. Failure to do so may result in disciplinary action. The rules also cover such points as morning and evening editions sold as a unit, duplicate circulation between morning and evening editions of a daily newspaper, predate editions, weekly or semiweekly editions of daily newspapers, and net press run by editions.

Audits and Re-audits

The Audit Reports include a comparative statement of the total net paid circulation as shown in the Publisher's Statements for the period audited and the findings of the auditors. Normally Audit Reports cover the twelvemonth period for which two semiannual Publisher's Statements have been released. Any difference between the net totals must be explained. Besides giving the A.B.C. auditors access to his books and records, the publisher must maintain a file of copies of all subscription offers, copies of contracts with solicitors, canvassers, subscription agencies or others through whom subscriptions are obtained. If, because of the absence, incompleteness, or inaccuracy of a publisher's records, it is impossible to make an audit, service on the publication is suspended and the publisher must agree to install and maintain an A.B.C. Circulation Record Book, to pay any extra expense involved, to issue no A.B.C. statement for the time being, and to continue the payment of dues during the suspension of service. In making an audit, the A,B.C. auditors have authority to take sufficient names at random from the subscription list and trace them through the original orders to the cash books or other records in order to make a verification test of the circulation. This is known as an Original Order Test. If in the opinion of the Bureau the publisher's records are inadequate to establish the facts relative to any phase of the circulation, the Bureau may make another kind of test by sending verification letters to subscribers or others involved. Unless the circulation is less than 100,000, not less than 500 letters shall be sent in such a test.

Report to Publisher

After an audit is made, a copy of it must be submitted to the publisher at least 10 days prior to its publication and distribution to members. The publisher, meanwhile, must not make any use of any part of such report until it is released by the Bureau to its members. If he finds anything in the Audit Report which he thinks is inaccurate, a publisher may file an objection with the Bureau relative to his Audit Report. The Bureau will correct any inaccuracies in its first draft but the report as finally released contains the data as the Bureau believes them to be. In other words, the release of the Audit Report is not subject to approval by the publisher.

If a publisher member desires the Bureau to make an outside investigation of some other paper's circulation, he must file a written request with the Bureau, together with evidence to support such a request. At the same time he must guarantee to pay the entire cost of the investigation if, after the investigation has been made, the complaint, in the opinion of the managing director, has not been justified. If the evidence submitted and the circumstances are such as to convince the managing director that the request should be granted, the investigation is ordered. If the special audit confirms the charges of inflation, the cost of the investigation is assessed against any or all papers involved, the managing director to determine the proportions. If the charges are not substantiated, the cost is borne by the complainant. If the Bureau should make a special investigation on its own initiative, the cost is assessed against the publication investigated.

Re-audits

A publisher member who questions the accuracy of an Audit Report of his publication or that of any other publication in the same class has the right to ask for a re-audit. He must do so, however, within 10 days of receiving the proof copy of his audit report or within 15 days of issuance, in the case of another publication. Further, he must give satisfactory evidence to warrant such a request. To back up such a request, the publisher making it must deposit with the Bureau an amount at least equal to the full annual dues of the publication for which the re-audit is requested. If the re-audit shows a total net paid average within 3 per cent of that reported in the original audit, the petitioner must pay the costs of the re-audit, but if not, his deposit is returned to him.

Publicity Restrictions

Members are limited as to the publicity they may give to A.B.C. reports. A publisher member may publish in his own or other publications or otherwise any figures or data from his own released Publisher's Statement to the Bureau or that of a competitor for the last regular statement period or from the latest Audit Report issued by the Bureau concerning his own publication. Publicity may not be given, however, to such statements or audits prior to their official release. Publisher members, if in good standing, may use the phrase "Member of the Audit Bureau of Circulations" in their advertising. If under suspension, however, claim of membership must be accompanied by the words " Under Suspension." Members are not permitted to use the A.B.C. trade-mark or to imitate its forms either as to wording or appearance. Misrepresentation of figures or data is subject to penalty. Changes, Although it has been in successful operation for more than 20 years, the A.B.C. is still in the process of change. Experience has shown that some of the rules need clarification or modification from time to time. No year has passed without some such changes.

In 1935, for example, membership on the board of directors was increased to 27, the two additional places going to newspapers. Another change concerned requests for investigations where inflated claims were suspected. Instead of being assessed against the complainant or the offending paper, as the case might be formerly, the rule was changed to read that where the complaint was justified the costs of the investigation were to be assessed according to the circumstances developed during the investigation.

Another definition which gave considerable trouble was one to cover the "city within a city" This was debated for some time. The revised rule, as adopted by the board of directors late in 1934, reads that " When a municipality in which a member newspaper is published is included in the arbitrary city zone of another city, each newspaper in the larger city shall set forth its circulation in the municipality arbitrarily included in the city zone of the larger city."

Outlook

The A.B.C. is without question the strongest force so far produced for the definition, determination, and realization of sound, honest, and accurate circulation standards. Its spread is shown by the fact that in 1935 all but 11 per cent of American daily newspaper circulation was so audited.

The membership as reported in 1936 was divided as follows : 2 national advertisers, 220; local advertisers, 25; advertising agencies, 129; daily newspapers, 1006; weekly newspapers, 39; magazines, 197; farm papers, 54; and business papers, 248. The number of daily newspaper members in 1935 was about 52 per cent of all daily newspapers. But 89 per cent of the total daily newspaper circulation was represented in the A.B.C. as against 75 per cent of the total magazine circulation. More than half of the newspaper members of the A.B.C. , however, have less than 15,000 circulation.

10

NEWSPAPER ADVERTISING

Newspaper advertising has rightly been called the foundation of all advertising. Its appeal is so general, the dependence upon it so widespread, and the acceptance of it so universal that its place as a social and economic force in modern life is assured and permanent. After 1900 it grew rapidly and later held its own in the face of the competition of other media, the effects of financial stringency, and the assaults of its critics. Crude and primitive advertisements appeared in the colonial press of America at least as early as 1704. Advertisements were solicited after a fashion, but the first publishers did not make the most of even their limited opportunities.

Some later publishers so far subordinated advertising to news that they left advertising out of their papers rather than increase the size or the number of pages. While Presbrey points out that the Pennsylvania Packet and Daily Advertiser, the first daily newspaper in America, owed its establishment in 1784 to the pressure of advertising, the fact remains that for many years after this the newspaper business office was still looked down upon and advertising continued to be a sort of side line. 2 Even so enlightened and progressive an editor as Charles A. Dana long maintained that properly written, edited, and managed, no newspaper need be larger than four pages to contain all of the important and interesting news of the day, besides what advertising was necessary. In the thirties the advent of the penny press marked a new day in American journalism. But the shackles were struck first from news and from circulation appeal and it was not until many years later that advertising began to catch up with these other newspaper departments. The earlier newspaper appealed to the classes rather than to the masses. With the appearance of the New York Sun and its successors, this situation was reversed, and they catered in a new way to large and hitherto neglected elements of the urban population. The growing place of the city newspaper was also furthered by the shift from a rural to an urban population, by the improvement in means of communication and transportation, and by the development of mechanical facilities adequate to the needs created by these changed conditions.

For more than a century and a half, American newspaper advertising grew slowly, its possibilities unrealized, its real power untapped. Display advertising as we now know it was undreamed of and relatively large users of space contented themselves with repetitions of dull and meaningless notices which for want of ideas or enterprise ran unchanged for long periods. It is something of a marvel that such advertising sold anything except the nostrums of the day in which respect, despite the later intervention of a beneficent government and an awakened social conscience, the consumers of the time were hardly more gullible than those of today.

GROWTH OF ADVERTISING

Until less than 50 years ago, American newspapers continued to derive a greater revenue from subscriptions than from advertising. The ascendance of advertising dates from the nineties when advertising revenue once for all passed that from circulation. It grew rapidly, although not uniformly, down to the outbreak of the World War. In the next 15 years under the lash of wartime conditions and the postwar boom, newspaper advertising soared to heights unimagined by even its most ardent advocates. Without exaggeration, the period between 1914 and 1929, from the standpoint of revenues and profits, might well be called the Golden Age of American newspaper advertising.

This amazing growth was anything but accidental. It was to a large extent, to be sure, a byproduct of the war which led to rapidly changing conditions. Business in general expanded to new dimensions. New and larger uses were found for all sorts of publicity and propaganda, much of it legitimate and necessary, some of it unsound, unjustified, and harmful. Advertising was a particularly useful part of this machinery, and it was swept along on the crest of the tide. In its later phases, in fact, it helped to swell the tide.

But there was something more advertising had come of age. Even without the war, it is likely that newspaper advertising along with other kinds was ripe for a remarkable development, although probably not in the same degree. In round numbers, the aggregate annual advertising revenues of American newspapers skyrocketed from around $175,000,000 in 1914 to about $800,000,000 in 1929. 1 At the same time, circulation and other income was rising slowly from somewhat less than $100,000,000 to nearly $300,000,000, a material increase but far behind the tremendous spurt taken by advertising. The war gave a mighty impetus to newspaper advertising of all kinds, but particularly to general (formerly called "foreign" or "national") advertising. William A. Thomson, director of the Bureau of Advertising of the American Newspaper Publishers Association, describes it in this way:

The sale of $24,000,000,000 worth of Liberty Bonds largely through a newspaper expenditure of some $16,000,000 was an unforgettable demonstration of the power of newspaper advertising to sway the reading public. Here was a dollar of advertising doing $1500 worth of business. The result was a marked increase in newspaper advertising on the part of the public service companies, financial houses, railway and steamship lines. Manufacturers whose production was curtailed by the war advertised to maintain the "good will" of their customers till better times. Others, who found their costs greatly increased, used newspaper advertising to select, and concentrate in, those markets that could be developed most economically. Immediately after the war, other factors came into play. War-time profits gave many manufacturers special funds to devote to advertising. High wages, rolling up an almost steadily increasing income level from 19 1 6 to 1 926, created new prospects for the advertiser. Luxuries became necessities; new products or improvements in old products followed hard upon the law of obsolescence. Installment selling, a mighty important factor at this time, extended the market even further until a very general ownership of washing machines, phonographs, pianos, vacuum cleaners, automobiles, and later radios, became month by month, common fixtures of the American home. It was natural that mass production, mass selling and mass advertising should go hand in hand. And it became equally natural that the daily newspaper should become the leading mass medium of industry. . . .

AFFECTED BY DEPRESSION

Like all other commercial and industrial enterprises, newspapers were inevitably affected by the great depression which began in October, 1929. There was this difference, however: newspapers weathered the ensuing storm far better than other forms of business, and relatively few of them were forced to suspend operation. The ultimate consequences, whether measured in terms of revenues, profits, advertising, or circulation, were appreciable. But because of their inherent soundness, wise methods of operation, the dependence of other forms of enterprise upon them, and the strength of their hold upon the public, they emerged from the blistering effects of the depression more stable and more essential as a social and economic agency than before 1929.

Newspaper advertising fell off sharply during the first years of the depression and then began to rise once more. Many marginal advertisers and others who suffered heavily dropped out of the advertising picture. Such linage losses were offset in part by the development of new sources of advertising revenue. Some newspapers reduced their rates or instituted bonus and rebate schemes to hold their advertisers. On the other hand, many general advertisers as well as retail advertisers increased, and even multiplied, their advertising outlays in the belief that economic salvation for them lay in that direction. Most of them were amply repaid for their faith. They found anew that sound newspaper advertising campaigns were not only a good investment but an absolute necessity.

The impressive thing about general advertising in the years following 1930 was that the newspapers more than held their share of the national advertiser's dollar. His outlay for magazine space shrank appreciably, his expenditures for billboard and car-card advertising dwindled sharply, and, by contrast, his investment in national radio network time had a mushroomlike growth. But in the face of general business conditions and conflicting trends, his dependence upon newspaper space remained highly favorable.

Stability and Strength

The steadiness and strength of the newspaper as an advertising medium are best shown by data compiled by the A.N.P.A. Bureau of Advertising. The outlay of the general advertiser for space or time fell from $510,500,000 in 1930 to $298,000,000 in 1933, then rose to $349,055,000 in 1934. The significant thing is that during these years the proportion of general advertising in newspapers held firm or even increased slightly. The figures, also shown graphically in the accompanying charts, follow:

Any way one looks at it, the newspaper as an advertising medium came out of the depression more secure, more necessary, more important, more useful, and more vital than before. From the standpoint of the newspaper itself, as advertising revenue fell off during those years, it made some adjustments, chief among them a fairly general increase in circulation rates. This led, as will be seen, to a corresponding gain in circulation revenue, but advertising remained the chief source of the income of the newspaper, and, despite what the critics may say, the chief prop for its editorial independence.

Advertiser and Reader Confidence

Whether he caters in greater or less degree to the general public, the advertiser emerged from the depression more dependent than ever upon the newspaper to publicize and circulate his business news. However much he may use direct mail, telephone solicitation, other publications, outdoor advertising, or that youthful giant, the radio, he is almost inevitably bound to the newspaper as his first line of advertising. As has been shown, this is increasingly true of general advertisers. Not only have many advertisers increased their appropriations for newspaper space, but still others have concentrated in newspapers to the exclusion of other media. In like manner, the newspaper reader, who happens also in large measure to be the ultimate consumer of most goods and services that are advertised, has come in still greater measure to pin his faith to newspapers. His confidence in the newspaper is shown by the fact that the total circulation of English language dailies in the United States stood at 38,155,540 at the close of 1935, according to the Editor & Publisher Yearbook. The total for 1935 represented an increase over 1934, 1933, and 1932, proof not only that circulation was on its way out of the depression before advertising, but that there is a definite and widespread public dependence upon, and faith in, the newspaper and its contents. Stated in another way, circulation in 1934 was 91.6 per cent of its all-time high in 1929-1930, where general (national) advertising was only 70.8 per cent of the figure for 1930.

Triple Role of Newspaper

One other point should be emphasized here. This is the growing recognition of the triple role of the newspaper as a purveyor of news, as an interpreter and critic of men and affairs, and as an advertising medium. This is a combination hardly available in any other medium, certainly not in the same degree. Women in particular have come to read the advertisements in the newspapers perhaps even more faithfully and more carefully than they do the news or even the society columns. All classes of readers have found it increasingly to their advantage to scan the advertising columns along with the straight news, feature, and editorial matter. This is especially true of retail or local advertising, and almost any sale or other special store event will serve as convincing proof of the effectiveness of intelligent well-planned newspaper advertising. As advertising standards have risen, newspapers have improved the appearance, the quality, the contents, and the appeal of newspaper advertising. On the whole newspapers take more seriously than is commonly supposed their responsibility to the public and to honest advertisers. Trade associations and other agencies have also contributed to these higher standards. The result is that newspaper advertising rightfully merits and enjoys the confidence of the advertiser, the patronage of the consuming public, and the recognition by competing media that for general utility, economy, and effectiveness it is without an equal.

Claims to Superiority

The reasons for this confidence are not hard to find. Practically all of the benefits of advertising in general are shared by newspaper advertising. In addition, it has certain special qualities of its own. Of all the forms of advertising, newspaper advertising has particular claims to effectiveness as a social and economic force. Its advantages may be summarized as follows :

- Mass Appeal. Taken as a whole, the total circulation of newspapers is significant enough to show the universality of the newspaper reading habit in America. No other one medium is so widely, so continually, so voluntarily, or so habitually accepted as the newspaper. It goes daily into the great bulk of the 30,000,000 homes in the United States, most of whose families are confirmed newspaper readers. It is at once visible, tangible, convenient, economical, and, consequently, effective.
- Concentration. The very fact that the newspaper is so widely accepted makes it possible both to blanket the country and to concentrate advertising effort. Individual newspapers cater to different groups of the population. A general advertiser is thus enabled to plan his advertising campaign effectively in terms of certain sections of the country or in terms of certain elements of the buying public as a specific target or objective. Under other circumstances, he can scatter his

appeal broadcast, shotgun fashion. Such concentration or flexibility is impossible in anything like the same degree with other media.

- Flexibility. The very nature of the newspaper makes for a flexibility and timeliness of advertising procedure and planning that are hardly possible with any other medium except possibly the radio. The frequency of issue of the newspaper enables the advertiser to change his plans overnight to take advantage of changed conditions. This is also reflected in the high degree of selectivity referred to in the preceding paragraph.
- Economy. In its appeal, its circulation, its flexibility, and its cost both to the advertiser and to the reader, the newspaper affords a medium which for economy of time, effort, and money is unsurpassed by any other. Its facilities are available to the advertiser in accordance with his needs and his budget.
- News Tie-up. A particular advantage of the newspaper as an advertising medium is the inherent relationship between its news and its advertising contents. Neither could exist satisfactorily without the other. A publication that was all news and no advertising would be prohibitive in price and would be lacking in a vital element. Similarly, a publication that was nothing but advertising would get relatively scant attention from the consuming public. The newspaper combines these two essential elements economically and conveniently as no other medium does.
- Public Confidence. The very bulk of newspaper sales is convincing proof of the public dependence upon and the public confidence in the newspaper. A relationship exists between the newspaper and its readers which is peculiarly close and intimate in many ways. This responsiveness gives the newspaper an advantage which is again peculiarly its own.

Newspaper advertising, then, is both flexible and timely; it affords either a concentrated or a general consumer objective; it is efficient and effective in terms of time, effort, and money expended in advertising campaigns; and it offers an appeal through a mass medium which has as yet no serious rival.

Weak Points

But newspaper advertising also has its tendons of Achilles. In America, despite the New York Times and the Christian Science Monitor, there is as yet no truly national newspaper. The very fact that the newspaper is so essentially, or at most, local or regional in character is sometimes a deterrent to advertisers who are looking for nationwide 'circulation. This objection can be met, of course, by using in combination strong regional newspapers like the Chicago Tribune, the Atlanta Journal, the Des Moines Register and Tribune, and many others. The graphic limitations of the newspaper constitute another weakness as an advertising medium. Owing to the inferior quality of newsprint, the necessity of using relatively coarse screened cuts, and the difficulties of using colór combinations at high press speeds, the newspaper has been unable to compete typographically with the better magazines on an even footing. The newspaper has been greatly improved in these respects, but, except for rotogravure, it is difficult to see how it can equal the quality printing of the better magazines.

The very frequency of issue of the newspaper is sometimes cited as a disadvantage in that it is so short-lived. A magazine, on the other hand, is apt to last much longer and to be read more than once. Yet by the same test, the radio is still more fleeting. The answer for both lies in the iteration and reiteration of the advertiser's message.

The criticism is still heard that American newspapers constitute a "kept press of business," i.e., that they are subservient to their advertisers, that they are primarily and chiefly mercenary, and that they have no real interest in their readers except to exploit them or to assist in their exploitation.

Such charges fall of their own weight when measured against the public service rendered by newspapers as a whole as well as by the increasingly painstaking and frequently expensive policies voluntarily adopted by newspapers to protect the reader-consumer from rapacious advertisers and others. The New York Times, the New York Herald Tribune, and the Scripps-Howard newspapers, to name only three, are conspicuous examples of publications which go to great lengths to guard against fraudulent and misleading advertising and otherwise to protect their readers. George Seldes, James Rorty, and other serious critics of the American newspaper cite instance after instance where the newspaper has bent the knee to the advertiser.

Undoubtedly many newspapers have yielded at some time or other to the pressure of the advertiser or their policies have reflected the outside connections of their owners. The newspaper, like any other human agency, is not infallible, and it would be difficult to find one that claims to be. But to condemn all newspapers because some of them always, or even many of them at some time, have been unduly tainted with the dollar sign is no more fair than a blanket denial of the charges would be.

The hopeful thing is that really reputable newspapers are conscientious, their scrutiny of advertising is increasingly watchful, and their independence of advertisers is greater each year. Any self-respecting newspaper knows that it can succeed only as it builds and maintains reader confidence. To reap and enjoy this, it must hold the reader above the advertiser.

The great and growing majority of newspapers are more careful and conscientious in such matters than they are usually given credit for being. Taken by and large, the disadvantages of the newspaper as an advertising medium are far outweighed by its advantages. After more than a century, the daily newspaper with its extremely low price is still the chief hope of the American advertiser and the chief dependence of the great bulk of its readers who comprise most of the consumers. Other media are useful to supplement or to pave the way for the newspaper's message. There is no sign at this writing that the newspaper will be supplanted by any other medium now in use.

Relative Merits of Papers

Some difference of opinion exists as to the relative merits of morning, afternoon, and Sunday newspapers for advertising purposes. It is claimed, for example, that the morning newspaper has a special appeal for businessmen and, conversely, that the morning newspaper is less satisfactory when it comes to reaching the woman reader who, it is well known, is a dominant factor in the family expenditures and purchases. It is argued that the afternoon paper is more likely to go into the home with more time for its perusal than is the morning paper. Sunday papers suffer from their very bulk and from the fact that potential readers may be motoring or golfing at the week end. Each argument is susceptible of a counterargument. The merits of a particular newspaper are apt to depend much more upon what kind of a paper it is, what clientele it caters to, and upon what its news, editorial, and business policies are rather than whether it is a morning or an afternoon newspaper. Examples of conspicuous success may be found in both fields, and, while it is true that afternoon newspapers far outnumber those published in the morning, it would be unfair and untrue to say that either has a marked claim to superiority as an advertising medium alone. In general, that newspaper which is read most and has the largest following in the home is apt to be best for advertising purposes.

Classifications

Newspaper advertising falls into five general classifications. These are (1) general display, (2) retail display, (3) classified, (4) legal, and (5) promotional or self-advertising. Each of these can be further subdivided in turn. They may be defined or described as follows:

1. General display is perhaps more commonly known as national or foreign display. This type of advertising either comes directly from national advertisers or, more often, through advertising agencies and has to do with nationally handled goods or services marketed or distributed through local outlets. Despite the effects of the depression, it is still an important source of revenue.

2. Retail or local display is the advertising of local department stores and other retailers. It is local in origin and is supplied directly to the newspaper by the advertiser or through a local advertising agency. The development of local display advertising has been highly profitable on the whole for both the retailer and the newspaper.
3. Classified is more often known to the reader or user as "want ads." It consists of relatively brief advertisements, usually set in small type under classifications which vary in number with the volume and variety of such advertisements. This type of advertising, properly developed, can be highly effective and profitable. Some newspapers are much more successful in developing it than are others.
4. Legal advertising includes announcements or reports required by law to be published, or sometimes optional at the discretion of public officials or boards, which relate to such matters as notices of election, proposals for bond issues, public improvement projects, petitions in bankruptcy, amendments to state constitutions, financial reports of political subdivisions, boards, and officers, and many other matters. The rates are usually fixed by law. This form of advertising is particularly important to small newspapers.
5. Self-advertising is better known as promotional advertising. It is a means by which newspapers call attention to their own offerings, facilities, merits, enterprise, and attainments. Still relatively new, it has emerged from the stage of infancy but is a long way from having attained full stature.

The methods of soliciting, handling, and servicing the various kinds of advertising vary with individual newspapers. The size of the newspaper, as measured by its circulation and its volume of advertising, is an important factor in determining the division of labor in the advertising department. Each major classification will be dealt with in detail in succeeding chapters. For years a two-way fight has been waged by newspapers over advertising. With one hand they have been engaged in competition with each other, and with the other they have been busy combating other media such as magazines, shopping guides, the radio, and direct-mail advertising. Some publishers have been converted to the sensible view that after all they have interests in common which are far better served by uniting against outside competitors than in cutting each other's throats. This does not mean that inter newspaper competition is outmoded, for it is not and never will be. But there is a growing tendency on the part of newspapers to make more common cause against other kinds of competitors.

Newspapers and the Radio

The radio offers a case in point. Along with the public, the newspapers first embraced the radio as a new toy or diversion, a novelty that opened the door to a whole new realm of entertainment. Acres of white space were freely given to publicizing radio programs and activities. When the radio developed rapidly into a serious advertising competitor, both locally and nationally, the newspapers reversed their attitude. Some of them took the extreme stand of not publishing even the barest program listings. Whatever the effect upon the broadcasters or the program sponsors, this was manifestly unfair to newspaper readers. Two results have become more and more apparent. Paradoxically, one is a marked tendency on the part of the newspapers and the radio to join hands, and the other is the development of radio-program advertising. The newspaper-radio alliance has resulted in the purchase, lease, or affiliation on the part of newspapers with 145 broadcasting stations in the continental United States. In such cases publishers have two strings to their advertising bow with the additional advantage of being able to use both media for promotional purposes.

Rotogravure and Comics

Two other channels of newspaper advertising have been greatly developed in recent years. One is the rotogravure section and the other the comics. The rotogravure section affords a particularly high-class medium for quality advertising. It puts the newspaper on a par with the best of magazine advertising. The well-nigh universal appeal of the comic strip and the comic supplement led naturally to their adaptation to advertising purposes. This was made possible in two ways. One was to shorten the comic page, using the remaining space for advertising. The other was to develop advertising with a strong personal appeal, printed in colors and frequently modeled after the comics themselves with characters and plot. There has been some objection to this on the part of a few newspapers as well as from readers. The practice, however, now seems well established. It is primarily to advertising that newspapers owe whatever typographical merit they possess. Advertisers were the first to see the practical possibilities of the better type faces, the effectiveness of better layouts and of a planned appeal to the eye of the reader, rather than the hit-or-miss methods formerly employed. Advertisers, too, have had a large hand in the development of better newspaper illustrations and the adaptation of color printing to newspapers. Printing in two or more colors, originally confined to the comic, magazine, and feature sections, has been developed to such an extent that hundreds of daily newspapers are equipped to offer color printing as a matter of ordinary service and routine.

Advertising Manager

From the standpoint of newspaper organization, the advertising manager is the key man in the advertising picture. He it is who sets the pace for the advertising department. It is to him that the publisher looks for results from the advertising department. It is his responsibility to keep the advertising sales staff on its toes, to strengthen and improve the position of the newspaper as an advertising medium, and to cooperate with other departments of the publication as well as with advertisers. To accomplish these ends he needs certain special abilities. Among these are salesmanship, leadership, energy, experience, vision and foresight, and a capacity for organization and administration. He needs to understand the points of view of the advertiser and the public as well as the problems of the newspaper itself. While it is not imperative that he be a " mixer" in the ordinary sense of the word, it is important that he get around, strengthen his contacts, and size up conditions for himself. Individual advertising managers are naturally apt to excel in one thing more than another. Some are better salesmen than they are administrators and vice versa. One who combined all of the qualities just listed would indeed be a rarity. Yet one such was the late Louis Wiley who personified the New York Times of the twentieth century almost as much as its distinguished publisher, the late Adolph S. Ochs, and who was even more frequently in the public eye. Perhaps as much as any newspaper business executive of his time his capacity, his vision, and his understanding extended to all parts of the newspaper.

Harvey R. Young, advertising director of the Columbus, Ohio, Dispatch, described some of the necessary qualities of the competent advertising manager, asserting that he should lead rather than drive his salesmen. Writing in Editor & Publisher, he emphasized the importance of the advertising manager's analyzing circulation so as to be able to know and explain fully "the advantages of all parts of the circulation, that out of the city as well as that in the city."

He defined the most successful newspaper advertising salesman as "the one who markets the circulation of his newspaper as intelligently and as carefully as successful retailers market their merchandise."

Advertising Distribution

Except for 1932 and 1933 there has been relatively little variation since 1920 in the distribution of advertising in American newspapers according to its major classifications. The division is shown by a Media Records report on the advertising returns for 1935 in 365 dailies in 95 cities, representing nearly half the total linage for the United States and Canada. The breakdown follows:

Future of Advertising. Stuart Chase believes that the newspaper of the future will be one which the consumer can read conveniently, devoid of what he calls the destructive "yammering" of competing advertisers whose products may be identical. They will be newspapers, he predicts, in which advertising will be devoted more to announcing new products or for sociological purposes such as safety and Red Cross campaigns. In that happy day, he also anticipates that the advertising revenue of the average paper may be as little as 10 per cent of the total, the reader paying the other 90 per cent. In this event he argues that "the freedom of the press will then be real," a condition which he insists does not exist now because " commercial considerations make it impossible."

It is doubtful whether all or any of these particular changes will come to pass, and it is debatable whether some of them should. It is likely that the Chase wish is father to the thought. To ask the reader, for example, to pay nine-tenths of the cost of his newspaper would be to make copy prices prohibitive for many readers. It would limit the usefulness and effectiveness of the newspaper and thus help to defeat the very ends it seeks to serve. But Chase is right when he holds that "Newspapers have a tremendous responsibility in regard to the misguided consumer," and that, despite the persuasiveness and not infrequently the irritation produced by radio sales talks, the public remains eye-minded rather than ear-minded. In the newspaper of the future, advertising will be more restrained in its claims and improved in appearance. It will deal more with the merits of the merchandise and services advertised and will pay less attention to competing lines. The newspapers of that day will assume far greater responsibility toward both consumers and advertisers. They will be more scrupulous in their advertising and business practices. This condition will be brought about by an awareness that common honesty in the long run is not only best but still pays the largest profits, by the pressure of publishing and advertising groups, by higher standards of practice adopted by both newspapers and advertisers, and to some extent by federal and state laws.

11

RETAIL ADVERTISING

The relationship between the newspaper and the retail or local advertiser has necessarily been closer and of longer duration than that with the general or national advertiser. The local publisher and the local advertiser are not only neighbors in the physical sense but there is a community of interest between them that does not exist in anywhere near the same degree with respect to the national advertiser. By contrast with the general advertiser, the retail advertiser has the advantage of being on the ground in dealing with the local newspapers. He knows local conditions at first hand, he can deal with the newspaper direct instead of through agents, and he has his own ideas as to the circulation and pulling power of local media. Such impressions and convictions are the result of firsthand observation and experience.

The newspaper, in turn, recognizes in the retail advertiser its best customer. The volume of advertising from this source is the backbone of the business of the newspaper. The publisher knows that whatever affects the conditions of local trade will inevitably affect his own business. It is distinctly to his interest, therefore, to place his facilities at the disposal of the local advertiser and to assist him in making the most of his business opportunities. The economic philosophy of this is simple: as local trade prospers the community at large benefits, and the newspaper profits. Retail advertising is as old as the American newspaper, yet, as in the case of general advertising, its real development has been achieved only in recent times. Despite the expansion of general advertising, the bulk of newspaper advertising continues to be local in character. Although its volume shrank, too, under the effects of the great depression that began in 1929, it held up better than did national advertising. The continued faith in, and dependence upon, newspaper advertising by the local merchant were important factors in enabling American newspapers to weather the depression as well as they did.

WANAMAKER'S INFLUENCE

John Wanamaker, the great Philadelphia and New York merchant, has been credited with showing both retail and general advertisers the real possibilities of newspaper advertising. His advertising feats attracted particular attention at the time of the Centennial in 1876. Presbrey says of him: "In this Wanamaker store in Philadelphia originated large scale advertising, the advertising that went into papers and large expenditures, produced a large volume of business and demonstrated for the directors' table of American business that advertising was a force worthy the attention of big minds. . . .

In the words of Joseph H. Appel, long associated with the merchant: "John Wanamaker showed the way to make business articulate so that it could establish confidence and good will between buyer and seller, consumer and producer. . . . John Wanamaker's example showed to manufacturers the use of advertising in effecting mass distribution, which demanded enormous mass production, with accompanying high wages, efficiency in manufacture and the great material prosperity of the United States. . . . The advertising by other stores and by manufacturers which followed when John Wanamaker 'showed the way' resulted in the enormous volume of advertising that makes possible America's great newspapers and magazines whose income is derived more than two-thirds from advertising and less than one-third from paid circulation."

The advertising principles of John Wanamaker were simple: "We advertise what we have for sale. We have for sale what we advertise. The people come and see that it is so." As Appel phrased it, he placed "truth on a business basis as the store had already placed business on a truth basis." As early as 1879, Wanamaker used a full page of newspaper advertising and in time this became his practice. This was not new in itself but the effective use he made of the space and the regularity with which he used it were innovations. Within a few years his example was widely followed. In fact other advertisers did not stop at imitating him but boldly helped themselves to the language and layout of his advertisements as well as to the ideas they contained. In one week in 1890, for example, the store reported "seventeen quotations found in the East and the whole advertisement copied bodily in the West." Wanamaker, in short, proved the value of persistent and largescale advertising. How much he was impressed by his achievement is shown by his own statement that "If I ever have a Columbus monument in advertising, it will be for the discovery that the advertising of constant benefit to merchant and customer is in the daily newspaper of known circulation." There were other strings to his bow, of course, besides advertising, but the American newspaper owes John Wanamaker a lasting debt for his pioneering in this quarter.

Department-store Advertising

The growth of department and specialty stores, taking their cue to some extent from Wanamaker, has paralleled that of the newspapers. As the stores have grown and prospered, the newspaper has expanded and profited. The two are interdependent to a large degree. It is doubtful whether either could continue to thrive or perhaps even to exist without the other. Channing E. Sweitzer, managing director of the National Retail Dry Goods Association, is authority1 for the statement that "The department and specialty stores, and the newspapers of this country have grown up together. In strong retail stores, large and small, newspaper advertising today is the spine of promotional activities, and it is hardly questionable whether many stores could exist without it and certainly newspapers could not. The support of retail advertising has largely helped to make it possible for the American press to perform public services unconceived years ago. The revenue from stores has provided, in a great measure, the means for the growth of newspapers, with globe-encircling press associations, wide-flung corps of correspondents, special writers, and a wide variety of features. Beyond this, retail advertising constitutes a strong element to the reader interest of modern newspapers, ranking, especially among women readers, as great in importance as the society and the sports pages."

Factors Governing Advertising

Various factors combine to govern the effectiveness of retail newspaper advertising. These include (1) the quality and quantity of the circulation of the newspaper; (2) whether the newspaper is a morning, afternoon, or Sunday publication; (3) the merchandising service and cooperation afforded by the newspaper; (4) competition; (5) seasonality; and (6) physical characteristics.

Circulation

Both the quality and the quantity of the circulation of a newspaper are important to the advertiser. It is no longer enough for a newspaper to have circulation in bulk. Over the years, the advertiser has become properly and increasingly concerned with the quality of the circulation represented in the white space he buys. The volume of circulation continues to be important, but it is of little use to the advertiser unless it can be definitely translated in terms of potential customer buying power. Gross circulation figures, therefore, are only one index of the probable value of a newspaper as an advertising medium. It is for this reason that newspapers break down their circulation figures in detail, so as to show the areas of direct returns, of delayed returns, and all other. In the case of daily newspapers, the first usually includes the city itself or city and suburban, the second the remainder of its trade basin, and the third all else. Even these categories are further broken down for the larger cities to show still more accurately the potential purchasing power represented by the clientele of the particular newspaper and, conversely, to eliminate doubtful elements or those with little or no buying power. A number of agencies have contributed to the careful and authentic appraisal of newspaper circulations in the larger cities. Individual newspapers have seen the value of such information and make frequent assays of their circulations for their own use and that of their advertisers, both retail and general. The A. B.C. has been another factor of growing importance for more than 20 years.

Morning vs. Afternoon Newspapers

For many years the morning newspaper was supreme. It had the largest circulation, carried the most advertising, enjoyed the greatest prestige, and wielded the most influence. Owing to changing conditions, it has been surpassed in recent years, despite conspicuous individual exceptions, both in numbers and in circulation by the afternoon paper. Today there are fewer morning than Sunday newspapers and the total morning circulation is smaller than that of either afternoon or Sunday papers. Each kind of newspaper is supposed to have a different "personality" from the advertising and editorial standpoints as well as from that of circulation. It has been said, for example, that the morning newspaper is a trifle slower in general speed of sales action than its afternoon rival, but has a greater power of repetition when a regular schedule is maintained. The argument is also offered that the morning newspaper has more of an appeal to the business man or businesswoman. Conversely, because they are apt to take it with them, it is contended that the life of the morning paper is briefer, and its advertising effectiveness limited accordingly.

There is no question but that the average evening newspaper gets more of a reading than does the average morning newspaper. It is more of a publication for home consumption than its morning rival. It is, therefore, more apt to be read by all the members of the family at a time when there is more leisure for reading and, consequently, for planning the shopping for tomorrow. Afternoon papers are called more dependable for direct advertising returns because of their size and timing as related to the reading hours and habits of the average family.

SUNDAY NEWSPAPERS

In Sunday papers it has been said that the ratio of returns from advertising is lower in proportion to their circulation than is the case with either morning or afternoon newspapers. This is explained by the fact that they are apt to show more waste circulation from the standpoint of the retail advertiser.

The very bulk of the Sunday newspaper is also cited as an argument against it on the theory that so much reading matter makes it well nigh impossible to give close attention to news, features, or advertisements unless the reader has a particular want to satisfy. Nevertheless the Sunday newspaper serves a definite advertising purpose, particularly for long-range copy, good will, and special events. In individual cases, it would be difficult to assign priority to any of these groups because so much depends upon management, skill, competition, local conditions, and other variable factors.

In point of total advertising during 1935, the Washington Star, an evening paper, was first with 21,837,189 lines, followed by the New York Times (morning) with 19,420,969 lines. Six of the first 10 were evening papers. On a six-day basis only, Sunday issues excluded, evening papers won 17 of the first 20 places. Despite this it would be unjust and inaccurate to say that morning newspapers like the Cleveland Plain Dealer and the Los Angeles Times have not a claim to superiority within their orbits just as their evening contemporaries have.

MERCHANDISING SERVICE AND COOPERATION

As far as advertising is concerned, the key to the publishing problem is not how widely the newspaper is distributed but how thoroughly is the paper used. From the business standpoint, the question is not how great is the paper's circulation or how great is its editorial influence, but are its advertising contents on a par with its news and editorial matter, and does the reader have the same confidence in the advertising that he has in the paper's news and opinions. It is obvious that advertising has little merit and the medium is of questionable value unless the reader is interested and served thereby.

It is the duty of the newspaper to assist both the reader and the advertiser with respect to advertising. Its function is to bring the reader and the advertiser together through the facilities it offers. Just as news and editorial excellence alone are insufficient, the task of the newspaper is not only to sell its white space to its advertisers but to aid them in making the best use of that space.

It has been pointed out that the newspaper can serve the reader through advertising in the following ways: (1) by assuring the accuracy of all advertising claims 'and statements; (2) by assisting readers to buy through the medium of a Shoppers' Service and Shoppers' Guide or merchandising certificates redeemable at any advertiser's; (3) by publication of a shopping list or advertising table of contents so as to simplify the shopper's problem.

In a similar manner, the newspaper can assist the advertiser in the following ways: (1) by an educational campaign through a series of talks to store customers, thus helping to reduce wasteful expense to the stores; (2) by help in bringing about better merchandising to back up an advertisement and thus eliminate much wasted advertising.

It is claimed that these methods would make the paper the shopper's favorite newspaper, would give its advertising much greater pulling power, would improve circulation, and would increase its prestige and power with advertisers, both retail and general. There are limits, of course, to the cooperation and assistance to be rendered by the newspaper. In determining these limits, the publisher will be guided by experience, by common sense, and by economic factors.

Competition

With the current tendency toward mergers, there are a growing number of American cities in which there is only one newspaper. As has been noted, there is a minimum number of newspapers in even the largest cities, as for example Cleveland, Pittsburgh, and Baltimore with three each and Chicago with only five of general circulation. This condition affects both the newspapers and the advertisers and is complicated further by the fact that in a number of cities where there are still two or more papers two of them are under the same ownership. This situation is fraught with possibilities of both good and evil. A monopoly offers the newspaper the possibility of greater profits and less expense, while the advertiser would benefit from better coverage at a lower cost. On the other hand, a newspaper which enjoys such a monopoly can be lulled into a false sense of security, and, if it presses its advantage too far or grows lax in its measure of service to readers and advertisers, it is apt to invite competition either through the establishment of other newspapers or through the diversion of its advertising into other channels. Where a newspaper enjoys such an advantage, then, it behooves it to make its reader-advertiser service so effective and so satisfactory that there will be no demand for a return to wasteful and expensive competition.

Seasonally

One of the reasons newspaper advertising was so slow in developing was that it was stereotyped and advertisers failed to realize the importance of timeliness. This condition has been almost entirely corrected, but newspapers still face the problem of seasonality. This results in seasonal fluctuations in linage which complicate newspaper operation and management. During the eight years from 1928 through 1935, for example, newspaper linage as measured by Media Records in 52 so-called key cities fell off from January to February, rose sharply in March, April, and May, dropped steadily from June into August, rose again to reach a new peak of fall buying in October, then tapered off through the holidays.

There were some exceptions, but these were the general trends. Newspapers have sought ways and means to counteract these seasonal effects, particularly that in midsummer. The line of attack has been through greater promotional efforts, closer merchandising tie-ups, and, in particular, the stimulation of advertising through seasonal discounts and space bonuses. Some newspapers have adopted a form of advertising contract which sets a minimum below which the advertiser may not go in any week or month as the case may be. These have been of some avail, but the problem is a long way from being solved.

Physical Characteristics

Arthur Brisbane is credited with defining the qualities of a good advertisement as follows : it must be seen, it must be read, it must be understood, and it must be believed. The appearance and the location of an advertisement, therefore, have much to do with its effectiveness. It is to the advantage of the advertiser as well as to that of the newspaper to insist, for example, upon certain restrictions as to typography, illustration, makeup, and position. These include limits upon the size and variety of the type faces, cuts, and borders, the nature of the composition involved, and the location of the advertising on the page. On some small newspapers, the advertiser still has his own way in such matters but these are the exception rather than the rule.

The advertising pyramid has long since been accepted as the standard form of advertising makeup. This type of makeup has its basis in both physics and psychology. It puts the largest advertisements where they properly belong and It places all advertising in the best general location with respect to reading advertising is built along both sides of the page with one or more news columns projecting toward the bottom of the page.

No way has yet been found to make the left-hand page as good from the standpoint of reading matter or advertising as the right-hand page. Again this is partly a matter of habit and partly because most readers are right-handed so that when the paper is opened it is natural to hold the right hand at arm's length rather than the left. Yet most editorial pages are on the left as well as first departmental pages such as sports and society on many newspapers. Few of the better newspapers now carry display advertising on page one, and there is a tendency to keep display advertising at a minimum even on pages two and three on some newspapers.

Rates

The rate structure is considered elsewhere, but the effect of rates upon advertising is worth passing attention here. Rates should be high enough to pay the publisher a reasonable profit in terms of his costs and his investment and the quality and quantity of the circulation. At the same time they should not be so high as to compel the potential advertiser to seek less expensive media. Generally, however, there is a lag between circulation and rates to the advantage of the advertiser.

Strong pressure was brought by advertisers in many cities in the depression years to compel newspapers to reduce their advertising rates on the grounds that circulation had fallen off and the prices of other commodities and services had been reduced. The fact was that most newspapers had not increased their rates in the seemingly prosperous days of 1929 in proportion to their circulation and pulling power and certainly not in proportion to other goods and services. Further, while there was some falling off in newspaper circulation, it proved to be largely temporary or fractional. In addition, experience showed that even where some newspapers reduced their rates as a result of advertiser pressure, only a few increased their linage thereby. Of 108 newspapers replying to a Newspaper Advertising Executives' Association questionnaire in 1933, 72 reported that they had made no reductions and 5 had even raised their rates. 1 Of the newspapers which had lowered their rates, 9 reported their linage improved or maintained as a result, two saw some beneficial effect in retail but not in general advertising, and 16 could see no improvement in linage as a result of the reductions. Still other papers gave "temporary" reductions or space bonuses or increased their cash discounts.

Newspapers are under constant pressure to make rate concessions in one form or another. They should be on their guard against such attacks. While they should be slow to raise their rates, they should not hesitate to do so where the facts and circumstances fully warrant it.

Combination Rates

In some cities where two papers are under the same management, the practice has developed of selling space in both papers in combination. This might include a morning and an evening newspaper or a weekday and a Sunday paper. This arrangement can be advantageous to both publisher and advertiser. Properly managed, it is a spur to advertising, swelling the volume, while it gives the advertiser the opportunity to take space in both publications at a combined rate which is appreciably less than the sum of the two normal rates. In some cases the combination rate is sold under pressure, and, while such a policy may be of temporary advantage to the publisher, especially where he has a monopoly, it leads to hard feeling on the part of advertisers and in the long run invites outside competition.

Out-of-town Advertising

If it is true that the home-town advertiser is the main support of the newspaper, there is some merit to his feeling that he is entitled to preferential treatment by the newspaper. Most newspapers will concede the point, but the difficulty is to know where to draw the line. This is particularly true in the case of smaller newspapers where every dollar of legitimate revenue may be important. Should they, for example, solicit or accept contracts from mail-order houses or from competing merchants in near-by towns or cities? The fact is that most of them do, and properly. The home-town merchant in turn would regard as ridiculous any proposition to confine his sales to local residents. While he should have all possible cooperation and preference, the local advertiser should strive so to conduct his business as to meet outside competition as far as possible.

PROPORTION OF ADVERTISING TO NEWS

This is a matter which concerns the publisher, the advertiser, and the reader alike. It is also a matter in which the government has an interest through the postal regulations. The proportion varies daily, weekly, monthly, seasonally, and yearly as conditions change.

In good times, the volume of advertising tends to increase somewhat at the expense of space available for news. In slack periods, the reverse is true, although, during the depression years, most newspapers were run on a "tight" basis, i.e., with restricted space for both news and advertising. In most newspapers advertising probably ranges between 40 and 60 per cent of the total space. An analysis of one large city newspaper showed only 45 per cent of the space given over to advertising, yet the paper was so highly departmentalized that space for news was at a premium. Despite the importance of editorial opinion and the development of advertising, the publishing of news remains the chief function of the newspaper. If the news is restricted unduly, the reader, the advertiser, and the newspaper all suffer eventually, and the government may step into the picture. Too many pages whose advertising content is unrelieved by news are apt to defeat their own purpose. Further, the government grants special postal rates to newspapers because of their usefulness and importance as a medium for the dissemination of news and information, not because of their advertising content. The government may, therefore, "look with disfavor" upon newspapers which fail to fulfill this function and in extreme cases may revoke the second-class mailing privileges.

Color Advertising

Color printing has been a logical and inevitable outgrowth of newspaper production. Owing to physical and mechanical limitations, newspapers were considerably behind magazines in this respect. This handicap was offset to some extent by the development of the newspaper rotogravure section. This has been followed in the last few years by marked improvement in color printing and in particular by its adaptation to advertising. Today probably a third of the daily newspapers of the United States are equipped to do such printing. Much of the advancement in this direction was due to pioneer work by the Chicago Tribune and a few other leading newspapers. Advertisers have been somewhat slow to take advantage of the possibilities of color owing chiefly to the higher rate, but even limited experience has shown that for certain kinds of advertising and occasions it has definite advantages in attracting the eye of the reader and enhancing the appearance of the advertisement.

Swatch Advertising

In 1934 and 1935 there was a wave of so-called "swatch" advertising in which samples of the materials used in goods and products advertised were pasted on the paper. This included such things as samples of shirting, curtains and drapes, and even leather goods. This necessitated handwork which in some cases was handled by the advertiser and in others it was farmed out to outside firms. Within its limits, it proved remarkably effective. Yet the physical difficulties of preparing and handling such advertising, the extra time and expense involved, and the limited use that could be made of it combined to prevent its spread. Further, the Post Office Department entered strong objections and a general ruling was finally issued forbidding the practice. The rule was later suspended temporarily but the innovation seems to have halted there.

Guaranteed Advertising

Reputable newspapers in recent years have assumed more and more responsibility for the advertising they carry. They have not only imposed restrictions upon the advertiser but, to an increasing degree, they stand ready to protect the reader in his dealings with the advertiser. This is markedly different from the early policy which was, in substance: "Let the buyer beware." The current practice was adopted, because it is to the advantage of the customer, the honest advertiser, and the newspaper itself. Newspapers have come to realize that it is to their interest as well as to that of the reader and the reliable advertiser to assume some degree of responsibility in this matter. One dishonest advertiser in a newspaper or one who is given to shady dealing is like one bad apple in a barrel in that he is apt to shake reader confidence in all advertisers and in the newspaper itself. The New York Herald Tribune went further perhaps in this respect than any other newspaper through the medium of its shoppers' bureau. Its policy was so broad as to guarantee absolute satisfaction to the purchaser of anything advertised in the Herald Tribune. If such a customer was dissatisfied for any reason, the paper stood ready to intervene in his behalf. The Tribune ran a column, "The Ad-Visor," conducted by Samuel Hopkins Adams, which attracted wide attention and had a healthy effect upon retail advertising.

Few newspapers are in a position to go as far as this. Others, such as the Columbus, Ohio, Dispatch, stand back of the advertising they carry in the following manner:

Guaranteed Advertising: The Columbus Dispatch will not knowingly publish a fraudulent or dishonest advertisement. In case of unsatisfactory dealings with Dispatch advertisers, every effort will be made by the publishers to secure an equitable adjustment.

Large vs. Small Accounts: A publisher is authority for the statement that, in almost any sizable city, 75 per cent or more of the retail display advertising comes from not more than a score of local advertisers. A glance at almost any representative newspaper will show that there is a large element of truth in his assertion. This situation raises several important questions such as: Does such dependence upon so few accounts put the newspaper too much in the power of the large advertiser? If these advertisers were to have serious financial difficulties or if they were to change to other media, what would happen to the newspaper? Have newspapers been remiss in not cultivating more small accounts? If there is to be more governmental regulation of business and more government in business with heavier taxes and -smaller profits, what then? There is no escaping the fact that there is some danger in a newspaper's being too dependent upon a few large accounts. If the publisher is not careful, an occasional large advertiser may attempt to dictate policies. This is much more apt to apply to the weak rather than to the strong newspaper, but the danger is there nevertheless. It is distinctly to the advantage of the newspaper, therefore, to develop small, as well as large, accounts as long as it continues to rely upon advertising as its chief source of income. These are cultivated in the central shopping areas but they have been largely neglected in neighborhood and suburban shopping centers. Such accounts not only yield additional revenue but guarantee the newspaper a larger measure of independence than where it must rely upon a relatively few large accounts. The Christian Science Monitor has shown what can be done with small accounts through intelligent and persevering application.

Publicity

Volumes might be written about publicity in its relation to newspaper advertising. It is the bane of newspaper publishing, a perennial topic at meetings -of editors and publishers. It is talked about, but, like the weather, little is done about it. Every newspaper is the target for advertising in the guise of publicity. Much of it comes direct to the editorial rooms, but an unduly large proportion, it must be confessed, clears through the newspaper business office. Such as passes muster there is apt to be sent to the editorial department marked, "B.O.M.," i.e., "Business Office Must" There seem to be two sides to the publicity question. Newspapers clearly follow no standard or uniform policy in the matter. There is no question but that some kinds of publicity are entirely legitimate such as that relating to certain phases of education, public health, and some governmental activities.

It would seem, however, that any "puff " which carries trade or firm names or which relates to the ordinary activities of business should be catalogued as advertising and treated as such. Yet many otherwise good newspapers not only accept but use such material as a matter of course. Smaller newspapers are more apt to be overly free with their space in this respect than are large ones. It is sometimes difficult to draw the line between publicity and advertising even when it refers to business men or to commercial activities. The advent of new motor-car models or the appearance of a new play, for example, are matters of legitimate reader interest which have a distinct news as well as advertising value.

Many newspapers accept certain kinds of publicity as a matter of course, using it in special departments of the paper. They are paid for it in a sense, however, from the fact that much higher rates are charged for the accompanying advertising. Entertainment and automotive advertising are two conspicuous examples of this practice. Publishers will never get anywhere in combating the publicity evil unless and until they stand together. Too many small publishers give lip service to the principle of "no publicity" but use it with alacrity if it is supplied by an advertiser. The first large cities whose newspapers joined forces against the common enemy were Atlanta and Los Angeles in the order named, followed by other cities including Nashville, Augusta, and Binghamton. In both cities, the plans were worked out by joint agreement of the publishers. Advertisers and advertising agencies were notified in advance under the joint signature of the papers, and instructions were issued on each paper for the uniform guidance of editorial and advertising executives.

In the case of Atlanta, the agreement was designed to halt a practice which " threatens the future interest of the public in the news columns" and tends to "weaken the value of the advertising columns." In general, the ban was aimed at all publicity stories and pictures "except in those instances where the subject discussed is one of such public interest that it would be deserving of comment in our newspapers without regard to advertising." It affected business, commercial, professional, and sports publicity including fashion and flower shows, cooking and garden schools, changes in personnel, store luncheons, entertainments and receptions, Santa Glaus stunts, Junior League and other "society" tie-ups, insurance, robots and trick automobiles, fairs and carnivals, travel and resorts, and local hotels.

Advance publicity on professional sports was restricted, but the actual coverage of such events was left to the discretion of the department. It was agreed to eliminate as far as possible the identification of persons in all types of stories which involved mention of the name of a commercial organization. Restrictions were likewise placed upon mention of the names of hotels, of the identity of companies making gasoline-price reductions, of undertakers in connection with ambulance runs to accident or crime scenes, and concerning ticket offices and prices relative to lectures, concerts, recitals, and other musical, educational, and sports events. The Los Angeles ban was similar in its purpose and scope. In neither case was it possible to eliminate all publicity. The two moves served to end much of the abuse that had grown up. In both instances the reaction of advertisers and the public was highly favorable. The examples set by Atlanta and Los Angeles could be followed profitably elsewhere to the improvement and benefit of newspapers and for the protection of readers and advertisers.

PROMOTING ADVERTISING

An executive of a newspaper which dominates its trade area once remarked before the market crash of 1929 that it could lock its front door, leaving the transom open, and enough advertising would fly in to keep the paper operating at a profit. Those days are gone, probably forever. Advertising, like other forms of merchandising, is on a different footing than it was. The competition is keener, space is bought on a more selective basis, advertisers are more critical of results, and new factors like the radio have entered the picture. This marks in reality a healthy condition, and it suggests that both advertising and newspapering have come of age. It is doubtful if any present-day newspaper could rest on its oars as described above or adopt the policy followed originally by the New York Times upon its establishment in 1851. This was to let the advertiser make the first move, if he wanted space he knew where to go for it. From sheer necessity, if for no other reason, the newspaper of today has to go after its advertising business. But in practice it is much more than mere going after business.

This something additional may be called promotion which in turn may be defined here as capitalizing upon ideas for new or additional sources of advertising. These may be applied to either retail or general advertising, but the former is likely to be more fruitful since it adapts itself better to this sort of cultivation. Seasons and anniversaries as well as special days and events lend themselves to such promotion. Various news departments may be developed or exploited with this in mind. These include daily, weekly, or seasonal departments, pages, or sections devoted to market and real estate news, garden and home activities and hints, amusements, travel, church announcements, commercial and professional activities and developments, and even death notices all form the basis for additional advertising. Both civic and commercial anniversaries, the opening of a new bridge, public building, or other similar improvements can be developed for legitimate advertising. Special pages devoted to the promotion of civic enterprises like community fund or traffic-safety campaigns can be sold similarly. The holidays, the holding of major conventions, or other meetings and events can be adapted likewise to "good will" or other special pages and sections. For even so short a period as a year, the files of Editor & Publisher show an astonishing variety of events and occasions that produced special advertising.

Much of this advertising justifies itself in the useful purpose it serves. Occasionally, however, it is prostituted by greedy newspapers or by high-pressure salesmen. The latter kind soon kills itself. One example of the former will suffice to illustrate the possibilities. An enterprising newspaper advertising man conceived the idea of an electrical refrigerator "show" similar to the well-known exhibits of new automobile models. The mezzanine of a downtown hotel was obtained for the purpose, the cooperation of the electrical dealers was obtained, the salesman lined up a large volume of exclusive advertising, and the dealers added materially to their sales and swelled the lists of future prospects. The same idea has been applied to radios as well as to other merchandise and services.

The more common of these special editions or sections may be published weekly, monthly, quarterly, semiannually, or annually. Those of the "anniversary" type can be adapted readily to circumstances. The anniversaries so observed may be those, for example, of the founding of a department store, the settlement of a community, the establishment of the newspaper itself, and so on. Where special sections are issued as supplements to a regular edition, a growing practice is to issue them in tabloid form. The kind of section or edition published will vary further with the newspaper, the time of year, and the community. What will produce only special pages or a small section in one instance may yield an entire edition elsewhere under different conditions. Taken by and large the special page, section, or edition is a fruitful source of additional revenue to the newspaper and, if properly promoted and conducted, serves a useful purpose for the advertiser and the reader.

Who Buys What

In recent years a new method of selling newspaper space has been developing. Owing to economic reasons, the old backslapping technique naturally wore itself out. Good fellowship was no longer a substitute for value received. The contemporary advertiser wants the facts, and the presentday newspaper is going to more and more pains to see that he gets them.

This development has put a premium upon what might be called the survey technique. Newspapers as well as advertisers want to know, in the language of one piece of newspaper promotion, "Who buys 'What ' and ' Where. ' " To obtain information as to consumer buying habits two courses are open: (1) the newspaper can undertake its own surveys or have them made by specialists who really know their business; (2) it can take advantage of official data contained in reports of the Census Bureau, the Department of Commerce, and other sources.

Such a survey is essentially a scientific job. It must be on that basis or not at all, as otherwise the newspaper will not really know whereof it speaks, and the advertiser will suffer accordingly. Much advertising is still wasteful because those responsible for it do not yet understand how to apply its basic principles and because too little is known about the market for which it is intended. From the standpoint of the newspaper, the only adequate solution lies in discovering and making available the essential facts about its market. Advertising claims made upon any other basis are built upon so much sand.

12

GENERAL ADVERTISING

General display advertising as distinct from retail display advertising has come of age since the World War. Formerly known as national or foreign advertising, it began at least as far back as Civil War times but the war-loan campaigns of 1917-1919 gave convincing proof of the directness, the effectiveness, and the relative cheapness of newspaper advertising for reaching the entire nation. Other media besides newspapers were used in the loan campaigns, but the press was the most effective and, considering its cost and its coverage, the most economical medium employed. Prior to the World War the full possibilities of what was then called national advertising were unappreciated.

Many advertisers were skeptical and the machinery for developing and handling accounts was in its formative stages. Not even the newspapers themselves were fully awake to the worth of their own medium in this respect and were neither staffed nor equipped to service national accounts. The automobile industry, for example, was notably doubtful as to the merits of newspaper advertising. Like many other important advertisers, its full conversion to the use of newspaper space dates after the World War. The marked preeminence of the newspaper as an advertising medium in the eyes of general advertisers has already been described. The fact that year after year the general advertiser puts nearly half of his total annual advertising outlay into newspaper space speaks for itself. That the newspaper stands alone in his estimation is further proved by the fact that he spends nearly half again as much upon it as for any other one medium.

A sharp decline occurred in nearly all lines of advertising as a result of the depression. The only real exception to this was the radio where special and unusual factors were involved. Yet despite the fact that the volume of general newspaper advertising shrank from $230,000,000 in 1930 to $145,000,000 in 1933, the 161 investment of general advertisers in newspaper space during the five years 1931-1935 inclusive was about $845,000,000 as against a total of $952,000,000 for all other media. It is almost axiomatic that a large advertiser is a heavy user of newspaper space. To put it another way, few such advertisers can afford to favor other media over the newspaper. A few still incline to the magazines or even the radio, but the great majority of heavy advertisers not only find the newspaper necessary but make their largest advertising investments in newspaper space.

In 1933, for example, the bureau of advertising of the American Newspaper Publishers Association reported that 19 American corporations spent $1,000,000 or more each in newspaper advertising. The first 9 averaged $4,500,000 apiece, and 8 of the 19 increased their newspaper advertising expenditures during the year. The report covered 342 advertisers all of whom spent at least $50,000 each on newspaper advertising during the year. Significantly, their outlays were divided as follows: newspapers, 59 per cent; magazines, 27 per cent; radio, 13 per cent. The proportions were almost identical with those for the previous year, indicating, as the report pointed out, "the relative stability of newspaper expenditure in the field of national advertising as a whole."

Individual advertisers using $1,000,000 or more of newspaper space included the American Tobacco Co., Liggett and Myers Tobacco Co., P. Lorillard Co., General Cigar Co., General Foods Corp., Kellogg Co., Standard Brands, National Biscuit Co., General Motors Corp., Chrysler Corp., Ford Motor Co., Colgate- Palmolive-Peet Co., Gillette Safety Razor Co., Socony Vacuum Corp., Standard Oil Co.

of Indiana, General Electric Co., R.K.O. Corp., and Goodyear Tire & Rubber Co. By groups, the largest users were: tobacco, foods, automobiles and trucks, toilet goods, gasoline and motor oils, druggists' sundries, movies, railroads, electrical appliances, soaps and cleansers, steamships, soft drinks, tires, finance, radios and phonographs. The one large exception was the R. J. Reynolds Tobacco Co., which had only a nominal newspaper outlay but which spent some $2,600,000 for magazine and radio advertising.

What It Is. In principle, such advertising is general rather than local in origin, character, and application. It differs from ordinary retail advertising in a number of respects. It usually originates at a central point and appears simultaneously in all parts of the country, e.g., the announcement of a new model automobile. Its appeal is usually in general rather than in detailed terms. It is designed to arouse interest and desire rather than to make the actual sale. It lays the ground work for the actual selling which is clinched by local retail advertising or by other means. Such advertising may be either regional or national as opposed to local in its scope. It may be prepared either by the advertiser himself through his own advertising department or in the office of an agency which specializes in such matters. For the most part the placing of such advertising is arranged by agents of both advertisers and newspapers. The advertising agency represents the advertiser, and the newspaper representative acts for the publisher. Unlike most retail advertising, general advertising usually comes in plate form supplied by the advertiser and brings a higher rate than retail advertising. Except where large individual newspapers or newspaper chains have their own representatives, both the advertising agency and the newspaper representative are paid a commission on all such accounts. In recent years there have been persistent attempts by large advertisers to break down the distinction between general and retail advertising.

They object to what many of them regard as the unjustifiable rate differential between the two kinds of advertising. For the most part publishers have been unmoved by such protests. The result has been that some advertisers have managed to attain by indirection what they were unable to get directly from the publishers. This was done by diverting considerable general advertising through retail or local outlets with a consequent saving to the advertiser and a loss to the newspapers. This led, in turn, to some advocacy on the one hand of a readjustment of newspaper rates in favor of the general advertiser and, on the other, to steps by newspapers to protect themselves against such inroads. Most newspapers have not only resisted such rate concessions but have extended the general rate to certain kinds of advertising even where it has to do with products or services sold locally at retail.

Beginnings

The makers of nostrums and patent medicines were the first to appreciate the possibilities of the newspaper as a mass medium. To them also was doubtless due part of the mistrust which some consumers still have of all advertising despite the efforts of ethical publishers and advertisers. John Wanamaker has been credited with demonstrating the real possibilities of advertising for general as well as retail advertisers. He was not the first advertiser to make large use of newspaper space, but he was probably the first to do it regularly and effectively by applying honesty, common sense, and plain talk to the innovations he introduced. Others followed the example he set in the seventies and eighties of the last century although they lacked something of his magic touch. National advertisers were handicapped by the almost utter lack of information about individual newspapers and by the absence of adequate means of handling their advertising.

For that matter advertising itself suffered from a sort of arrested development. From the standpoint of the advertiser, the newspaper situation was almost chaotic. No authentic lists of newspapers were available, while at best circulation was merely "claimed" or "estimated," and nothing was known as to its quality. Advertising rates, even where quoted, meant next to nothing as few publishers expected to get what they asked and many of them were glad to take whatever they could get and risk the credit at that.

General Agent

The first general agent came into the picture about 1840. He was primarily a broker who bought newspaper space in quantity lots and disposed of it as best he could but chiefly to his own advantage. He brought the publisher and the advertiser together, but his services stopped at that point.

He had previously bargained with the publisher for his space, usually for whatever it would bring. This was, in fact, little more than a primitive sort of barter system in which the advertiser, so to speak, bought "a pig in a poke" while the publisher either took merchandise or printing supplies in trade or gave unbelievably heavy discounts off his quoted space rates.

This chaotic condition was explained by the fact that so-called national advertising was something whose possibilities not even the publisher himself foresaw and for which he was, therefore, unprepared. Because of the lack of both authentic and adequate information about newspapers and their circulation, the advertiser, too, was at a disadvantage. As the middleman who made up his own list of newspapers, the details of which were long a closely guarded secret, the general agent profited both ways. If he was not authorized to sell space at his own figure, he contracted for it at the lowest possible rate and sold it at the highest possible figure, pocketing the difference. Thus space worth $2000 might yield the newspaper as little as $600, the difference going to the agent.

Credit risks were taken for granted. It was assumed that the average loss because of bad credit was 25 per cent and this was, consequently, figured in advance. If the advertiser's credit was good, he was usually entitled to a 25 per cent discount so that the publisher was out of pocket either way. The agent's commission was normally 25 per cent, hence, at most, the publisher eventually received half of the published rate. But this was the exception rather than the rule. In addition, the agent rendered none of the services to the advertiser and to the newspaper that are now taken for granted.

Special Agent

The general agent who stood between a group of newspapers on the one hand and the advertiser on the other began to give way by 1889 to the special agent who represented a limited number of newspapers. For the first time their interests became primary rather than incidental with an agent, and the function of the special agent was to sell space on its merits in the newspapers he represented instead of for whatever it might bring. The first advertising agency is said to have been opened by Volney B. Palmer in Philadelphia in 1840. The secrecy and mystery of the private lists of newspapers with circulation information of doubtful value were exploded once for all in 1869 with the publication over the protests of other general agents of the first issue of Rowell's American Newspaper Directory.

L. H. Crall, generally credited with being the first modern newspaper representative, opened his office in 1875 and began to sell space for the Cincinnati Times, the Cincinnati Enquirer, the St. Louis Globe Dispatch, the Chicago InterOcean, and the Milwaukee Sentinel The publishers of those newspapers agreed to pay him 15 per cent commission on such advertising as he could produce. Out of this idea grew the modern newspaper representative who looks after the interests of the newspaper exclusively.

Special Representative

The special representative is employed by newspapers at strategic business and manufacturing centers where large or numerous advertising accounts are likely to be placed. He may be in the emplcy of individual newspapers or groups of newspapers on a straight salary or on a commission basis. He may represent one newspaper or several score of newspapers. There is no limit to the number as long as they are noncompetitive and he is able to represent them adequately and diligently. He must know advertising, and he must know his newspapers and their territory. Armed with convincing market and circulation information and prepared on behalf of the newspapers he represents to afford all the reasonable merchandising and advertising service that may be required, it is his business to sell the merits of the newspapers he represents to advertisers or to advertising agencies with accounts to place. In reality the old general agent has been replaced by two functionaries : the special representative who is the agent of the newspaper and the advertising agency which serves the advertiser. The representative counsels the publishers for whom he acts and solicits a share in the general advertising accounts as they are placed. The agency gives the advertiser expert advice and professional assistance in the planning, preparation, and placing of advertising. Both the representatives and the agencies dealing in general or national accounts are to be found in strategic centers like New York, Chicago, St. Louis, Atlanta, New Orleans, San Francisco, and Los Angeles. There are about 175 recognized newspaper advertising representatives in the "United States, while of several thousand advertising agencies nearly 500 are accredited by the American Newspaper Publishers Association. The rise of the special representative afforded the newspapers individual representation, aided them in maintaining their advertising rates, improved their collections, furthered the preparation of market data and made expert advice available to the publishers. Concurrently advertising agencies became less concerned about buying space at bargain rates and gave more attention to serving the advertiser directly by preparing his copy and helping to plan his sales campaigns. The special representative helped to stabilize the business and showed the publishers how national advertising could be developed at a profit to the paper. At the same time the advertising agency was showing the advertisers how to buy space more wisely and use it more effectively.

The special representative is a very valuable factor in improving publishing and advertising conditions. While he represents the publisher and therefore naturally has the publisher's point of view, he is in a position to take a broader view than the individual publisher on specific problems. This is because he has the interests of several principals at heart. He can see how they all would be affected if the pet plan of one of them should be made effective generally. In this way he acts as a balance wheel. His detached viewpoint is valuable to the particular publisher with whom he feels himself forced to disagree, for he can save his principal from making disastrous mistakes. The special representative today is a specialist in every sense of the word. Paul Block & Associates, for example, represent 19 large newspapers, including Mr. Block's own newspapers, maintain offices in seven cities, and employ more than 60 trained newspaper solicitors in a total personnel of nearly 200. The 24 Scripps-Howard newspapers are represented by their own national advertising department with sales offices in eight cities. All its employees work on salary instead of commission. The Hearst newspapers are represented by the Hearst International Advertising Service with Rodney E. Boone as manager and with offices in 11 cities. In the general field, it is the task of these special representatives "to be able to furnish the advertisers, the advertising agencies, and space buyers the same information pertaining to a city and newspaper that the local representatives of a newspaper would furnish a local department store or any other local advertiser." By reason of the dual development of functions of the special representative and the modern advertising agency, space buying has been put on a scientific basis and guesswork has been largely eliminated. Dependable facts and information about newspapers are readily available, authentic data concerning a given trade area are to be had as a matter of course, and general advertising is more profitable for both publisher and advertiser.

ADVERTISING AGENCY

Although nearly a century has passed since the advertising agency first appeared, it was only after the turn of the century that general newspaper advertising became a force to be reckoned with and, as described, only since America's entry into the World War that it attained anything like its present proportions. As the general newspaper representative grew into the special representative the advertising agency took on new characteristics also. Even as late as 1910, no merchandising service was provided for advertisers, the A.B.C. had not been organized, newspaper advertising rate cards were unstable, the volume of so-called national advertising was small, and the newspapers themselves were not organized to handle such advertising. That all of this was changed in the next decade was due to a number of factors, one of the most important of which was the expansion of the advertising agency to something like its present proportions. In the early days, as the veteran E. E. Calkins described it, "advertising agents, even the biggest and best, did little to help their clients with copy, and nothing at all with art and typography. What they were concerned with was rates, buying and selling space. White space was sold like white flour buy in the cheapest, sell in the dearest, market. Agents accumulated space by various devices and sold it to customers as chance offered." George P. Rowell was a pioneer in this field at a time when authentic information concerning the names of newspapers, their advertising rates, their circulation, and the size and character of their place of publication was practically unknown. In the same way, J. Walter Thompson, founder of the agency of that name, pioneered in the magazine field. In the new scheme, the space buyer in the advertising agency, as Calkins put it, became the key man who "knew to the fraction of a decimal point just how little the newspaper publisher could be bullied, bribed or cajoled into accepting for his space. The two great unsolved mysteries of the advertising business were the real circulation of the medium, and the actual bed-rock cost of its space."

Conditions were unsatisfactory in other respects. Not only did a sort of trial-and-error method prevail with respect to rates but there was about as much variety typographically. How advertisements were set depended largely upon the ideas and facilities of the individual papers. Column widths varied considerably. Mechanical, advertising, and business policies differed with individual papers. National advertisers were irked by local rules but the patent-medicine advertisers, the first large national advertisers, obtained uniformity by using plates. It is plain that the newspapers were slow to appreciate the possibilities of national advertising. Calkins set the decade 1900-1910 as the period of growth of the advertising agency, but it was a steady rather than a sudden development. "Plan, copy, art, typography, intelligently composed lists of mediums, the 15 per cent commission, stabilization of rates, research and merchandising," he testified, "became part of the agency service in the years before the World War. Today few business organizations are better equipped, more efficient or more progressive than the first rate advertising agency."

The newspapers, he pointed out, eventually saw the light with the result that there was "a flood of information about circulation, territory, local trade conditions, a miniature picture of the milieu the newspaper served. Rates were fixed and the elephantine rate card . . . was transformed into a simple price list that anyone might understand." Newspapers, in short, became the principal advertising medium, a position they have maintained despite the competition of magazines and, more recently, the challenge of the radio. Modern advertising, Calkins observed, is amply supplied with methods, resources, and techniques with the result that it is "vaster, more pervasive, infinitely more interesting than fifty years ago, more necessary but more expensive, relatively less effective because of sheer ubiquity, but gaining something from that, too." Because of "injudicious rivalry and slavish imitation, excess, extravagance, brag and vulgarity," it is vulnerable to such critics as Chase, Schlink, and Rorty to whom the public is inclined to lend a ready ear. "It is up to the advertising agent, to his taste, his sense of proportion, his realization of which side his bread is buttered on," Calkins concluded, "to use the facilities he has created and developed so that the buying public will find advertising its most dependable guide."

Agency Commission

Years ago the compensation of the advertising agent who places an account was fixed at 15 per cent. Although this arrangement is in general use, its validity is challenged by some of the largest advertisers who argue that it is based upon "an outworn conception" of advertising. It is defended by the agencies and is accepted by most advertisers and used by practically all newspapers. The critics of this system point out that in the beginning the agent was a mere seller of space but that over the years he has tended to become, in the language of one of them, "a confidential partner of the advertiser." They concede that the commission system, based on a percentage of the money spent, was right and proper when the agent was simply a broker of space bought and sold. But they contend that conditions have changed and that the function of the agent as well as his relation to the advertiser has changed also.

Their objection to the commission system is something of a piece with their feeling against what seems to them unwarranted discrimination in rates. The whole matter of the commission system and agency relationships has been the subject of several special studies in recent years. The American Newspaper Publishers Association at its 1922 convention in principle confirmed the commission arrangement and opposed any rebating of commissions to the advertiser. With the marked increase in general advertising by large advertisers and under the stress of the depression, the question was raised anew in 1932. This led to a study by Professor James W. Young, of Northwestern University, which it was hoped would be definitive. When the Young report, presented in May, 1933, upheld the agency system in general, the Association of National Advertisers declined to accept it and undertook one of its own, which resulted in the Haase report.

1922 Resolution

The resolution adopted by the publishers at their 1922 meeting read as follows:

Whereas, the purpose of the publisher in allowing a differential to the recognized advertising agent is to enable said agent to render adequate service to the advertiser; therefore be it Resolved, By the American Newspaper Publishers Association in convention assembled, that the advertising agent cannot render adequate service in return for inadequate pay, and that inadequate service does not lead to the success of the advertiser. Therefore the publisher pays for service he does not get when any portion of the differential is turned over to the advertiser ; and be it further Resolved, That the splitting of the differential in any form directly or indirectly by the advertising agent with the advertiser is immoral and destructive to the best interests of the advertiser, the publisher and the agent, and should not be permitted to continue. Young Report.

This report reached three main conclusions: (1) that the present method of advertising agency compensation "is the most practicable one for maintaining the true and longrun interests of all advertisers and all publishers"; (2) that the rate of commission "is not excessive for the structure as a whole"; and (3) "that all advertisers and publishers should bear, in proportion to volume, a share of both the direct and indirect costs of the structure."

The study by Professor Young brought out wide differences in the results achieved by various advertising agencies under varying conditions. For example, one account which used more than $1,000,000 worth of space in 1931 was shown to have been handled at a net loss to the agency of $37,700. It developed that even in a given agency two accounts of about the same size may yield widely varying rates of net profit, or that the same account, handled by different agencies, may produce materially different rates of net profit, or that in a given agency the same account may vary widely in profit from year to year. It was found that the costs and profits of agencies vary in part according to the nature of the product advertised, in part by the, nature of the media used, in part by the degree of success of advertising at the particular moment, in part by the temperament and organization of the advertiser, and in part by other factors.

The Young report emphasized that the use the advertiser makes of his space is much more important than the cost of the space. In the face of criticisms that agency commissions are unsound, uneconomic, and unfair, a poll of 92 leading advertisers made by Professor Young disclosed that only 19 believed them to be excessive, 25 others were somewhat dissatisfied, while 67 were "entirely satisfied or at least content."

A.N.A. Report

The Association of National Advertisers declined to accept the Young report and authorized a study of its own. Among the objecting advertisers were such important ones as General Motors Corp., Chrysler Corp., Procter & Gamble, General Foods Corp., R. J. Reynolds Tobacco Co. It was argued that the data gathered for the Young report were insufficient to justify the conclusions, that the report gave too much attention to periodicals and not enough to newspapers, and that it did not clarify the legal relationship of the agent with the advertiser on the one hand and the publisher on the other.

The result was the Haase report whose conclusions follow: (1) the advertising agent is the agent of the advertiser only and as such owes him, undivided loyalty; (2) the advertiser pays the agency and his money flows through the agent to the medium ; (3) the present rate of compensation was set by agents, and the owners of advertising mediums, influenced and guided in their decision by agents, are not of prevailing importance in determining the rate; (4) the chief fault of the discount (commission) system is its seeming rigidity; (5) the discount (commission) system has been modified in actual business practice, four basic arrangements now being in use; and (6) the advertiser is free to make any terms he wishes with the advertising agent who cannot, legally or ethically, obligate himself to the advertiser if he is already bound to the publisher.

The attitude of the advertisers was summed up in these words: " Any agent or owner of an advertising medium can, with perfect safety, set the terms upon which he will do business, but when he undertakes to prescribe a course of conduct for businesses other than his own, then he is confronted with the highly important question of restraint of trade." The advertisers, in short, argued that the advertising agent is no longer a middleman but is solely their agent and that as such it is entirely right and proper for them jointly to fix the basis on which they will do business without interference by the newspaper or other medium.

ADVERTISING SERVICE

From the hit-and-miss methods of a generation ago, advertising has taken on some of the aspects of a fairly exact science. If the medium, the message, the methods, and the time are right, the results of a well-planned advertising campaign can sometimes be forecast with surprising accuracy. Unlike formerly, advertising is no longer sold on the basis either of bulk or sentiment. It is a well-established fact that quality circulation backed by intelligent merchandising service form a well-nigh unbeatable combination.

Consumer studies are made by the newspapers themselves, by advertising interests, and by independent agencies. They are frequently as revealing to the newspaper as they are convincing to the prospective advertiser. They cover a variety of matters such as reader and consumer habits, factors that influence buying, and a thorough and detailed analysis of the market afforded by given newspapers including such things as purchasing power, income, wholesale and retail outlets, bank clearings, home ownership, automobile registrations, and other pertinent factors. Results have also been determined on the basis of what is known as "advertising penetration" which shows to what extent the advertising has been effective in terms of reader consciousness. By a properly scientific study of the market and the medium, sales potentials can be worked out for certain kinds of goods. Individual newspapers like the New York Times, the New York Sun, the Chicago Tribune, the Cleveland Press, and the Los Angeles Times to name only a few go to considerable effort and expense to provide adequate merchandising service for their advertisers, both general and retail. This includes dependable market data, lists of outlets, local tie-ups, etc. Such papers maintain their own research staffs or they may arrange with outside agencies for special studies and surveys for their own information and for the benefit of advertisers. The Editor & Publisher Yearbook lists nearly 500 daily newspapers which offer merchandising service.

The R. L. Polk Co. also makes such surveys and studies. It has conducted independent newspaper and market analyses, e.g., in New

York City and Columbus, Ohio. A new type of scientific analysis of local market conditions discloses not only where a given product is sold but how much a given market will absorb. This plan, sponsored by Major Market Newspapers, Inc., provides "sales potentials" for various kinds of merchandise by "putting the microscope" on local sales markets.

By this method, it is claimed that manufacturers, distributors, and dealers can be shown what the potential market amounts to and can then be sold on advertising schedules adequate to cultivate the market. It is also claimed that a study of the potential sales data as compared with actual sales may show a market high in potential sales greatly underadvertised, indicating either that the dealer setup needs strengthening or that not enough local advertising is being used to enable the dealer to get his share of the business.

Not all newspapers are in a position to go into such great detail concerning their circulations and markets as it is only the largest papers which are financially able or which need to go to, such lengths. But even small papers find it both necessary and profitable to afford some such cooperation to the advertiser either directly or through the representative of the paper. Even these same small papers can assemble and organize circulation and market data to this end to their profit and that of the advertiser.

Standard Advertising Contract

For the sake of uniformity, mutual understanding, and helpfulness, a Standard Advertising Contract is in use. Based upon experience, it bears the approval of the American Newspaper Publishers Association, the American Association of Advertising Agencies, and other publishers' associations. It was revised in 1933 so as to clarify it and bring it up to date. In the revised form the conditions affecting terms of payment were reworded to make it plain that the publisher will "hold the agency solely liable for payment, " thus avoiding any possibility of imposing double liability for payment on the advertiser. Also included was a statement that the agency "will not rebate to its client any part of the commission."

Further, all provisions for terms of guarantee of .circulation were eliminated.

Parties to the contract are not permitted to change the conditions except that portions may be crossed out before the order is sent to the publisher. All special conditions must appear prominently on the face of the contract. The standard conditions follow:

1. Terms of Payment.

a. The agency agrees to pay and the publisher agrees to hold the agency solely liable for payment for the advertising covered by this contract. The agency personally agrees to pay for advertising covered by this contract at the office of the publisher or his authorized representative on or before the last day of the month following that in which the advertising is published unless otherwise stipulated on publisher's rate card on which this contract was based, or when cash discount is deducted but payment date not specified on the publisher's rate card, on the 15th day of the month following. Bills must be rendered not less often than monthly, but failure to do so shall not constitute breach of contract.

b. The agency agrees to pay in the manner specified in paragraph (a) for all drawings, composition, cuts or mats if furnished by the publisher at the request of the agency provided it is the practice of the publisher to charge for such service.

c. Cuts and mats shall be sent to the publisher prepaid. If they are not, the publisher may accept them, and pay transportation and import charges and the agency shall promptly reimburse the publisher.

d. If at the end of the advertising period named in the contract or upon prior termination of the contract for any cause, the agency has not used the full amount of advertising contracted for, the agency shall pay to the publisher such additional sum on all advertising so published as shall be equal to the difference, if any, between the amount due at the rate named in the contract and the amount due at the rate applicable to the quantity of space used, according to that schedule of advertising rates of the publisher on which the contract was based, and upon such expiration or termination said additional sum shall become immediately due and payable. Short rate bills must be rendered within sixty days after the expiration of the contract period, otherwise the publisher agrees to a settlement at the rate named in the original contract. Unless otherwise expressed on the face hereof, this contract may be canceled by the agency, or less space used, in accordance with the provisions of this paragraph.

e. Any bill rendered to the agency by the publisher shall be conclusive as to the correctness of the items therein set forth and shall constitute an account stated unless written objection is made thereto by the publisher or the agency within sixty days from the rendering thereof.

f. The publisher reserves the right to cancel the contract at any time upon default by the agency in the payment of bills, or other breach, or in the event of any material violation on the part of the agency of any of the conditions herein named; and upon such cancellation all advertising done hereunder, including short rates or other charges under this contract, and unpaid, shall become immediately due and payable. In case of delinquency in payment or impaired credit of the agency the publisher shall have the right at any time to change the requirements as to terms of payment for further advertising under this contract as he may see fit.

g. In all cases where date of payment is material, unless otherwise stipulated the postmark date on the envelope properly addressed to the publisher or to his representative shall be considered the date on which payment was made.

2. Rates.

a. All rates shall be published. There shall be no secret rates, rebates, or agreements affecting rates. All rates shall be furnished agencies if requested.

b. "Publisher's rate card" shall be understood to mean that schedule of advertising rates of the publisher upon which this contract is based.

c. The rate stated in the contract is the minimum rate at which an equal or less amount of space, for the same class of advertising, to be published in a like position, under the same conditions, within the same period of time, can be secured.

d. If additional space is used within the period covered by the contract, where the publisher has a schedule of graduated rates, any lower rate shall be given if earned, according to the publishers rate card on which this contract is based.

3. Advertising Material.

a. The subject matter, form, size, wording, illustration and typography of the advertising shall be subject to the approval of the publisher but unless otherwise authorized in advance no change shall be made without the consent of the agency.

b. If the publisher is unable to set any advertisement in the type or style requested, he may set such advertisement in such other type or style as in his opinion most nearly corresponds thereto, and the advertisement may be inserted without submission of proof unless proof before insertion is requested on the face of the order.

c. Where cuts, electrotypes or material furnished by the agency occupy more space than specified in the contract or insertion order, publisher should immediately communicate with the agency for definite instructions. If the publisher is unable to secure definite instructions from the agency, the advertising shall be omitted.

d. If agency has contracted for a series of insertions in a publication, and before closing date insertion order and copy for next issue have not been received by publisher, publisher shall notify agency and follow agency's instructions.

e. Advertisements ordered set in "space as required' shall be measured from office ad rule to office ad rule.

4. *Proof of Insertion.*

a. The page containing the advertising or, at the request of the agency, a copy of each issue in which the advertising appears, shall be mailed or otherwise supplied to the agency, which shall be deemed to have received such copy or page unless the publisher is notified in writing of the non-receipt thereof within thirty days after the date of publication. The publisher may mail or otherwise supply an affidavit of publication in lieu of a second copy or page containing the advertisement. Failure to forward or furnish such copy, page or affidavit shall not constitute a breach of contract.

5. *Circulation.*

a. Unless the publisher is a member of the Audit Bureau of Circulations, the agency shall be entitled, upon request, to a statement of net paid circulation verified by a certified public accountant, or in lieu thereof to the right to examine the publisher's circulation books.

b. Omission of Advertising.

c. Failure of the publisher to insert in any particulər issue or issues invalidates the order for insertion in the missed issue but shall not constitute a breach of contract. In newspapers the advertising must appear in all regular editions issued on the date for which the advertising is ordered. Advertisements omitted from any particular edition or editions must be reported to the agency and if received in time and omitted through fault of publisher must be made up or adjusted unless otherwise instructed. Unless otherwise stipulated, the publisher shall have the right to omit any advertisement when the space allotted to advertising ,in the issue for which such advertisement is ordered has all been taken, and also to limit the amount of space an advertiser may use in any one issue.

6. General.

a. The agency agrees that it will not rebate to its client any part of the commission allowed by the publisher.

b. In dealing with agencies, the publisher shall follow a uniform policy to avoid discrimination.

c. Unless later date is specified in publisher's rate card, advertising shall begin within thirty days from the date of this contract, or contract becomes null and void.

d. A waiver by the publisher of any default or breach by the agency shall be considered as a waiver of any subsequent default or breach of the same or any other provisions hereof.

13

CLASSIFIED ADVERTISING

Judged by present-day standards, the first paid advertising to appear in an American newspaper was classified advertising. In fact, much of the early advertising published in the colonial newspapers would now come under the head of classified advertising. It is perhaps significant that this initial paid advertisement was placed by a printer. It appeared in the third issue of John Campbell's Boston News-Letter, dated May 1-8, 1704, as follows:

AT Oysterbay, on Long Island in the Province of N. York, There is a very good FuUing-Mill, to be Let or Sold, as also a Plantation, having on it a large new Brick house, and another house by it for a Kitchin & workhouse, with a Barn, Stable &c. a young Orchard and 20 acres of clear Land. The Mill is to be Let with or without the Plantation; Enquire of Mr. William Bradford Printer in N. York, and know further. Until the idea of display advertising dawned some years later, all advertising appeared in this form. Much of it had to do with announcements by merchants, the departure of vessels for distant points, rewards for the return of runaway servants, the sale of slaves, and similar items. It was all very informally lumped together under the general heading of " Advertisements," the individual announcements being identified by twoline initial letters. By its miscellaneous nature as well as by its lack of display, it definitely resembled the classified advertising of a much later day.

As recently as a century ago, the advertising carried by newspapers was still in this form. In patterning his newspaper after the English penny press, Benjamin Day, founder of the New York Sun, seized upon the idea of a large volume of small advertisements for the dual purpose of interesting the reader and producing revenue. As Presbrey describes it, "Petty wants of various kinds, and offers to exchange, were encouraged and gave additional reader interest to the paper. Help-wanted advertisements especially were solicited on the character of the Sun's circulation and were obtained in increasing number. These appeared under a classification of ' Wants. ' Two or three lines in length, and not the kind of advertising for which space could be sold by the year, such advertisements paid a one-time rate of fifty cents." To these were added presently similar advertisements of theaters and museums, excursions, and marriage and death notices.

IMPORTANCE OF CLASSIFIED

From these crude and haphazard beginnings, classified advertising has developed into one of the most important departments of the newspaper. To the layman it is "want " advertising. It is that but it is a good deal more, as a glance at any good classified section will show. Some idea of the magnitude of the business can be had from the Media Records report that out of a total of 1,901,000,000 lines of advertising carried during 1935 by 365 papers in &5 leading cities, 300,247,167 lines were classified advertising, or a little less than one-sixth. With the total value of all advertising in these papers estimated at $400,000,000, their income from classified alone is said to have been somewhere around $75,000,000. Individual newspapers have developed classified advertising in varying degrees, and the development has been anything but uniform. Many of the smaller newspapers in particular have failed to cash in on the full possibilities of classified as an important source of added revenue as well as an important service to their clientele. Yet, by its own admission, one newspaper in a city of 10,000 paid for a new, modern, and unusually well-equipped plant out of its profits from classified advertising alone in five years.

One hundred forty newspapers in the United States and Canada each exceeded 1,000,000 lines of classified during 1935. The Chicago

Herald and Examiner was first with a total of 4,829,654 lines of classified, of which 3,555,968 lines were published on week days and 1,273,686 on Sundays. Others in the first 10 were: Los Angeles Times, Detroit News, Chicago Tribune, New York American, Toronto Telegram, Los Angeles Examiner, San Francisco Examiner, New York Times, and the Toronto Star.

Selling Classified

For a long time classified advertising was treated as a sort of stepchild in the newspaper business office. That day is happily past and classified advertising is now recognized and treated as a specialty, which it is. Many newspapers, in fact, now start their advertising salesmen with a " course" in the classified department. As a matter of fact, newspapers which have highly developed their classified pages probably devote as much talent, energy, and ingenuity to this phase of the business as to any other.

Hit-and-miss methods of selling classified are distinctly outmoded. The value of trained personnel, of right principles, and sound methods has long been recognized. This was summarized by H. W. Connell, at that time classified advertising manager of the San Antonio Express and News, in a bulletin of the Southern Newspaper Publishers' Association as follows:

The efficient management of a classified advertising department is one of the most complicated that the business offers. It requires an up-to-date knowledge of rate scaling, a thorough acquaintance with classification making, typography and makeup, an understanding of classified credit and collections, a constant vigilance to eliminate fraudulent announcements, and one of those odd persons called classified advertising manager who is happy to devote at least 12 hours a day of his time to its operation. It has been said that the only problem about classified advertising is to make it profitable. But to be profitable, it must be used, it must be read, it must give results and satisfaction, and the price must be right. These accomplishments are within the reach of small as well as large newspapers. In fact, some of the smaller dailies make a much better showing with their classified departments than do their large contemporaries. Take the Janesville, Wis., Gazette, for example. By the persistent use of the right methods some years ago, it boosted its classified section from four columns to two pages daily.

A stable classified section like this guarantees the paper a steady income at a good rate, besides increasing the usefulness of the paper to its community. Such an accomplishment, it has been said, calls for the psychology of selling small space, training telephone solicitors, and writing original promotion copy. The Gazette put its own house in order and then proceeded to comb its territory for all possible sources of classified business. It put in a sound system of solicitation, billing, promotion, layout, and classification and changed its promotion to meet changing needs. It used four girls to solicit classified advertising by telephone and supplemented them with one or two men on the street. It watched all possible leads for new business, scrutinizing the day's news, exchanges, and old issues. It put a premium on six-month and yearly classified accounts and paid the girls a bonus for contracts.

Telephone Solicitation

Classified advertising is peculiarly adapted to telephone solicitation, but selling by this method calls for expertness. Girls are much better for this purpose than men. They need, however, to be taught the principles of salesmanship, to use positive statements but to avoid argument, and particularly to cultivate a smile in the voice. The telephone, too, opens a much wider field to the solicitor with respect to both time and distance. Such selling is not limited to ordinary business hours, and the solicitor can reach distant prospects within a few seconds and at a minimum of expense. The mere fact that the prospect is listed in the telephone book is in his favor as it is an index that his credit is good.

Trained Ad Takers

Many papers stress the fact that trained personnel is available to assist in the writing of classified advertisements. The average person knows in a general way what he wants to say in an advertisement, but, frequently, he does not know how to say it the best or most economical way. It is a definite service to the user and to the reader, therefore, to train competent help in the classified department. It has been estimated that the cost of training a competent girl for such work runs from $400 to $500, hence it will pay the newspaper to keep the labor turnover at a minimum. The New York Herald Tribune has gone a step further at this point in helping the classified user with the issuance of a booklet on "How to Answer a Want Ad."

Classified Promotion

It is one thing for a newspaper to get classified advertising. To get the reader to pay attention to it is another problem. To this latter end all sorts of devices are in use. Many papers make a practice of putting desirable comics and features in the classified section, relying upon their pulling power to get the reader to look at the classified ads themselves. A check of 30 newspapers, referred to elsewhere in this connection, revealed that the crossword puzzle, which remains a perennial newspaper favorite, and individual comics or comic strips were used most frequently for this purpose. Other features used included news pictures and the contract-bridge lesson. Various promotional schemes are also used to lure the reader into the classified columns. One of the most common, because it is most effective, is to run an office advertisement with plenty of white space to show the specific results obtained by classified users. Another is to call special attention by means of a box or by an office ad used elsewhere in the paper to particular values or bargains offered in that day's classified columns. Still another is to offer free movie or other amusement tickets daily to a given number of readers whose names, chosen at random from the city or telephone directory or some similar source, are sandwiched between ads in the classified section. Another frequent device is to use timely streamers or banners across the top of the classified pages. These not only add to the appearance of the pages but can be useful promotionally.

Apparently there is no limit to the range or ingenuity of classified advertising promotion. Whatever forms it takes, it is one of the fundamentals of the business. No newspaper ever built up its classified department without promotion, or maintained or enlarged it without continuing its promotional campaigning.

The Chicago Tribune several years ago added 250,000 lines of classified in one year through a combination promotion. This included intensive newspaper and radio promotion, the introduction of an ad-writing service, the proper use of investigations and surveys, strong sales solicitations, the addition of news pictures to the Sunday classified section, a "hidden want ad" competition, and a friendly approach to advertisers on the part of the entire sales force. The ad-writing service aided greatly in building good will and in improving the advertising copy. The news pictures were added because the surveys showed that readers are greatly interested in them. The radio promotion was built around human-interest stories told by want-ad takers in 150 broadcasts over WGN, the Tribune station. The San Francisco Examiner put on a real estate classified promotion campaign on the theme, "Golden Ground around the Golden Gate. In pressing this campaign, the Examiner used the following: broadsides to every real estate dealer, company, and corporation in San Francisco and 26 near-by towns and cities announcing the campaign; daily display ads, four columns by 10 inches deep; radio talks by real estate men; presentations by salesmen and reprints of promotional material; page one boxes, used every other day on page one, part two; frequent news stories; window cards for cooperating dealers; rack cards; souvenir reprints of radio talks; streamers to spot the real estate columns.

A number of newspapers, including the San Antonio Express and Evening News and the Rochester Democrat & Chronicle have given free want ads to children, the purpose being, of course, to impress their elders with the usefulness and effectiveness of classified advertising. The Express and Evening News offered free want ads to children under 16 who wished to sell, acquire, or trade anything during a given month.3 It was called the "Children's Store," and the offer was limited to children who brought their own copy. The ads were limited to 23 words for a week's insertion. The advertiser's name or telephone number was required with each ad. The Democrat & Chronicle a few months earlier ran a free barter column for children.

The Janesville, Wis., Gazette, referred to above, found it profitable to establish friendly relations with auctioneers in connection with the farm auctions. It gave an annual dinner for the auctioneers in its territory, it paid them a commission on classified business they produced which ranged from $8 to $17 per auction, and the Gazette also provided food at auctions which were advertised in the paper. This policy not only paid in advertising and in good will but contributed toward a 3000 gain in circulation which justified an increase in advertising rates.

Classified Rates

It is a general rule in newspaper offices that the classified advertisement should yield enough to cover its cost, including the white space used and a proportionate share of the overhead, plus a reasonable profit. In general, the rate is somewhat higher than the average open rate and probably somewhat less than the general rate. It is usually also based on a sliding scale with the result that the rate falls as the number of insertions increases.

The classified rate varies considerably. The transient or irregular advertiser generally pays a higher rate than the steady customer. The cash customer pays less than the charge account. Some classifications are charged at a lower rate than others as, for example, Rooms for Rent and Situations or Employment Wanted. Most papers fix a minimum charge regardless of the number of words or lines in the advertisement.

Two systems of classified rates are in general use. One is the line rate, in which the cost to the user is determined by the number of lines in his advertisement, regardless of the number of words. The other is the word rate in which, similarly, the user pays so much per word just as in a telegram, regardless of the number of lines the words make. The argument as to which is the better arrangement has been going on for years with no sign of settlement. A survey made in 1935 covering 717 papers revealed that 354 operated on the word rate and 352 on the line rate, while some used one method for local classified and the other for foreign.

Each will be examined in some detail.

The Word Rate

The chief advantage of the word rate is that it simplifies computation. This is particularly useful for the transient user and the small professional advertiser who are the backlog of all classified advertising and who rarely know how many lines their advertisement will make. Further advantages of the word rate as described by James McGovern, of the Pittsburgh Press, in an address before the Newspaper Classified Advertising Managers' Association follow: it eliminates unintelligible abbreviations, costly oversets and undersets, and while tending to reduce the inch value, would more than make up in good will, in popularity, and in acceptability and probably in increased gross revenue any loss so sustained.

By contrast, he argued, the line rate is a source of antagonism, misunderstanding, and complaint, and is responsible for most of the serious complaints and adjustments in the classified department. These, he explained, "originate invariably in the inability of the ad takers to quote the exact number of lines an ad will occupy, and the antagonism created in the advertiser's mind when we endeavor to explain the impossibility of squeezing a 20-word ad into two lines of space. Unintelligible abbreviations thrive under such conditions, resulting in reader confusion and eventual loss of reader interest."

The Chicago Herald and Examiner, national pacemaker in classified advertising, uses the word rate. 3 It based its sales-promotion campaign for several years on such themes as "Economy Want Ads "A New Plan of Figuring Your Want Ad Cost," and "Easy to Read

Easy to Figure." Its rate structure was designed to undersell that of competitors and yet by producing multiple insertions to reduce the composition and bookkeeping costs and thus to make the volume high and the rate profitable.

It also aimed at a high Sunday volume by putting a premium on a seven-time order and giving the customer the privilege of making one entire change of copy in that time. Where a large advertisement was placed for the Sunday issue, a six-time order called a "rate-holder" of 12 words was permitted the advertiser, thus making a seven-time order.

The Herald and Examiner's campaign was also based on the principle: "Get the want ad before it becomes a voluntary ad." To this end, a house-to-house canvass was made and classified ads in opposition papers were followed up promptly. For promotion, the newspaper, billboards, radio, and direct mail were used.

Similar policies are followed by other important papers, such as the Indianapolis TimeSj the Washington News, and the Baltimore Post. The first named had the lowest seven-time rate of any of the local newspapers yet standardized at 3 cents a word. It put the emphasis on four- and seven-time orders by offering the public one extra insertion with a three-time order or two extra with a five-time order; in other words, four insertions for the price of three or seven for the price of five. It reported its voluntary business from classified increased 300 per cent in six months.

Similarly, the Washington News with a basic rate of 2% cents a word, offered 16 insertions for the price of 10. A criticism of these bargain offers is that in effect they amount to unwarranted price reductions.

The critics point out that the publishers are seeking additional revenue, yet by this method they sacrifice revenue for linage. An objection to the word rate itself is that it does not readily take into account the extra space consumed by oversize type, centered words, catalogue listings, and the like. The objectors feel strongly on the question for, as one of them predicted, "If the publishers of the country don't scotch this movement they will live to regret it."

The Line Rate

Stout arguments can readily be marshalled in favor of the line rate. These may be summarized as follows: it means a higher net rate per inch to the paper than the word rate; it eliminates the problem of long words; it is simpler for the accounting department; it is useful for comparison with display rates; it conforms to the current general practice of computing space in terms of lines.

One problem in connection with the word rate is that many classified advertisements run over into an extra line by only one or two words. These additional words yield little extra revenue while the remainder of the line is a total loss. On the line basis, the entire line is paid for since the space is used even though it is not solid composition. An example cited by Loyal Phillips, at that time classified advertising manager of the Omaha World- Herald is a case in point.

He reported that a newspaper survey revealed 51 advertisements in one column with a total of 112 words in the terminal lines of the advertisements or about 2.2 words each. For these, the paper received an average of 5 cents a word at the word rate or $5.60 for the 51 lines.

On a corresponding line rate, it would have received $12.75, so that the use of the word rate here meant a loss of $7.15 per column or about 35 cents an inch.

Oversets can be greatly reduced or eliminated by the proper operation and use of the line rate. One paper reduced the oversets to only six in 1000 advertisements. This was achieved by counting 35 letters, spaces, and punctuation marks per line instead of 38. In addition, clerks and solicitors were penalized 25 cents for each overset. No abbreviations were permitted under this system.

Classifications

While classifications are fairly well standardized, they vary greatly in number with individual newspapers. In general, the larger the newspaper the greater the number of classifications. The largest number found by the author in a survey of 30 representative newspapers of all sizes was 153 in the case of the Chicago Herald and Examiner.

Some newspapers number their classifications, and some still print their classifications daily, while others do not. In some cases newspapers print a classification list in the Sunday issue but not on week days. The Herald and Examiner prints a small index in the upper outer corner of each classified page for that page alone for the convenience of users.

The number of principal classifications need not exceed 10. For all ordinary purposes, all such advertisements can be included under one of the following heads: Announcements, Employment, Real Estate, Business Services, Financial, Livestock, Merchandise, Automotive, and Miscellaneous.

Most newspapers break several of these up into major subdivisions as, for example, Real Estate, which becomes For Rent or For Sale, and Employment which becomes Help Wanted and Position or Situation Wanted. Each of these is further subdivided according to the policy of the individual newspaper and the volume of such advertising.

As an additional service to users, a number of newspapers such as the Detroit News, the New York Times, and the Chicago Herald and Examiner maintain an extensive "Lost and Found" service.

An effort is made to bring losers and finders together and a permanent record is kept of articles advertised in their columns as lost. Another service to users is to run a daily listing of the box numbers to which replies have been received together with the number of such replies in each case.

Guaranteed Results

One kind of classified promotion that appeals to the user of such advertising is to guarantee the results. One month a year, for example, the San Francisco Chronicle has used this sort of campaign as a means of getting new business.

The scheme is simple: to renew classified advertisements placed on a weekly basis for an added week if the results are not satisfactory. The Chronicle began this practice in 1931.

In 1933 experience showed that about 30 per cent of the copy was run for the second week. Similarly, the Mobile Press and Register invited advertisers to run their copy for seven consecutive days with an offer to repeat it for an additional week if results were not obtained within three days. That this type of promotion is not adopted by more newspapers might be taken to cast some doubt upon its validity.

Classified Censorship

One of the best ways for a newspaper to build reader confidence in its classified columns is to exercise strict control over those columns and to adhere to rigid standards as to what will be accepted for them. This should apply to the entire section but in particular to the "Help Wanted" and " Business Opportunities" classifications.

Opinion seems to be agreed on this point. The notice carried by the Cincinnati Enquirer illustrates the general practice: "All advertisements are restricted to their proper classification, style and type. The Enquirer reserves the right to edit or reject any advertisement."

"Uncensored classified is a deadly poison and not too slow to destroy the good will of any newspaper," according to C. M. Carroll, former president of the Association of Newspaper Classified Advertising Managers. "The same man who would rip things open if his editors permitted publication of polluted news or his advertising manager accepted a fraudulent display advertisement, is frequently unaware that his readers confidence is being viciously undermined by the wrong kind of three- and four-line advertisements. ... In the interest, first, of the public and, second, of the newspaper as a commercial enterprise, the same vigilance that walls the news and the display advertising must be maintained towards the agate columns."

Similarly, Norton Cole, of the Syracuse Post-Standard, told the New York state division of the National Association of Classified Advertising Managers that "The good advertisement is the one that an advertising salesman would answer himself or give to one of his best friends to answer."

And A. H. Van Duyn, formerly of the Oklahoma City Daily Oklahoman, added, "... if you do put in a strict censorship, put it in for everyone or no one. There must be no exceptions for friends or any one else.

What little linage you may lose from chiselers will probably be more than made up by reputable advertisers with increased respect for your medium." The abuses for which censorship is a remedy are covered under a code of ethics adopted by the Newspaper Classified Advertising Managers' convention in 1934, later indorsed by the Newspaper.

Advertising Executives' Association. Under this code the newspapers would bar:

1. That which intentionally causes the loss of money to readers either directly or indirectly.
2. That which causes injury to health or morals of readers.
3. That which evades or fosters the evasion or violation of any law, municipal, state, or national.
4. That which criticises, directly or by implication, an individual, race, creed, religion, organization, institution, business, or profession.
5. Using newspaper classified advertising in such a way as to destroy the confidence of either or both readers and

advertisers in classified advertising, or any legitimate business or professional activity.

6. Requesting misclassification of advertisements when such misclassification may be, or is, detrimental to the newspaper or detrimental or unfair to advertisers using classifications requested.

In addition, newspapers were advised to bar outright or to censor rigidly: personal advertisements from fortune tellers, clairvoyants, or astrologists when such services are illegal or the advertisers obviously are unable to perform a valuable service; homework ads; help-wanted ads calling for deposits, money or kits; beauty ads; out-of-town school ads; Mexican divorce ads.

Of 130 newspapers queried in a. survey reported by Editor & Publisher, 63 said they had a definite censorship code for classified advertising and 67 others disclosed that they censored copy according to their individual judgment. 2 Some newspapers operate jointly in this respect, others individually, and some in cooperation with outside agencies such as the local Better Business Bureau.

Individual newspapers go still further to protect themselves, the legitimate advertiser, and the reader. Some have standing offers of rewards for the apprehension of persons misusing the classified columns. The Chicago Herald and Examiner, for instance, carried a standing notice to the effect that it would pay $100 for "the arrest and conviction of an advertiser fraudulently obtaining money through want ads published in its columns." It paid $100 to a woman, for example, who exposed another who had sold her an "Oriental" rug through its want ad columns.

Others carry standing notices either in box form or in italics like the following:

Washington Star: The Star makes every effort to have the advertisements appearing under its Help Wanted Classifications contain accurate statements of the nature of employment being offered. Advertisers are requested to cooperate in this regard, and those answering advertisements will please notify the Classified Department of the Star of any misleading statements.

Chicago Tribune: The Tribune does not knowingly accept Help Wanted advertisements which misrepresent the nature or terms of employment, or advertisements for Sales Help which do not indicate the type of product or service to be sold and the form of compensation. Report any misrepresentations or requests for a cash bond, deposit, or investment for samples not stated in the advertisement to the Tribune, Superior 0100, Local 328 (for complaints only).

New York Times: Three business references required of all advertisers in the Business Opportunities columns.

Cleveland Press: The Press, in accordance with a ruling established many years ago to safeguard its readers, does not accept advertisements for children to board unless properly licensed by the Department of Public Welfare. (Homes accepting child with parent require no state license.)

A similar notice is carried by the Cleveland Plain Dealer under the classification, Children Boarded. The Christian Science Monitor publishes the following notice under the general heading of Local Classified: Advertisements under this heading appear in this edition only. Rate 30$ a line for one or two insertions, 27^ a line for three, four and five insertions within a week, and 24j a line for six or more consecutive daily insertions.

Minimum space three lines, minimum order four lines. (An advertisement measuring three lines must call for at least two insertions.) An application blank and two letters of reference are required from those who advertise under most of these headings. Write or call for detailed information.

The Detroit News runs a number of standing heads. Under "Wanted Male Help" and " Wanted Female Help" it announces: The Detroit News does not knowingly accept in this classification advertisements which misrepresent the form of compensation. Do not include original or valuable papers of recommendation when "answering box ads. Report any violation of this rule or any request for a cash bond, deposit or investment for samples not stated in the advertisement to The Detroit News, Randolph 2000, Classified Advertising Manager.

Its notice under "Business Opportunities" reads: The Detroit News does not knowingly accept in this classification advertisements which misrepresent in any form. Report any violation of this rule where fraud or misrepresentation of copy is proven to The Detroit News, Randolph 2000, Classified Advertising Manager. It follows a similar policy with respect to machinery and supplies, and automobiles. The Chicago Tribune goes a shade further in regard to the latter. It makes the following offer: The Tribune does not knowingly accept automobile advertising which misrepresents the year of the car.

If you wish to confirm the year model of a used car advertised in its columns, secure the serial number (which determines the year model) and telephone the Tribune, Superior 0100, Local 328, for verification.

TYPOGRAPHY

Most newspapers have rather definite restrictions on the typography and makeup of the classified section. This is done to insure some degree of uniformity, to prevent some advertisers from literally blotting out others by the use of type that is too large or too black, and to control the "color" of the page.

Although agate is the standard classified type size, much larger type sizes are permitted, particularly in display classified. But in such cases the type is limited to light faces or to inline or outline faces. The Chicago American for example, permits type faces as large as 48 point as well as italic in 12 and 14 point in display classified. Most papers also put some limitations on the use of cuts in the classified section. The survey previously referred to disclosed that 45 per cent of the papers queried permit the use of cuts. Of these about two-fifths require that they be screened while the remainder publish them as ordered. Display Classified. This is a hybrid sort of advertising. It is really quasi-display advertising in the classified section. It consists of advertisements which have a particular appeal on the classified page but differ from other classified advertisements in size and typography. It is peculiarly adaptable for such purposes as real estate, used cars, and personal loans. It is restricted as indicated above, however, with respect to type sizes and faces as well as illustration. It lends itself particularly to long-time classified contracts.

Collections

The sheer volume of classified advertising multiplies the difficulties of bookkeeping and collecting. The bulk of the insertions are small advertisements that run two or three times and then stop. It is important, therefore, not only to check the validity and the legitimacy of the advertisement but the credit rating of the advertiser before publication. It has been said that collecting for want ads is more important than getting the business originally. Collections are sometimes difficult to make from persons who failed to get the results they expected or to which they thought they were entitled and who are, therefore, reluctant to pay. One method of handling accounts is to divide them between professional, i.e., regular users and the so-called "T and T" telephone and transient users. The latter are said to comprise about 35 per cent of the total. Naturally, the chief difficulty in collections comes from this quarter. It has been recommended that persons placing advertisements under any of the following classifications for the first time be required to pay cash as experience shows them to be poor credit risks: Business Opportunities, Situations Wanted, Personals, Legal Notices, Oil and Mining, Board and Room. When they have established credit, the requirement can be waived. The Los Angeles Evening Herald & Express ' operates a "copy and censorship" desk where all advertisements are checked for credit and to detect fraud or misrepresentation.

Transient accounts are usually billed upon the expiration of the advertising. In some cases a cash discount is given if the bill is paid within 10 days. The subsequent procedure that might be followed is: (1) duplicate invoice mailed 15 days after expiration; (2) phone call 25 days after expiration to get promise of payment; (3) first collection letter 30 days after expiration; (4) second letter 40 days after expiration; (5) third letter 50 days after expiration; (6) fourth letter 60 days after expiration. In some cases the customer's account is permitted to run until his credit limit is reached when he is notified by phone or by mail.

ROUTING COPY

Two or more copies of all classified advertisements are usually made on forms provided for the purpose, the number depending upon the size of the paper and the system it follows. The copies are in different colors for purposes of identification. After being checked for accuracy, for legitimacy, and for credit, one copy goes to the composing room, one goes to the billing department, and the third may be kept for 30 days or more in the classified department itself. If any disputes, controversies, or questions arise they will usually crop up within a few days. It is usually unnecessary, therefore, to keep more than one permanent record on file.

14

THE RATE STRUCTURE

The matter of rates has long been a pressing and difficult newspaper problem. A newspaper has only two things to sell: white space to the advertiser and the printed paper to the reader. At first the reader supplied most of the income to the newspaper, but, as advertising developed, the advertiser became the principal source of revenue and circulation income became secondary. Since 1929, this situation has changed somewhat but the sale of advertising space is still the chief financial prop of the newspaper. All things considered, copy prices for newspapers are far better stabilized and standardized than are the rates for advertising space.

This is because fewer factors enter into the copy price of the newspaper than into its advertising rates. Except on Sunday and in a few instances on Saturday, the copy price of a given newspaper is always the same regardless of the number of pages it contains. Thus a reader who gets a 14-page paper on Saturday or 18 pages on Monday for his 2 cents may get an issue of 48 pages or more on Friday for 2 cents.

The copy price is generally based upon such factors as what the reader is able to pay, what he is willing to pay, what he is used to paying, and upon what rival newspapers charge. At one time there was a direct relationship between the copy price and advertising. In fact, it was the custom for some years in the United States to give the yearly subscriber the additional privilege of advertising space without extra charge. The merchant paid $40 for a year's subscription to a given newspaper and in return received a copy of each issue, plus the right to advertise his wares or services. It is only in recent years that scientific cost finding has come to play a real part in the determination of advertising rates. Even now many newspapers, particularly the smallest ones, fix their rates by various rules of thumb. This situation has been inherited from the earliest newspaper times, but it is also partly a matter of professional negligence and even ignorance. After allowing for the variable factors involved, there is no question but that the advertising rates of some papers are too high, and, more frequently, those of others are too low. In the one case the advertiser is not getting his money's worth, and in the other the publisher is not receiving what he should.

Newspaper advertising rates and the policies that determined them have varied greatly from time to time. Early in the seventeenth century, as Presbrey points out, the advertiser was permitted to name his own price. This applied to the public registers under James II and Charles I. Some years later the rate for an " advice," as advertisements were called, depended not upon the amount of space used but upon the occupation or station in life of the advertiser. For a workman the fee was 4s., for a bookseller 5s., for a physician 10s., and, in the case of land to be sold, it was Id. per sterling of value. At the beginning of the eighteenth century the customary charge by London newspapers was Is. regardless of the number of lines, but the advertisements were usually from 8 to 10 lines deep. Fixing the rate at 2d. per line led to an increase in the size of advertisements. In the United States a fairly general practice was to give unlimited space for $32 a year.

The advent of the penny papers a century ago led to gradual changes in advertising rates, policies, and practices. The "square" was made the unit of advertising space, ranging from 10 to 16 lines deep. Six lines in The Sun in 1839, for example, sold for $30 a year, or $3 a month, or $1.75 a week, or 50 cents a day. Similarly, The Herald charged $30 a year for one square, or $3 a month, $1.25 a week, 50 cents a day. About 75 years ago, the advertising agency entered the picture. Although it has since played an important role in the brokering of advertising, it was anything but a stabilizing influence at first. In some ways it was responsible, in fact, for making a bad situation worse. Under the prodding of advertising agents, much newspaper space was sold for what it would bring. Publishers advertised one rate and sold through agents at a much lower rate and even then received only a fraction of the proceeds As a result, the rate situation was thoroughly chaotic in the period after the close of the Civil War.

Presbrey describes it as follows:

Newspapers had rate cards but the price the paper eventually got depended upon how badly it wanted the business and how well the advertiser or agent could bluff. A first demand by the paper for $500 might, before the bargain was struck, be reduced to $50. Ink, newsprint, type and other material used in newspaper making were accepted in payment for space, and this gave opportunity for a new crop of agents, who made bargains at both ends and sold the acquired space for cash. Ink manufacturers and type founders usually had space to sell in the papers they served, and they, too, were advertising agents in a way. When the newspaper could get neither cash nor supplies it sometimes would accept anything it could get clothing, household articles, foodstuffs even and sell or give these commodities to its employees. This was known as "swap" advertising. With such demoralization in rates it was possible for the shrewd space broker to make a very good living. Newspaper rate cards were based upon an expected loss of 25 per cent from bad credits. Sure pay usually resulted in at least that much off the card rate. The agent's commission was 25 per cent. If he did not get more than that he was not as smart as his confreres, for most of them managed to get a good deal more. The agent who had the best knowledge of a newspaper's financial condition and the business methods of the men who managed it, and knew whether "No" meant just that or was subject to change, was the man who made the most money.

A few newspapers, like the New York Herald, refused to pay any commission, but others paid as much as 75 and even 80 per cent. Space worth $2000 might yield as little as $600 to the newspaper. According to Rowell, one of the pioneers in the field, agents themselves were sometimes authorized to fix the rates, and the newspaper would regard itself as bound thereby. While newspapers doubtless suffered from this lack of a sound general policy with respect to advertising rates, they were also at fault in another matter. Until fairly recent years, the circulation figures and other information concerning the circulation of a publication were regarded as anything but the business of advertisers or competitors.

It was the custom of newspapers, as has been described, to present "estimated" or " claimed" circulation figures. In many cases such figures were obviously padded for the purpose of impressing or, worse, of deceiving the advertiser. Some publishers probably did not really know what their paid circulation was because the same laxity prevailed in respect to circulation as to advertising. Since the organization of the A.B.C. in 1913 this condition has been greatly improved. While a minority of dailies are members of the A.B.C., a large proportion of the really important papers belong to it, and its influence has been felt throughout the publishing and advertising industries to the advantage of both. Through this agency, advertisers have a sound, tangible yardstick by which they can measure and analyze the circulation of daily newspapers which are A.B.C. members. The situation sometimes arises, especially in the larger cities, where one or more competing papers bear the A.B.C. stamp and the rival or rivals do not, which may lead to the suspicion that the latter are unable or unwilling to meet so rigid a circulation test. The A.B.C. yardstick goes well beyond the requirements of the so-called "government report" or sworn statement made by the publisher to post-office authorities as to his average daily net paid circulation for the preceding 12 months. It makes two things definitely possible: to determine whether advertisers are getting their money's worth in terms of circulation in. the advertising space they buy and to compare the circulations of different newspapers which are A.B.C. members.

How Advertising Is Sold. Advertising has been sold in various units, including the page or fractions of a page, the column inch, the square, and the line. Even these units vary with the size of the format used by a given publication. Magazine space is still quoted on the basis of a page. Some newspaper space, too, is sold by the page or half or quarter page, but even in such cases the rate is generally quoted on the basis of a line.

The column inch, as the name suggests, is that space one column wide and 14 lines deep. The line, which is the most common unit of advertising space now in use, is a line of agate type. Each of these units has some disadvantage. An obvious objection to the page or fractional page is that it is too large a unit for many advertisers whose business or whose purse does not justify the use of such space. This is also true to some extent of the column inch and of the square.

In addition, the latter is a rather arbitrary unit which, in the mind of the layman or the person unfamiliar with advertising, suggests nothing specific or tangible by which he can visualize it. The line, being roughly 3-4 inch, is small enough to suit the purpose of close measurement and is a unit which the layman can understand and visualize. Its disadvantage is that while it is fixed in respect to depth or point size, it still varies somewhat in length. This is due to the fact that although agate is a fixed type size, 5-4 point, newspaper column widths are not standardized.

They may be 12 or 12 ems and in some cases 13 ems wide. In terms of space this makes a difference of 4, 4.16, or 8.33 per cent, respectively, in the area sold. As between individual newspapers, the advertising rate will vary according to: (1) the volume of circulation; (2) the quality of the circulation; (3) competition; (4) production costs; and (5) prestige of the newspaper itself.

As between advertisers, the line rate quoted by most newspapers will vary according to: (1) whether they are general or retail advertisers; (2) if the latter, whether they are large, regular users of space; (3) the position of the advertising; (4) the kind or classification of the advertising; (5) whether color is used; and (6) the kind and amount of advertising or merchandising service given.

BULK CIRCULATION

Other things being equal, the newspaper with the largest circulation generally gets the highest rate for its advertising. A newspaper with 100,000 circulation is obviously a far better advertising medium ordinarily than one with 25,000 circulation because it reaches four times as many potential customers of the advertiser. But even if the quality of the two circulations is the same, which is rare, the advertising rate of the larger paper is not in direct proportion to its circulation. That is to say, as the volume of circulation increases, the line rate rises also but not in direct proportion, for otherwise the rates for publications with extremely large circulations would be prohibitive.

Because of this rate differential in favor of bulk circulations, it is sometimes definitely to the advantage of advertisers to concentrate their messages in a few large newspapers rather than to spread their advertising in many small newspapers with a combined equal circulation. To illustrate, two great metropolitan newspapers have a combined circulation of about 2,200,000. The open line rate of the one is $1.65 and that of the other is $1.40, or a total of $3.05. Five other leading newspapers have a combined circulation approximately equal to that of the two and with a combined open line rate of $4.49. In other words, to reach 2,200,000 newspaper buyers through the two newspapers costs approximately 50 per cent less than to get the attention of an equal number of prospective customers through the five newspapers cited.

Quality Circulation

The quality of circulation is frequently much more important to the advertiser than the volume of circulation. This is particularly true if the advertiser handles only quality merchandise or if he is dependent upon a small, select clientele of relatively high purchasing power. The circulations of some large newspapers are spread over such expanses of territory as to make them of doubtful value to the retail or local advertiser. Other factors are involved, of course, and it is unwise to generalize too far. Most retail advertisers, however, prefer concentrated circulation of proved quality to bulk circulation with slower and less certain returns. With the general advertiser, the situation may be different, and extensive coverage may be distinctly to his advantage. To illustrate again, newspapers like the New York Times, the New York Herald Tribune, and the Christian Science Monitor appeal to the cream of the newspaper reading public from the standpoint of intelligence and potential purchasing power. As a result, the returns to their advertisers are frequently higher than from competitors with larger circulations. This will depend, of course, to some extent upon what is advertised as well as upon other factors. But in consequence of this reader confidence and their proved value to the advertiser, such newspapers are in a position to enjoy somewhat higher rates than some of their competitors. The Christian Science Monitor, for example, has an open rate of 80 cents a line for all editions, based on a circulation of 126,000. By contrast, another Boston newspaper with 361,000 circulation has a flat rate of only 60 cents a line. Much of the circulation of the Monitor, of course, is outside of Boston, but the fact remains that it is preferred or quality circulation and for this reason the Monitor is in a position to charge more for its space.

Competition

How much competition a newspaper has from other newspapers and to some extent from other media is also a factor in determining rates. In recent years an increasing number of newspapers in smaller cities have achieved a monopoly as far as local competition is concerned. This has been brought about by purchases, mergers, and the elimination of weaker papers. In some instances two dailies remain, but they are under joint ownership. It might be supposed that where a newspaper enjoys such a monopoly, it is in a position to fix highly favorable rates.

This is true to some extent and such newspapers have an advantage just as any monopoly is apt to. But they must be on their guard against pressing their advantage lest their steady advertisers find the rates irksome to the field looks so inviting as to attract the attention of possible competitors. Where local newspapers are jointly owned or managed, it is a common practice to offer the advertiser- what are known as combination rates, which are lower than the sum of the Individual rates of the two papers. This is also done with daily and Sunday papers similarly operated. This encourages the use of more advertising space. It has the advantage of economy for the advertiser and more revenue for the newspaper.

In cities where there is newspaper competition without the likelihood of a merger, the existence of the other paper or other papers is always a deterrent to widely different rates. One newspaper cannot afford to have its rates so high that, regardless of its claims to preference as an advertising medium, advertisers are compelled in self-defense to use a less effective competing medium.

If such competitors are anywhere nearly equal in their net paid circulation, their rates are apt to approximate each other. Further, unless it makes an appreciable gain in circulation or can demonstrate some other distinct advantage, one newspaper cannot arbitrarily raise its rates without the possibility of losing accounts to its rival or rivals. Rate adjustments are sometimes made by mutual agreement among the newspapers concerned. Where it is possible, such a procedure is to their mutual benefit.

Production Costs

These are perhaps the most variable factors involved in determining rates. So many elements enter into the costs of production that it is difficult to catalogue them. In this respect newspapers are somewhat like individuals in that one seems to thrive on a modest budget, lays something aside for a rainy day, always meets his financial obligations, and, without making a splurge, seems to be able to afford everything necessary to a comfortable living. On the other hand, his neighbor with a comparable income and similar obligations has difficulty in making ends meet, he does not always buy wisely or well and, generally speaking, leads a sort of hand-to-mouth existence.

So with newspapers. Even through the depression which began in 1929, some publications had the foresight to trim their sails before the economic storm struck in all its fury. In the years that followed they had to retrench, of course, but they continued to show a profit. On the whole, as has been pointed out, newspapers generally made a good showing by contrast with other kinds of enterprise during this period of stress. Regardless of external conditions, the production costs of newspapers will vary greatly. One is housed in a costly plant in an expensive location, while its immediate competitor is content with a more modest layout in a cheaper location. Besides the initial outlay this involves such important factors as return on the investment, maintenance and depreciation, and realty taxes and assessments. Of two competing newspapers of comparable size, one may have an efficient plant well operated while its rival sutlers from an inefficient layout and from poor management.

One newspaper may have a circulation which calls for long hauls and a large outlay for transportation, including both equipment and manpower. Its rival, on the other hand, may enjoy the advantage of a concentrated circulation which it can handle at much less expense with a consequently larger margin of profit. It is fundamental, therefore, that in determining their advertising rates and in fixing their copy prices, newspapers should do so on the basis of exact cost finding. It is at this point that newspaper management frequently breaks down, and publishers proceed more or less by rule of thumb. To arrive at the proper rates to charge, the publisher should first determine his average costs over a period of reasonable length and build thereon in terms of circulation and the factors discussed above.

These costs should include the following: labor, based on a careful study of the expense and production in each department, especially the mechanical; materials; new equipment; overhead, including maintenance, depreciation, taxes and assessments, dividends on preferred stock, interest on and retirement of notes or bonds, if any, and interest on investment. To this should be added a reasonable profit commensurate with the business done, the risks taken, and the services rendered. Because of the business hazards involved in newspaper publishing, it has been held that 16 per cent constitutes a reasonable profit.

Prestige

Among the nearly 2000 dailies published in the United States are a number which are conspicuous for their editorial excellence, for news enterprise, for public service, or for the high returns they yield to the advertiser. The resultant prestige which they enjoy is reflected in reader confidence. This is an intangible quality which takes time to cultivate but which, once attained, the newspaper must hold and seek to improve. This prestige is made up largely of confidence in the medium on the part of both readers and advertisers. It is reflected to some extent in good will and is one of the most valuable assets a newspaper can have. A newspaper which has proved its superiority over the years to the definite satisfaction of both readers and advertisers is in a highly enviable position which should be reflected to some extent in its rate card.

ADVERTISING DIFFERENTIALS

General vs. Retail Advertising

Almost without exception, newspapers maintain a sharp rate differential between the general or national advertiser and the retail or local advertiser. There are a number of reasons for this practice, chief of which is the fact that the newspaper pays commissions to its representative who solicits the business as well as to the advertising agency, representing the advertiser, which buys the space. The mechanics of this arrangement will be examined in more detail but it suffices here to say that as a rule the differential is not much more than enough to offset the commissions involved. There is considerable debate as to the soundness of this practice. General advertisers are exerting increasing pressure upon the newspapers in an effort either to bring about the adoption of a basic open rate applicable to all advertisers or at least to lessen the gap between the two rates. They argue in substance that there is no valid reason why they should pay a higher rate than the retail advertiser and that the present general practice is unwarranted discrimination.

The situation has been complicated by the fact that an increasing volume of general advertising has been placed in recent years through local outlets. These may be owned or operated by the manufacturer who is also the general advertiser.

They may have a working or even a contractual arrangement with him, and in many instances it is no doubt true as newspaper publishers and advertising managers assert that sharp practice occurs which amounts to downright rate evasion at the expense of the newspaper. This comes about through the placing of general advertising through retail advertisers, thus getting the benefit of the local or retail rate.

The situation is further aggravated by the fact that general advertisers who refrain from or who are not in a position to effect such rate evasions find themselves at a disadvantage with more fortunate or less scrupulous competitors and at the same time are unable to obtain any appreciable concessions from the newspapers to offset this.

It would be rather difficult to show just what the differential is in dollars and cents between the general and the retail rate. Most newspaper advertising rates that are given in such media as Standard Rate & Data Service, the Editor & Publisher Yearbook, and the Ayer Newspaper Directory are open or general rates. Even where retail advertising rate cards are available so many factors enter into the advertising contract that it is hazardous to generalize about the rates. But in most cases it is probable that the general or open rate is at least 40 per cent higher than the retail open rate.

At least two major suggestions have been made to solve this difficult and irritating problem. One is to equalize or adjust rates so as to eliminate or minimize the gap between them. The other is to set up special classifications. These may vary somewhat in form but each has its special advocates. The existing system, of course, still has its defenders.

Rate Equalization

What amounts to an equalization of general and retail rates has been worked out by individual newspapers in different ways. This may take the form of reducing the general rate to the level of the retail rate plus the agency commission, or of abolishing the local rate on some classifications, Perhaps the most conspicuous convert to rate equalization was the St. Louis Post-Dispatch which abolished the differentials between retail and general advertising except for the amount of the agency commission, thereby enabling agencies "to buy display advertising, whether general, automotive, or financial, in the Post-Dispatch on the same net basis as retail advertisers."

The change involved an increase of 1 cent a line on all local advertising in the weekday issues and reductions ranging as high as 6 cents on general advertising where a sliding scale replaced the old flat rate. Sunday rates were lowered on both sides. In commenting on the change, George M. Burbach, advertising manager of the Post-Dispatch was quoted as saying: "We are making no apology for past rate cards. We felt that rate differentials previously in force could be justified by good arguments. Under present conditions, however, we feel that there is no more reason to charge the national advertiser one rate and the local advertiser another rate, than there would be to sell apples from one side of a cart at one price and from the other side to buyers at a different price."

A comparison of the new rates of the Post-Dispatch follows: This move by the Post-Dispatch attracted wide attention. Locally, the Globe-Democrat followed suit with reductions applying to contracts but with no change in its retail rates while certain special classifications remained on a flat basis but at the new reduced rate. The Star-Times pointed out that it had narrowed the gap between retail and general rates in 1932. The Kansas City Star congratulated the Post-Dispatch in promotion advertising but called attention in good humor to the fact that "the Kansas City Star has been good in the matter of local-national rate differentials for half a century, whereas the reform of the Post-Dispatch dates back a month."

Elsewhere, the Post-Dispatch move was commended by agency men and by large general advertisers. Other publishers were bombarded with pleas and arguments to do likewise. David Stern, the New York-Philadelphia-Camden publisher, was one of these. In reply, he cited the low milline rates of his papers and contended that milline rates rather than differentials were the important thing. 3 He pointed out that his New York Evening Post sold space on the guaranteed basis of 205,000 circulation at 30 cents a line, making a milline rate of $1.46 which, with the lone exception of the Philadelphia Bulletin, he emphasized, "is the lowest milline rate of any standard-size evening paper in the United States."

Similarly, his Philadelphia Record brought 45 cents a line or a milline rate of $1.50 on the basis of 300,000 circulation which with the exception of the Chicago Tribune, he commented, "is the lowest milline rate of any standard-size morning paper in the United States." He pointed out further that no newspaper in the United States guaranteed a lower milline rate than his two and that there were 30 United States dailies with a milline rate lower than that of the Post-Dispatch whose scale, he added, gave rate decreases to all advertisers using 5000 lines or more a year with increases for all advertisers using less than 5000 lines. The Post-Dispatch declined to comment on this.

The Wilkes-Barre Times-Leader and the Wilkes-Barre Record abolished rate differentials between retail and national advertising on automotive, electrical, and financial advertising "as well as advertising coming from all types of local distributors of nationally advertised products." This involved no change in rates but a discontinuance of local rates on specified types of advertising, all of which must now pay the general rate regardless of whether they are placed locally, directly, or by agencies. Commissions or discounts on these classifications are limited to recognized agencies. In varying forms this plan has been adopted by a large number of newspapers. It was also urged before the A.N.P.A. convention as affording at least a partial solution of the rate differential problem. A survey revealed that at least 120 dailies have a single rate for all automotive advertising, whether general or retail, besides clauses in their contracts with the retailer forbidding him to pass on his rate to firms from which he buys goods. The Janesville, Wis., Gazette set its general rate at 6 cents a line gross, less 15 per cent agency commission and 2 per cent for cash. Its retail rates were advanced to a point where, on the average, they would meet the net national and in some cases would be higher.

Classifications

A classification rate system has also been advocated as a solution of the general-retail rate question. John E. Finneran, Scripps-Howard advertising director, declared that the advertising brokerage system is costing the newspapers millions of dollars through diversion of retail rates. This comes about, he charged, through (1) buying of space by retailers who bill the distributors at the price the retailers pay; (2) charging manufacturers more than the retail but less than the general rate; (3) the retailer paying the retail rate but charging the manufacturer the general rate, pocketing the difference himself. As a solution, he suggested that classification rates be set up for certain products such as mechanical refrigerators, radios, automobiles, gasoline, tires, etc.

This would result, in effect, in retail, classification, and general rates. Actually, this is simply an extension of the policy that now prevails locally with respect to amusement, political, and other special classifications. As a further curb on diversion, it has been variously suggested that general copy placed through a retailer be limited to 20 per cent of his total space in any one day if the retail rate is to apply.

CONFLICTING VIEWPOINTS

One point of view in this perennial controversy was brought out by John Benson, president, American Association of Advertising Agencies, speaking before the Inland Daily Press Association. He said, in part: What do we agencies expect the publisher to do? We expect no miracles to happen. But we do expect of the publisher a new policy in his rate making, a trend away from widening differentials and more regard for the welfare of national advertising. We think he should treat his customers alike and give them all a fairly equal chance to win.

We expect him to abandon the idea of looking to the national advertiser to recoup losses in the retail field. We expect him to protect the advertising agency as the developer of business for him, have firm rates and stick to them. We believe he should earn and hold the confidence of his local contemporary, so that they can cooperate.

Similarly, Walter A. Burke, Pacific Coast regional executive of the A.A.A.A., declared at a meeting of the Northern California Newspaper Advertising Managers' Association that the existing system of differentials had brought about an unbalanced rate structure that resulted in discrimination, placed an unnatural burden on the advertising of one group, reduced the advertising effect of the space used, encouraged the extension of special allowances in other directions, and cheapened the value of newspaper space in the eyes of retailers because offered so cheaply. He also warned that newspapers would have to look to some other source of revenue if the current trend resulting from widening retail-general rate differentials continued.

Remarks of Irl W. Brown, of the Texas Daily Press League, before the Texas Press Association convention, represent the opposite viewpoint. He argued that the general advertiser was not justified in claiming the same rate as the local advertiser when the former does nothing, he said, to build up local interests, pay local taxes, contribute toward meeting local payrolls, or create local values. As against this the local advertiser continually helps to promote local interests. The Texas publishers were also cautioned that "if you cut your national rate your local rate has got to come up, and your local advertisers can not afford to pay the rate based upon a large circulation, much of which lies outside the local trade territory.

LARGE VS. SMALL ADVERTISER

Another common practice among newspapers is to give the steady retail advertiser who is a large and consistent user of space the benefit of a preferential rate. This is usually based upon what is known as the sliding scale.

The theory behind this is that a large customer is always a preferred customer. Since he is regular in his use of space, the sales and other overhead expense incident to handling his account is less than on small individual accounts each of which calls for sales effort and expense. Such a policy encourages the use of more space.

While this is the general practice, it should be noted that it applies only to retail or local advertising. A few newspapers, however, believe in a flat scale as being fairest to all advertisers, easiest to administer, and simplest to apply. Within limits the Robinson-Batman Act, described in the following chapter, represents an attempt to end some discriminatory practices by legislation. To illustrate the sliding scale, a large newspaper has a weekday open rate of 90 cents a line. An advertiser signing a contract to use 5000 lines a year is entitled to a discount of 1 per cent. For 10,000 lines the discount is 2 per cent, for 15,000 it is 3 per cent, and for 25,000 it is 4 per cent. Above this figure the discount increases as follows:

Thus by applying the discount at 100,000 lines, the 90-cent rate becomes 79.2 cents. Similar discounts are given for space in the Sunday paper for which the rates are frequently higher than for the daily because of a considerably larger circulation. In lieu of the space discounts just described, what are known as time discounts may also be given.

These are, in effect, a premium or .concession for regularity of advertising. An advertiser is not ordinarily eligible for both space and time discounts simultaneously. In addition to these, it has been the practice of some newspapers during the depression to offer "temporary" or "interim" discounts as a further incentive to both volume and regularity on the part of the advertiser.

All of these devices, as a matter of fact, are inducements to the advertiser to use more space and to use it regularly. In these ways, the newspaper endeavors to encourage the use of advertising space and, to some extent, to minimize the seasonal fluctuations that occur in advertising.

POSITION ADVERTISING

Many variations in rates come about through the position or location occupied in the paper by the advertising. The larger the newspaper the more detailed and complicated are its position rates. The smaller the paper the fewer are its rules apt to be in this respect. Advertising which is placed anywhere in the paper without special consideration as to location is said to be "R.Q.P.," i.e., run-of-the-paper advertising.

Unless it qualifies for space or time discounts, such advertising is paid for at the paper's open rate. An advertisement has "full position" when it is next to editorial or other reading matter on two sides, and "half position" when there is reading matter on one side. "Island" advertisements, now rarely seen except in small newspapers, are those entirely surrounded by reading matter.

Since the object of all advertising is primarily to attract the attention of the reader, many advertisers seek to make certain that even the casual reader will see their advertising message by specifying preferred locations in the paper. For this preferred treatment the newspaper properly charges extra.

These locations may be on a given page or in a given department or section of the paper or in a special position on a page. For advertisements of less than a page, the easiest way to attract the attention of the reader is to place the advertising at the top of a column or next to reading matter, or both.

It may also be next to or following reading matter, or the reverse. In this connection it is a common practice to require such advertising to be at least a certain size. For example, one metropolitan paper fixes 14 lines as the minimum space acceptable for a designated page, and 28 lines as the minimum for a designated position. Further, it gives no discounts on position, rates which are in addition to the regular rates.

Most large newspapers in the United States no longer accept first-page display advertising. There are a few exceptions, however, such as the Wall St. Journal and the Boston Transcript. First-page advertisements of a few lines, known as " readers" or "liners," are still accepted by even such papers as the New York Times. These also call for a higher rate. Other pages in the paper which call for such advertising surcharges usually include first and last section pages, the more important inside news pages such as pages two and three, the page opposite the editorial page, and departmental pages or sections such as sports, amusements, markets, financial, women's, and society.

One metropolitan paper has an open rate of 68 cents a line. Its position charges, per line extra, are as follows: Not sold. Many papers, particularly smaller ones, add a fixed percentage to the open rate as a surcharge for position advertising. The rate card of one, chosen at random, reads, "preferred position 35%."

Another, somewhat larger, adds surcharges as follows: next to reading, 15 per cent additional; following and next to reading, 25 per cent extra; pages two or three, 25 per cent; sports, social, or back page, 25 per cent. Still another, apparently with limited facilities or space, advertises: "Position not guaranteed but placed following or next to reading matter when possible. The Cleveland Plain Dealer charges 25 per cent extra for next to-reading position and 50 per cent extra for first-following-and next-to-reading.

Classification

Most large newspapers vary their rates to some extent according to the kind of display advertising carried. In some cases these display classifications are few, and in others the lists are rather long. Generally speaking, amusements, including sporting events, and financial and political advertising pay higher rates, while a few, such as for bona fide charitable agencies and schools, are charged at somewhat less than the open rate. The higher rate is charged partly on the theory of what "the traffic will bear" and in the case of amusement and automotive advertising because of the practice of running free publicity matter with it. Lower rates may be accepted for some classifications either because the advertisers are presumably less able to pay the regular rate or as a matter of inducement.

Color

A growing number of American newspapers have installed facilities for color printing. As an additional effective means of attracting reader attention, these newspapers offer the advertiser the option of one or more colors besides black. As a rule the use of color is limited to full page or other large advertisements. Surveys are cited to show that color advertising outpulls black and white advertising of similar size and character by 53 per cent.

The claim is therefore made that since the surcharge for color is only 15 to 30 per cent, depending upon position and other factors, the use of color gives a "readership bonus " of from 23 to 38 per cent. Such advertising is ordinarily confined to the largest advertisers, but many small newspapers are now equipped to provide color for advertising. The extra charge is justified, of course, by the fact that each additional color calls for separate plates and special inking.

Special Service

Most newspapers render every possible service to the advertiser and cooperate with him fully. Necessarily there is a limit, however, to how far the newspaper can go in such matters, both in fairness to other advertisers and in justice to itself. For example, if a newspaper not only assists an advertiser to plan his campaign but through its art staff supplies him with drawings and has special cuts made, such service may properly be regarded as extra and an additional charge for it is entirely in order.

RATE YARDSTICKS

So many elements enter into the fixing of newspaper advertising rates that it is necessary to have some means of comparing the rates of publications whether they are direct competitors or not. A number of formulae have been devised to this end, but none of them is entirely satisfactory. As in other lines, "figures can lie and liars can figure" and each publication is naturally interested in interpreting its rate and circulation to its own best advantage. The yardsticks in use are the milline, the truline, the purline, and the mil-unit.

The Milline. This is the advertising rate of any publication in terms of 1,000,000 circulation. It is equally applicable to magazines and to a limited extent to the radio. It makes possible a comparison of two media whether they are alike or diverse. It yields a ready answer, but the difficulty is that the answer is frequently too simple and does not take into account all of the factors involved.

Bibliography

Baker, C. Edwin: *Advertising and a Democratic Press,* Princeton NJ: Princeton University Press, 1994.

Beasley, Maurine Hoffman, and Sheila Gibbons: *Taking Their Place: A Documentary History of Women and Journalism,* Washington, DC: American University Press, 1993.

Bliss, Edward: *Now the News: The Story of Broadcast Journalism,* New York, Columbia University Press, 1991.

Cook, T.: *Making Laws & Making News*, Washington, DC: Brookings, 1989.

Danky, James P.: *African-American Newspapers and Periodicals: A National Bibliography*, Cambridge, MA: Harvard University Press, 1998.

Graber, Doris A.: *Processing the Newspaper,* N.Y., Longman, 1984.

James D. and W. David Sloan: *Historical Methods in Newpaper,* Hillsdale, NJ: Lawrence Erlbaum, 1989.

James, Philip: *African-American Newspapers and Periodicals: A National Bibliography*, Cambridge, Harvard University Press, 1999.

Kitano, Harry: *The Ethnic Press of Newspaper in the United States,* Westport, CT: Greenwood Press, 1987.

Kolodzy, Janet: *Writing and Reporting Across the Newspaper,* Llanham, MD: Rowman & Littlefield, 2006.

Kolony, James: *Convergence Journalism: Writing and Reporting,* Llanham, MD: Rowman & Littlefield, 2006.

Norris, Pippa: *Women, Newspaper and Politics*, Oxford, Oxford University Press, 1997.

Ross, Karen: *Making the Local News: Local Journalism in Context,* London, Routledge, 1998.

West, Darrell M.: *The Rise and Fall of the Newspaper,* Boston MA: Bedford/St. Martin's, 2001.

INDEX

□□□